Praise for *A Meditator's Life of the Buddha*

In this work, Bhikkhu Anālayo applies his consummate knowledge of the textual collections of Early B[illegible]e task of constructing a biograph[illegible]on his life as a meditator. The boo[illegible] picture of the Buddha's life, but [illegible] exercises attached to each chapter it enables the rea[illegible] the Buddha on his quest for enlightenment and beyond, into his mission as a teacher and through to his parinirvāṇa or passing away. While offering a scholarly portrait of the Buddha, this book is also a testament to the overarching unity of the various early Buddhist schools in their conception of the Buddha's life, a unity that coexists along with a rich diversity in their detailed narrations about particular events in that life.
Bhikkhu Bodhi, scholar and translator

A Meditator's Life of the Buddha explores the remarkable inner journey that transformed Siddhartha Gotama into a fully awakened Buddha. It traces the unfolding of the Buddha's path from his going forth and discovery of the path, to the triumphant night of his full awakening, four and a half decades of compassionate teaching, and concludes with his final meditation.

This book is simultaneously a biography of a great man, an insightful study of Early Buddhism, and a practical guidebook for serious meditators. Each chapter offers readers a rare, and often surprisingly intimate, account of how the Buddha met real-life situations. We learn how he faced difficulties and overcame fears, struggled to abandon defilements, prioritized his commitments, mastered concentration states, recognized the significance of insights, and experienced the great peace that finally characterized his life as an awakened one. It is an inspiring guide that will accelerate the reader's own journey of awakening. Highly recommended, and sure to inspire dedicated meditators!
Shaila Catherine, author of *Focused and Fearless: A Meditator's Guide to States of Deep Joy, Calm, and Clarity*

The Buddha's life story provides an implicit support for one of the most important of early Buddhist meditation practices, the contemplation of the Buddha. Anālayo's highly original approach to the familiar story is to present his material in the form of an explicit guide to this practice, laid out in 24 stages, which follow what we know of the Buddha's own meditation practice. Anālayo brings his formidable scholarship to elucidating what this consisted in, drawing on discourses preserved in Pāli and Chinese that have a reliably early provenance. The extremely useful exercises with which each chapter concludes ground the scholarship in a fervent awareness of the goal, represented by the Buddha, which we should always have in mind in our own practice.
Jinananda, author of *Warrior of Peace: The Life of the Buddha*

Anālayo is both an outstanding scholar and a devoted practitioner, and this account of the Buddha's life through his engagement with meditation may be his ideal subject. We need more accounts of the Buddha's life that draw out what the early texts say, distinguishing that from the legends that came later. Anālayo's mastery of both the Pāli and the Chinese sources, as well as the scholarship that surrounds them, makes him an unrivalled authority in this, and an attentive guide to the Buddha's explorations of the mind and meditative states. In another person's hands all this knowledge could have made *A Meditator's Life of the Buddha* an exercise in scholarship, but Anālayo's heartfelt engagement with the material and his dedication to meditation practice is evident on every page.
Vishvapani, author of *Gautama Buddha: The Life and Teachings of the Awakened One*

A Meditator's Life of the Buddha

Also by Anālayo

Satipaṭṭhāna: The Direct Path to Realization
The Genesis of the Bodhisattva Ideal
A Comparative Study of the Majjhima-nikāya
Excursions into the Thought-world of the Pāli Discourses
Madhyama-āgama Studies
Perspectives on Satipaṭṭhāna
The Dawn of Abhidharma
Compassion and Emptiness in Early Buddhist Meditation
Saṃyukta-āgama Studies
Ekottarika-āgama Studies
The Foundation History of the Nuns' Order
Mindfully Facing Disease and Death: Compassionate Advice from Early Buddhist Texts
Buddhapada and the Bodhisattva Path
Early Buddhist Meditation Studies
Dīrgha-āgama Studies
Vinaya Studies

A MEDITATOR'S LIFE OF THE BUDDHA

Based on the Early Discourses

Anālayo

Windhorse Publications

Windhorse Publications
169 Mill Road
Cambridge
CB1 3AN
UK

info@windhorsepublications.com
windhorsepublications.com

As an act of Dhammadāna, Anālayo has
waived royalty payments for this book.
The index was not compiled by the author.

Cover design by Dhammarati
Cover image: Sandstone figure of the Buddha, Sarnath, fifth century AD; © The Trustees of the British Museum.

Typesetting and layout by Ruth Rudd
Printed by Bell & Bain Ltd, Glasgow

British Library Cataloguing in Publication Data:
A catalogue record for this book is available from the British Library.

ISBN: 978-1-909314-99-3

CONTENTS

ABOUT THE AUTHOR

Born in 1962 in Germany, Bhikkhu Anālayo was ordained in 1995 in Sri Lanka, and completed a PhD on the *Satipaṭṭhāna-sutta* at the University of Peradeniya, Sri Lanka, in 2000 – published in 2003 by Windhorse Publications under the title *Satipaṭṭhāna: The Direct Path to Realization.*

Anālayo is a professor of Buddhist Studies; his main research area is early Buddhism and in particular the topics of the Chinese *Āgamas*, meditation, and women in Buddhism. Besides his academic pursuits, he spends most of his time in meditation under retreat conditions and regularly teaches meditation. He presently resides at the Barre Center for Buddhist Studies in Massachusetts.

ACKNOWLEDGEMENT

I am indebted to Bhikkhu Bodhi, Bhikkhunī Dhammadinnā, Ann Dillon, Linda Grace, Michael Running, Syinchen Shi, and Matt Weingast for commenting on a draft version of this book.

PUBLISHER'S ACKNOWLEDGEMENTS

Windhorse Publications wishes to gratefully acknowledge grants from the Triratna European Chairs' Assembly Fund and the Future Dharma Fund towards the production of this book. Windhorse Publications also wishes to gratefully acknowledge and thank the individual donors who gave to the book's production via our "Sponsor-a-book" campaign.

Triratna
European Chairs Assembly

FutureDharmaFund
Transforming Self and World

MEDITATIVE EXERCISES RECOMMENDED IN EACH CHAPTER

FOREWORD BY JACK KORNFIELD

You hold in your hand a wonderful gift, offered to Western readers from my accomplished and respected friend, Bhikkhu Anālayo. In *A Meditator's Life of the Buddha*, Bhikkhu Anālayo, a visionary scholar and acclaimed translator, shows us with text and story, exercises and practice, how the life of the Buddha can directly inspire our own spiritual journey.

For many in the newer generations of Western students, a deep connection to the Buddha comes only after some period of practice. Initially, most Westerners are drawn to the transformative teachings of the Dharma, to the clear understandings and the powerful practices it offers. Invariably their lives are uplifted by them. Usually their relationship to the Buddha grows more slowly. This is in great contrast to the lifelong spirit of devotion and love for the Buddha that permeates his followers across Buddhist Asia.

For me, a connection to the Buddha came truly alive when I travelled to Burma, after my first years practising as a monk in the forest monasteries of Thailand. My supporters at the centres of Mahāsi Sayādaw and Sunlun Sayādaw insisted I visit the Shwedagon, the enormous and marvellous pagoda in the centre of Rangoon. My mind was already quiet and my heart tender from long months of meditation. Walking the wide polished marble path between the main stupa and the hundreds of temples set around the stupa, I was informed that the stupa contained the hair and the walking stick of the Buddha, brought from a temple in India many centuries ago.

Whether it was literally true or not, I was filled with rapture and inspiration. Before this moment the Buddha had seemed like a distant archetype, noble and inspiring, but somewhat unreal. In this moment, I understood that this man was real, like us! A human, a remarkable one, who lived and walked and taught the great wisdom that has been passed on through generations.

Later in Bodh Gaya and Sarnath I could feel the same immediate connection to the Buddha as a living man who walked among us. The power of his teaching became connected to the earthly sense of the living Buddha and this presence has nourished and empowered my practice and life. My love and devotion have grown deeper over the years.

For many Western meditators, respect and appreciation for the Buddha grows with the deepening of their practice. At those times when the mind becomes profoundly focused and still, we can begin to experience the clarity and purity described by the Buddha. As our consciousness becomes malleable and well trained, we open with awe to a small taste of the flawless purity of the Buddha's mind that gave birth to these teachings.

Whatever the stage of our practice, this book is an invitation to explore and deepen our own connection to the Buddha. There is magic in it, for it opens us to the vastness of human possibility. Traditionally Buddhists begin by taking refuge in the Buddha. The Buddha's life and his awakening offer us a precious jewel, a model for all who follow his teachings. So powerful were his realization and enlightenment that they have touched and transformed the lives of billions of humans for 2,600 years. And the blessing is that the freedom pointed out by the Buddha is available to each of us.

Bhikkhu Anālayo has laid out this volume in an integrated and friendly way. Each of the chapters details a meditative dimension of the Buddha's awakening and teaching that can resonate with our own path. And each chapter then provides meditative reflections and contemplations that will deepen our understanding and dedication.

From the first, we are invited to consider the motivation for our spiritual journey. Like the Buddha, we too will have seen the inevitable sorrows and entanglements of life, and we too can sense the possibility of freedom. From the very beginning of reflecting on our deepest intention, to the very end of the path, opening to the liberation teachings of emptiness, freedom, and Nirvāṇa, we are skilfully led to follow the Buddha's journey of meditations with our own practice.

Among the many important themes from the Buddha's life, two that can especially inspire our practice are those of fearlessness and wholesomeness.

Developing fearlessness does not mean there will be no fear, but that journey of awakening is so important and compelling that we willingly dedicate ourselves to the truth in spite of the difficulty. Our life is short. What is liberation beyond birth and death? In Zen this question is called the Great Matter. Genuine spiritual practice requires us to bring a fearless awareness to examine our body and mind and our human condition. It is by courageously seeking the truth that we can awaken to timeless freedom and vast compassion.

Yet notice carefully, in these teachings, that, while suffering is the starting point, it is not the end of the journey. We are inspired to discover what is beyond suffering. In this we are invited by the Buddha's example to establish and dwell in a healthy mind and heart. Awakening is filled with joy and well-being – freedom brings a peaceful heart.

Cultivating profound well-being is possible for each of us. Turning towards the wholesome and fostering a healthy mind and heart are a critical dimension of our practice. A common misunderstanding found in modern mindfulness teachings is that by simply observing experience with mindfulness all will be transformed. But there is more to mindfulness than this. The wisdom in this book helps us to realize that wise mindfulness recognizes what is present, and then guides us from unwholesome to wholesome states. We can learn to see clearly and then, in response, tend, direct, refine, and transform our own mind.

Developing a mind and heart suffused with wisdom and *mettā* allows us to live with freedom wherever we are. Bhikkhu

Anālayo shows us how the Buddha embodied this spirit, ever responsive to those around him. There is an immediacy, decorum, grace, open-handedness, and profound compassion in his tending of all he touched. We are invited to bring these same qualities alive in our own Dharma life.

Read this book slowly.
Savour it and let it sink in.
Make it a manual of practice.
Use the reflections to deepen your journey.

May the teachings, stories, and practices here
bring you the blessings of the Buddha.

With *mettā*,

Jack Kornfield
Spirit Rock Center
24 June 2017

He fared rightly, meditating and reflecting;
With his unperturbed purity
He invariably smiled and had no anger;
Delighting in seclusion, he attained the highest;
Fearlessly, he invariably focused on what is essential:
The Buddha.

INTRODUCTION

The following pages offer a study of meditative dimensions of the Buddha's life, based on a combination of extracts from the early discourses and discussions. With the title *A Meditator's Life of the Buddha* I intend to convey not only that in this book I focus on the Buddha as a meditator, in the sense of concentrating on his meditative experiences and practices, but also that my target readership is other meditators. In this way, I hope to provide inspiration and guidance for those who have dedicated themselves to meditation practice aimed at progress to awakening. In so doing, my intention is to present one possible way of understanding selected aspects of the life of the Buddha according to how these are portrayed in the early discourses, certainly not the only one, let alone the only correct one, in such a way that they can serve as an inspiration and guide for fellow meditators.

A substantial number of biographies of the Buddha have already been compiled by others, which allows me to focus on selected topics in the knowledge that a more comprehensive coverage of his life is readily available. Besides not attempting to offer a complete coverage of the Buddha's life, my approach also differs from other biographies known to me by focusing on only meditative aspects of the Buddha's life. Besides this thematic focus, I also employ source material only from the Pāli discourses and their parallels.[1] Comparative study of this type of text

1 A biography based on translations of source material from the Pāli discourses and *Vinaya* can be found in Ñāṇamoli 1972/1992.

enables a reconstruction of the earliest stages in the history and development of Buddhism. My use of only the early discourses as sources for constructing a life of the Buddha means that some elements of the traditionally well-known hagiography fall outside the scope of my source material (although I will discuss such tales when this seems opportune). Examples are the story of the future Buddha's departure at night after seeing the members of his harem asleep, or his confrontation with Māra's army on the eve of his awakening.

Although my presentation differs to some extent from traditional accounts of the Buddha in this respect, a central aim of the present project is to encourage a traditional practice whose potential has to my mind not received the attention it deserves among modern-day Buddhist practitioners. This is recollection of the Buddha, a topic that I explore in more detail in the conclusion to this book.

Similar to my book on *Mindfully Facing Disease and Death*, the main body of the present book also has twenty-four chapters. Twelve chapters cover the period up to the Buddha's awakening and another twelve chapters deal with selected aspects of the ensuing period from the moment of his awakening itself up to his final meditation. Each of these twenty-four chapters concludes with suggestions for meditative practice or reflection.

In Chapter 1 I begin with the future Buddha's motivation to go forth; in Chapter 2 I turn to his moral conduct and how he faced fear. In Chapters 3 to 5 I cover his development of concentration: his overcoming obstacles to concentration, his attainment of absorption, and his cultivation of the immaterial attainments under the tuition of Āḷāra Kālāma and Uddaka Rāmaputta.

The Buddha's time of asceticism is the theme of the next three chapters, 6 to 8. The discovery of the path to awakening and the strong determination to pursue this path are the topics of Chapters 9 and 10. In Chapters 11 and 12 I study the first two higher knowledges, and in Chapter 13 the event of awakening itself.

The decision to teach is the topic of Chapter 14, followed by three chapters, 15 to 17, dedicated to the first teaching with which the Buddha set in motion the wheel of Dharma.

In Chapter 18 I take up the Buddha's decision to honour the Dharma, followed by his skilful teaching activities in Chapter 19, and his penetrative seeing through views and his dwelling in emptiness in Chapters 20 and 21. In Chapter 22 I study the Buddha's daily conduct. The Buddha's way of facing old age, disease, and death is the topic of Chapter 23 and his passing away of Chapter 24. In the conclusion I turn to recollection of the Buddha, a meditation practice that in one way or another underlies the entire book.

As in the case of *Mindfully Facing Disease and Death*, the majority of the passages chosen are based on Chinese originals and, with a few exceptions, are here translated into English for the first time. The choice to rely on passages from the Chinese *Āgama*s reflects the fact that several English translations already exist of the corresponding Pāli versions. By translating their Chinese counterparts, my intention is to allow the reader to compare the parallel versions in English translation and get a first-hand impression, beyond the selected observations that I provide regarding variations between them.

In my translations I replace abbreviations found in the original with the full passage, marking the fact that this part has been supplemented by putting it into italics.[2] I hope this will enable the reader to decide between the alternatives of doing a full reading in a more contemplative spirit or else jump the repetitions and read on for information. When I supplement text to enable a better understanding of a somewhat cryptic Chinese passage, I use square brackets [ ] instead of italics, and for emendations I employ angle brackets ⟨ ⟩. In order to avoid gendered terminology, I translate equivalents of the term *bhikkhu* with "monastic". In my translations I employ Pāli terms for the sake of ease of comparison, without thereby intending to take a position on the language of the original used for the Chinese translation. Exceptions to the use of Pāli are terms like Dharma and Nirvāṇa, both of which are now commonly used in English publications.

The quote I have chosen as an introductory verse to this book stems from the *Madhyama-āgama* parallel to the *Upāli-sutta* of

2 In order for this to work, in translated passages throughout Indic terms are not in italics.

the *Majjhima-nikāya*.[3] It forms part of a series of verses spoken by the former Jain follower Upāli in praise of the Buddha. Each of the qualities highlighted in this verse could potentially serve as a starting point for recollecting the Buddha.

The first line, according to which the Buddha "fared rightly, meditating and reflecting", aptly sums up the Buddha's progress to awakening, where meditative practice and reflection combined together enabled him to discover the path to liberation. The Buddha's post-awakening "unperturbed purity" made him one who "invariably smiled and had no anger". This throws into relief the beauty of a purified mind, where there is no longer any scope for anger to arise and whatever happens can be met with the smile of compassion. The Buddha "attained the highest" precisely because of his "delighting in seclusion", whereby he set an example to be emulated by those who wish to reach the highest themselves. The last line mentions the Buddha's fearlessness and highlights that he "invariably focused on what is essential". This reflects a recurrent trait of the Buddha evident in the early discourses, which show him to have had a clear-cut focus on what really matters.

I hope that in what follows I will be able to do justice to this recurrent trait of the Buddha's teachings by presenting a selection of passages from the life of the Buddha in such a way as to combine a focus on what is essential from a meditative perspective with the type of information that helps to make him come alive in his progress from struggling with defilements and obstructions to becoming the supreme guide of those willing to train themselves through meditative cultivation in order to realize Nirvāṇa.

3 The translation is based on MĀ 133 at T I 632b21 to 632b23 (which continues after "the Buddha" by noting that "his disciple is Upāli"), parallel to MN 56 at MN I 386,24 (translated Ñāṇamoli 1995/2005: 491) and Sanskrit fragments in Hoernle 1916/1970: 29 and SHT III 872, Waldschmidt et al. 1971: 122f; for a comparative study of the verses see Anālayo 2011: 331. The Chinese original does not mark the tense of the verbs. Since at the time of Upāli's delivery of these verses the Buddha was still alive, some of the verbs (like the reference to his smiling) would probably best be rendered in the present tense (unlike his having fared rightly, which does require the past tense). I have opted to render all of them in the past tense, however, in the hope that this will make it easier for current readers to employ the verse for recollection.

I

THE MOTIVATION TO GO FORTH

The future Buddha's motivation to go forth is my main concern in the present chapter. I begin with a substantial excerpt from a discourse that describes his luxurious upbringing as well as his insight into the basic predicaments of human existence. This description is found in a discourse in the *Aṅguttara-nikāya* and its *Madhyama-āgama* parallel, which is the version I translate here.[1]

> I recollect that, a long time ago, being at home with my father Suddhodana, I would spend the four months of the summer season up in the main mansion without any other men, with only women for my entertainment. From the beginning [of this period onwards] I would not come down. When [after that time] I wanted to go out and visit parks, thirty renowned horsemen were selected to mount carriages and escort me in front and at the rear, to attend and follow my lead, not to mention others [who were attending on me]. I had power like this, being of such superbly delicate [upbringing].[2]

1 The translated passage is taken from MĀ 117 at T I 607c25 to 608a18, parallel to AN 3.38 & AN 3.39 at AN I 145,14 (translated Bodhi 2012: 240f, referred to as discourse 39).

2 AN 3.38 at AN I 145,14 also mentions the spending of four months with only female companions, but does not refer to being escorted out to a park on an occasion which the context suggests took place after the four months of the summer. AN 3.38 additionally draws attention to the excellent food given even to workers and servants at Suddhodana's home.

I also recollect that, a long time ago, I saw field workers who were taking a rest in their fields. I went under a rose-apple tree and sat down cross-legged. Secluded from sensual pleasures, secluded from evil and unwholesome states, with [directed] awareness and [sustained] contemplation,[3] with joy and happiness born of seclusion, I attained the first absorption and dwelled in it.[4]

I thought: "Uninstructed ignorant worldlings, who are themselves subject to disease and not exempt from disease, are disgusted and humiliated on seeing other people who are sick, which is not wanted and not enjoyable.[5] They do not examine themselves."

I further thought: "I am myself subject to disease and not exempt from disease. If I were to be disgusted and humiliated on seeing other people who are sick, which is not wanted and not enjoyable, then that would not be proper for me, because I am also subject to this." Having examined it in this way, the conceit that arises due to being without sickness ceased in turn on its own.

I further thought: "Uninstructed ignorant worldlings, who are themselves subject to old age and not exempt from old age, are disgusted and humiliated on seeing other people who are old, which is not wanted and not enjoyable. They do not examine themselves."

I further thought: "I am myself subject to old age and not exempt from old age. If I were to be disgusted and humiliated on seeing other people who are old, which is not wanted and not enjoyable, then that would not be proper for me, because I am also subject to this." Having examined it in this way, the conceit that arises due to [young] age ceased in turn on its own.

[I further thought: "Uninstructed ignorant worldlings, who are themselves subject to death and not exempt from death, are disgusted and humiliated on seeing other people who are dead,

3 For a discussion of the significance of how the factors of the first absorption are rendered in the *Madhyama-āgama*, in comparison with their counterparts *vitakka* and *vicāra* in Pāli discourses, see Anālayo 2017b: 123ff.

4 AN 3.38 does not report the prince's attainment of the first absorption.

5 AN 3.38 at AN I 145,23 first takes up old age and then turns to disease.

which is not wanted and not enjoyable. They do not examine themselves."]

[I further thought: "I am myself subject to death and not exempt from death. If I were to be disgusted and humiliated on seeing other people who are dead, which is not wanted and not enjoyable, then that would not be proper for me, because I am also subject to this." Having examined it in this way, the conceit that arises due to being alive ceased in turn on its own.][6]

On being healthy, uninstructed ignorant worldlings are proud, conceited, and become negligent. Because of sensual desires, their ignorance grows and they do not cultivate the holy life.

On being young, uninstructed ignorant worldlings are proud, conceited, and become negligent. Because of sensual desires, their ignorance grows and they do not cultivate the holy life.

On being alive, uninstructed ignorant worldlings are proud, conceited, and become negligent. Because of sensual desires, their ignorance grows and they do not cultivate the holy life.

A substantial difference in relation to the early part of the passage translated above is that the *Aṅguttara-nikāya* discourse does not refer at all to the bodhisattva's experience of the first absorption.[7] I will return to this topic in Chapter 9.

Compared to the last part of the extract from the *Madhyama-āgama* version, which describes how ignorance grows on being healthy etc., the *Aṅguttara-nikāya* parallel is more detailed. It additionally notes that worldlings engage in evil conduct and for this reason are reborn in hell, and that monastics disrobe and return to the lower life, all of which the Pāli discourse reckons

6 The passage on death seems to have been lost in MĀ 117, hence I have supplemented it here. That this is a case of loss can be seen from the ensuing part, which clearly covers the three predicaments of disease, old age, and death. The same can also be seen in a set of verses that in MĀ 117 follows the part translated above, which at T I 608a20 begins with the line: "being subject to disease, being subject to old age, and being subject to death". This makes it safe to conclude that the absence of the treatment of death in the present part of the discourse must be the result of an error of transmission. AN 3.38 does cover old age, disease, and death (in that sequence).

7 Here and elsewhere, the term "bodhisattva" refers to the Buddha during the period preceding his awakening and does not yet carry the connotations it came to have in later times.

to be due to being intoxicated with being young, healthy, and alive.[8]

Alongside such differences, the *Madhyama-āgama* and *Aṅguttara-nikāya* versions agree closely in throwing into relief the contrast between the average worldling and the bodhisattva's reaction to witnessing old age, disease, and death. A crucial difference here is that, whereas worldlings "do not examine themselves", the bodhisattva realized his own vulnerability to becoming old and sick, and the certainty of having to pass away. He did not allow his present youth, health, and being alive to distract him from recognizing this state of affairs.

In later hagiography this basic insight finds expression in the legend according to which during pleasure outings the bodhisattva happened to see for the first time in his life a diseased and an old person, as well as someone dead.[9] Alongside narrative embellishment leading to the implausible depiction of the bodhisattva as being up to that moment completely ignorant of these fundamental aspects of human life, the tale in a way serves to make the same point as the passage above. Confrontation with old age, disease, and death is what motivated the bodhisattva's going forth. The same finds expression in the *Ariyapariyesanā-sutta* and its *Madhyama-āgama* parallel, in which the Buddha depicts his "noble quest" to freedom from these predicaments of human life. The relevant passage in the *Madhyama-āgama* version proceeds in this way:[10]

> Formerly, when I had not yet awakened to supreme, right, and complete awakening, I further thought like this: "I am actually subject to disease myself and I naively search for what is subject to disease. I am actually subject to old age *myself and I naively search for what is subject to old age. I am actually* subject to death *myself and I naively search for what is subject to death. I am actually* subject to worry and sadness *myself and I naively search for what is subject to*

8 AN 3.39 at AN I 146,22.

9 See the discussion in Anālayo 2013b: 110f.

10 The translated passage is taken from MĀ 204 at T I 776a26 to 776b5 (translated Anālayo 2012b: 25f), parallel to MN 26 at MN I 163,9 (translated Ñāṇamoli 1995/2005: 256); for a comparative study of this episode see also Anālayo 2011: 171–4.

> *worry and sadness. I am actually* subject to defilement myself and I naively search for what is subject to defilement.
>
> "What if I now rather search for the supreme peace of Nirvāṇa, which is free from disease, search for the supreme peace of Nirvāṇa, which is free from old age, *search for the supreme peace of Nirvāṇa, which is* free from death, *search for the supreme peace of Nirvāṇa, which is* free from worry and sadness, *search for the supreme peace of Nirvāṇa, which is* free from defilement?"
>
> At that time I was a young lad, with clear [skin] and dark hair, in the prime of youth, twenty-nine years of age, roaming around well adorned and enjoying myself to the utmost. At that time I shaved off my hair and beard, while my father and mother were crying and my relatives were displeased. I put on monastic robes and went forth to leave the household life out of faith and to train in the path, maintaining purity of livelihood in body, and maintaining purity of livelihood in speech and in mind.

The *Ariyapariyesanā-sutta* differs in so far as it also mentions being subject to birth. It also does not give the exact age of the bodhisattva and has no counterpart to the last sentence on cultivating purity of livelihood and conduct. Alongside such variations, however, the two versions clearly agree in depicting the Buddha's quest as an existential one, based on the realization of being subject to predicaments like old age, disease, and death. These feature as aspects of the noble truth of *dukkha* in what according to tradition was the first teaching delivered by the Buddha after he completed his quest, a topic to which I will return in a subsequent chapter.[11] Clearly, recognition of the predicament of old age, disease, and death was central in inspiring the Buddha's quest and eventual awakening.

From the viewpoint of the modern-day living situation, particularly in the West, this might require some reflection in order to sink in fully. Hospital amenities, homes for the elderly, and the impressive degree to which death has been made as unnoticeable as possible can at times make it easy to overlook one's basic vulnerability to these three predicaments of human life. Yet the occurrence of any disease serves as a reminder of

---

11 See below p. 143.

the limitations of the human body.[12] The only way to avoid old age is to die when still young, hardly an attractive solution. Conversely, with the full impact of old age the body can reach a condition where death becomes almost a relief. In dependent arising (*paṭicca samuppāda*), old age and death in fact form a compound, perhaps reflecting that either the one or the other, if not both, will certainly manifest. In fact, in a way old age is gradual dying. Contemplating the above, it becomes possible to allow the facts of old age, disease, and death to stand out in their full significance and thereby become a motivating force for directing one's life in a way that takes these indubitable facts into account.

As a side note, it may be worth mentioning that the *Ariyapariyesanā-sutta* and its parallel both report that the bodhisattva's mother cried when he went forth.[13] This is to some extent unexpected, since according to tradition she passed away seven days after he was born.[14] Closer study of other passages related to this issue makes it fairly probable that the above reference is to the Buddha's foster mother, Mahāpajāpatī Gotamī.[15]

This passage is of interest not only because of the reference to the mother's crying, at first sight puzzling, but also in so far as it shows that the motif of the bodhisattva's secret departure at night is a later development of Buddhist hagiography, similar to the tale of his encounters with a sick and old person as well as a corpse. Instead of a secret departure at night, the above passage conveys the impression that he went forth with the knowledge of his parents and relatives, who reacted with displeasure and tears when he carried this out.[16]

These two hagiographic tales of the bodhisattva's outings and his secret departure at night could have had their origin in pictorial depictions of his insight into the human predicament

---

12 See in more detail Anālayo 2016b: 220–3.

13 The corresponding passage in a Sanskrit fragment parallel, 331r6, Liu 2010: 144, speaks of relatives in general who cried.

14 This contrast has already been noted by Bareau 1974: 249.

15 See in more detail Anālayo 2015b: 433–5.

16 Vijitha 2015: 61 points out that, contrary to the traditional hagiographic account, "Siddhartha's renunciation was not a secret. He renounced worldly life before his parents and relatives."

and his renunciation of sensual pleasures.[17] The employment of a kind of canvas carried around to deliver teachings is already reflected in the early discourses, making it quite possible that such depictions could have been in use at a comparatively early time.[18] On this assumption, such depictions might then have been taken literally by later generations.[19]

A poetic expression of the bodhisattva's insight that spurred him to go forth can also be found in a few verses in the *Attadaṇḍa-sutta*, found in the *Aṭṭhaka-vagga* of the *Sutta-nipāta*. Of this part of the *Sutta-nipāta*, a Chinese parallel has been preserved, which proceeds as follows:[20]

The whole world was [to me as if] all ablaze,[21]
All the ten directions [seemed to me] out of order and without peace.
Being conceited of themselves, they do not give up craving,
Because of lack of vision, they hold on to it with their ignorant minds.[22]

Do not create the entanglement of being in quest for the darkness of *dukkha*!
I contemplated it all and my mind did not delight
In that which leads to suffering and pain. I saw the dart,
By becoming still, one sees what is challenging and is able to endure it.[23]

---

17 Here I follow a suggestion made for the tale of the bodhisattva's encounters by Weller 1928: 169.

18 See Anālayo 2017c: 278.

19 Thomas 1927/2003: 58 concludes that "the story of the four visits to the park is only a historicising of a canonical passage which knows nothing of these events. The events have been merely built up out of the meditation on old age, sickness, and death. We find the same state of things in the story of the Renunciation."

20 The verses are found in T 198 at T IV 189b16 to 189b21 (translated Bapat 1950: 80), parallel to Sn 937 to 939 (translated Bodhi 2017: 315). That these refer to the bodhisattva's pre-awakening insight seems implied in T 198 at T IV 189b13 and Sn 935.

21 Instead of being ablaze, according to Sn 937 the whole world is without essence.

22 The second half of Sn 937 instead describes that, wishing for a dwelling place for himself, the bodhisattva did not see one that was not occupied.

23 Sn 938 proceeds quite differently; a common element is the idea of seeing a dart.

> Following this dart of pain, obstinately and without leaving it behind,
> Cherishing this dart, one runs all over the world.
> Honouring proper view, one pulls out the painful dart.
> One's tribulations are forgotten and one no longer runs [around].[24]

The first stanza brings out vividly the agitation caused by seeing the all-pervasiveness of old age, disease, and death, which according to an explanation given in the *Niddesa* is the implication of the reference to the different directions being in turmoil.[25] This stands in contrast to the conceit and ignorance depicted in the *Madhyama-āgama* passage translated at the outset of this chapter. The conceit of being young, healthy, and alive is inseparable from ignoring the inevitable fact of old age, disease, and death, an ignorance that provides the fertile soil for craving to grow.

The second stanza's reference to a quest for the darkness of *dukkha* relates to the basic distinction drawn in the *Ariyapariyesanā-sutta* and its *Madhyama-āgama* parallel between two type of quests, an ignoble one and a noble one. Needless to say, the noble quest is what motivated the Buddha to go forth, to remain still, as the verse says, instead of running around, thereby becoming able to see the challenging truth of *dukkha* and learn to endure it.

The third stanza again plays on the basic contrast also made in the other passages translated in this chapter. According to the *Niddesa*, the "dart" stands for lust, hatred, delusion, conceit, views, sorrow, and perplexity.[26] How to go about pulling out this dart will be the topic of the next chapters.

EXERCISE

As a practical exercise, I suggest making an effort to recognize manifestations of old age, sickness, and death around us throughout the day. For such recollection it would be relevant

---

24 Sn 939 makes basically the same point in a briefer fashion.

25 Nidd I 410,18, which adds that the same also stands for being subject to birth, impermanence, and *dukkha*.

26 Nidd I 412,23.

that the *Ariyapariyesanā-sutta* and its *Madhyama-āgama* parallel agree in considering various forms of wealth and possessions to be subject to old age, disease, and death.[27] This implies that these three predicaments can be noticed in various material things, not only in people or other living beings. All beings and things are bound to get old, bound to lose their functionality gradually, and bound to break apart in the end.

Based on such an extended scope of observation, the next step is to realize the inevitability of being ourselves subject to ageing, illness, and passing away. Given this inescapable predicament, how should we best formulate our own "noble quest"? In view of mortality and the vulnerability of this body to becoming old and sick, what is really worth dedicating ourselves to? How can we best prepare for facing these inevitable predicaments of human life? What would best be the central motivation that gives direction to our life and informs our daily activities and meditation practice? Engaging in such reflections can become a way of following the example of the Buddha-to-be.

27 MN 26 at MN I 162,12 and MĀ 204 at T I 776a7.

II

MORAL CONDUCT

With this chapter I turn to the future Buddha's moral conduct, which he undertook after having gone forth. This is described in the *Bhayabherava-sutta*, the Discourse on Fear and Dread, and its *Ekottarika-āgama* parallel. As the title of the Pāli discourse indicates, the topic of fear is central to the exposition. The relevant passage has its place after a brief exchange between the Buddha and a visiting brahmin on the difficulty of dwelling in seclusion. Here is an extract from the *Ekottarika-āgama* version:[1]

> At the time [when I was still a bodhisattva], I had this reflection in turn:
>
> "Any recluses or brahmins whose bodily conduct is impure and who frequent secluded dwellings and solitary places with impure bodily conduct, their efforts are in vain, their practice is not genuine, [they will experience] fear as well as evil and unwholesome states. But I now frequent secluded dwellings and [solitary] places with a bodily conduct that is pure. To frequent secluded and quiet places with any impure bodily conduct is not found in me. The reason is that my bodily conduct is now pure."
>
> I am very much a leader for arahants who have purity of bodily conduct and who delight in secluded dwellings, caves, and [solitary] places. Like this, brahmin, seeing in myself such

1 The translated passage is taken from EĀ 31.1 at T II 665c2 to 665c19 (translated Anālayo 2016a: 14f), parallel to MN 4 at MN I 17,11 (translated Ñāṇamoli 1995/2005: 102f); for a comparative study see Anālayo 2011: 38.

> purity of bodily conduct, I delight in secluded dwelling places, [experiencing] increasing joy.
>
> At the time [when I was still a bodhisattva], I in turn had this reflection:
>
> "Any recluses or brahmins, whose [verbal and] mental conduct is impure, or whose livelihood is impure, and who frequent secluded dwellings and solitary places, even though they practise like this, yet [their practice] is not genuine, they are filled with all [kinds] of evil and unwholesome states. That is not found in me. The reason is that now my ⟨ ⟩[2] verbal and mental conduct, as well as my livelihood, is pure. Whatever recluses or brahmins, who have ⟨ ⟩ verbal and mental [purity], as well as purity of livelihood, they delight in staying in seclusion and in dwelling with purity in [solitary] places. That is the case with me. The reason is that I now have [purity] of ⟨ ⟩ verbal and mental conduct, as well as purity of livelihood."
>
> I am very much a leader for arahants who have ⟨ ⟩ verbal and mental [purity], as well as purity of livelihood, and who delight in staying in seclusion and in quiet places. Like this, brahmin, given that I have ⟨ ⟩ verbal and mental [purity], as well as purity of livelihood, when staying in seclusion and quiet places I [experience] increasing joy.

The *Bhayabherava-sutta* similarly highlights the importance of having pure moral conduct in its bodily, verbal, and mental dimensions, as well as purity of livelihood, in order to be able to dwell in seclusion without giving rise to fear and dread. This reflects a recurrent emphasis in early Buddhist thought on the need to establish a sound foundation in ethical conduct for meditation practice to be successful.

In my book on *Mindfully Facing Disease and Death* I took up the relationship between moral conduct and fear at the time of disease and death.[3] Of relevance here is that the observance of the precepts can become a way of making a gift of fearlessness to

---

2 Here and below, the use of ⟨ ⟩ signals an emendation. The text repeats "bodily", which I have not translated on the assumption that this is a textual error, as bodily conduct has already been covered in the preceding paragraph.

3 Anālayo 2016b: 79.

others. By pledging oneself to refrain from conduct that inflicts harm on others, such as killing, stealing, etc., one becomes someone whom others do not need to fear. Having made such a gift of fearlessness, one in turn gains fearlessness when sick or on the verge of death, through being free from regret. It is the dimension of freedom from regret that is similarly relevant in the present context.

Besides, the reference in the *Bhayabherava-sutta* and its parallel to seclusion as a situation that can easily encourage the arising of fear reflects an idea pervasive in the ancient Indian setting, according to which nature is seen as dangerous and threatening.[4] The *Ākaṅkheyya-sutta* and its *Madhyama-āgama* parallel list absence of fear among a range of wishes a monastic might have,[5] confirming that this was an issue among monastic disciples, presumably in particular among those who lived in secluded settings.

A discourse in the *Aṅguttara-nikāya*, of which unfortunately no parallel is known, brings out in what way external nature can become fearful to one who lives in seclusion.[6] Being all alone in the forest, one might be bitten by a snake, a scorpion, or a centipede, or else one might be attacked by a lion, a tiger, a leopard, a bear, or a hyena, and because of that one's life might come to an end. Even if one should not encounter a dangerous animal, one might fall sick and, being alone and without support, pass away because of this. Yet another potential source of sudden death could be criminals who have escaped to the forest and might kill one. Such were potential dangers of dwelling in seclusion in the ancient Indian setting.

---

4 See, e.g., Schmithausen 1991: 29 and 1997 as well as Boucher 2008: 54.

5 MN 6 at MN I 33,26 (translated Ñāṇamoli 1995/2005: 115f) and MĀ 105 at T I 596a3; see also AN 10.71 at AN V 132,17 (translated Bodhi 2012: 1427) and for a survey of the listings in these versions as well as in another parallel, EĀ 37.5, Anālayo 2011: 47f.

6 AN 5.77 at AN III 101,5 (translated Bodhi 2012: 709f). Although this *Aṅguttara-nikāya* discourse does not appear to have a parallel, this could simply be the result of the somewhat accidental distribution of discourses among the *Āgamas* where, in particular in the case of the *Ekottarika-āgama* preserved in Chinese, only a fraction of the discourses have parallels in the *Aṅguttara-nikāya*. In other words, absence of a parallel does not in itself automatically imply that a discourse is late.

The *Aṅguttara-nikāya* discourse's survey of potential sources of danger when alone in an ancient Indian forest makes it clear that the problem of fear does not refer only to regret experienced from within, but also to dread aroused by external causes. The *Bhayabherava-sutta* and its parallel explicitly take up this topic, reporting how the bodhisattva, having established a firm foundation in moral conduct and thereby removed internal causes for the arising of fear, faced fear arisen due to external causes. The relevant passage from the *Ekottarika-āgama* proceeds in this way:[7]

> While I was staying in secluded dwellings, if at that time the branch of a tree broke, or a bird or an animal ran by, I had this reflection: "This is [what causes] great fear in a forest." Then I further had this reflection: "If fear comes, I will seek a means to prevent it from coming again."
>
> If fear and dread came while I was walking, then at that time I did not sit or else lie down, determining to discard that fear and dread, and [only] afterwards did I sit down. Suppose fear and dread came while I was standing, then at that time I did not walk or else sit down, determining to discard that fear and dread, and [only] afterwards did I sit down. If fear and dread came while I was sitting, I did not walk [or else stand], determining to discard that fear and dread, and [only] afterwards did I walk.[8] If fear and dread came while I was lying down, then at that time I did not walk or else even sit up, determining to discard that fear and dread,[9] and [only] afterwards did I sit up.[10]

The *Bhayabherava-sutta* similarly describes how, on hearing some unexpected sound in the forest, the bodhisattva would face the arising of any fear by remaining in the same bodily posture. This exemplifies a basic attitude that is particularly salient in mindfulness training, where one learns to stay aware

7 The translated passage is based on EĀ 31.1 at T II 666a28 to 666b9, parallel to MN 4 at MN I 20,37.

8 The translation is based on adopting the variant "walking" instead of a reference to "sitting", which seems out of context.

9 The translation is based on adopting a variant without an additional character that is also not found in the previous passages.

10 The translation is based on adopting the variant "sitting" instead of a reference to "lying down", which seems out of context.

of what happens without immediately reacting to it. In the present case this is the arising of fear, which is met simply by remaining with mindfulness of the body in the present moment, rather than allowing apprehension of what might happen next to take control of one's mind. When hearing an unexpected sound in the forest, a natural reaction would be to change one's posture in order to be able to find out what is about to happen and be able to meet any potential source of danger to the best of one's ability. Or else one might at least wish to get a little bit away or undertake some other bodily action to distract oneself from the fear. Instead, whenever fear arose, the future Buddha made it a practice that he would quietly remain with mindfulness of the body in the very posture in which he had been, when the fear arose, until it naturally subsided.[11] In this way the mind stays quietly in the present moment with what is, instead of leaning into the next moment out of a concern with what will be.

In a way the same attitude of standing still also informs moral restraint, inasmuch as when faced with one temptation or another, one rather decides to stay put, so to speak, instead of reacting in an unwholesome manner. In fact the significance of the future Buddha's moral conduct goes beyond the topic of fear, as it established the indispensable foundation for his meditative practice and eventual gaining of awakening. From the viewpoint of early Buddhist thought, without building up a firm foundation in this way, sustained progress in meditation and the gradual liberation of the mind from defilements can hardly be expected. This is not just because agitation due to regret and a bad conscience tend to interfere with mental composure and tranquillity. Another dimension of the same is that one's overall conduct needs to be in line with the goal of one's aspirations in order to be able to lead to it. Every single step taken against the pull of defilements, even if it only manifests as maintenance of

11 Giustarini 2012: 529 comments on the present passage in MN 4 that "an absence of physical movement promotes a state of equanimity which in turn allows the overcoming of fear. Physical stillness and stability seem to be able to inspire mental stillness and stability, which are helpful remedies in counteracting and eventually eradicating fear." On mindfulness of the body see also Anālayo 2013b: 55–61 and 2017b: 39–43.

basic ethics, is in line with and therefore a step closer to the final goal of total freedom from defilements.

For the purpose of establishing such a foundation by way of moral restraint, a discourse in the *Saṃyutta-nikāya* and its *Saṃyukta-āgama* parallel offer a helpful reflection. In the case of abstaining from killing, the Chinese version describes the following reflection:[12]

> "If someone wishes to kill me, that is not enjoyable to me. What is not enjoyable to me, for another it is also like that. [So], how could I kill another?"
>
> Having had this reflection, one undertakes not to kill living beings and does not enjoy when living beings are killed.

The *Saṃyutta-nikāya* version explains that such a reflection motivates one to abstain from killing, to encourage others to abstain in the same way, and to speak in praise of such abstention. The two versions apply the same principle to other types of moral misconduct. Although the principle underlying this reflection itself probably needs no further comment, I would nevertheless like to draw attention to the fact that this involves both compassion and mindfulness.[13] It is precisely by establishing a flexible and open attitude through mindfulness that one can put oneself mentally into the situation of another, based on which compassion naturally arises and stops one from doing what is harmful to others.

Besides mindfulness and compassion, another source of inspiration for keeping the precepts is that one thereby emulates the conduct of a Buddha and his arahant disciples. This comes to the fore in a discourse addressed to a female householder, versions of which are found in the *Aṅguttara-nikāya* and in the *Madhyama-āgama*. Here is the part relevant to the topic of killing from the *Madhyama-āgama* discourse:[14]

---

12 The translated passage is taken from SĀ 1044 at T II 273b16 to 273b18, parallel to SN 55.7 at SN V 353,29 (translated Bodhi 2000: 1797); for a Gāndhārī parallel see Allon in Glass 2007: 12.

13 On various dimensions of compassion in the early discourses see Anālayo 2015a: 5–74.

14 The translated passage is taken from MĀ 202 at T I 770b25 to 770c2, parallel to AN 3.70 at AN I 211,18 (translated Bodhi 2012: 298f).

> For their whole life arahants, "worthy ones",[15] refrain from killing, abandon killing, giving up knife and stick [out of a sense of] shame and scruple, with a mental attitude of *mettā* and compassion, with empathy for all beings,[16] including insects; they purify their minds from killing living beings.
>
> For my whole life I also refrain from killing, abandon killing, giving up knife and stick [out of a sense of] shame and scruple, with a mental attitude of *mettā* and compassion, with empathy for all beings, including insects; I am now purifying my mind from killing living beings.
>
> In this respect I am similar to arahants, not different from them.

A minor difference in the *Aṅguttara-nikāya* version is that insects do not find explicit mention. The same difference recurs among other parallels to this discourse extant in Chinese translation, two of which do not mention insects,[17] whereas another two parallels mention worms and insects.[18]

The basic principle underlying this reflection serves to highlight that by abstaining from killing, and by extension refraining from other types of unwholesome conduct, one is emulating the conduct of arahants. However much at present one's mind may seem far removed from total freedom from defilements, at least inasmuch as moral conduct is concerned, one can indeed come to be "similar to arahants, not different from them". Needless to say, every single moment one cultivates being similar to arahants in this way is yet another step closer to becoming one of them oneself.

Besides extending the above reflection to other dimensions of moral conduct, the *Aṅguttara-nikāya* discourse and its *Madhyama-*

---

15 "Worthy one" is the literal meaning of the term arahant. The Chinese original uses two phrases that both correspond to arahant. The first of these is a phonetic rendering and the second a translation of the term, which rendered literally would be "true person". My translation as "worthy one" reflects the underlying Indic term rather than its Chinese rendering.

16 Although the couplet of Chinese characters used in this part of the original means more literally "benefit", it can also serve to render *anukampā* and this sense seems most appropriate to the context.

17 T 89 at T I 913a25 and EĀ 24.6 at T II 625b15.

18 T 87 at T I 911a18 and T 88 at T I 912b6; on this type of difference see also Martini 2012: 60 note 38.

āgama parallel also bring in the six recollections, *anussati*, one of which is precisely to recollect one's own moral conduct. The *Madhyama-āgama* version describes this in the following manner:[19]

> One recollects one's own morality: "[My morality] is not deficient, not defective, not defiled, not corrupted; it is extensively and widely [undertaken] without expecting a reward, as praised by the wise. I am well endowed with it, well inclined towards it, well undertaking it, and well upholding it."
>
> One who has recollected one's own morality in this way will in turn gain the ceasing of any evil pondering, and will also gain the ceasing of any defiled, evil, and unwholesome state.

The *Aṅguttara-nikāya* discourse and its *Madhyama-āgama* parallel agree in comparing the effect of such recollection to cleaning a dirty mirror through appropriate means until it becomes shiny and bright. This illustration makes it clear, I think, that such recollection is not meant only for those who already have completely pure moral conduct. Instead, recollection of one's morality is of relevance to those whose situation is similar to a dirty mirror, in the sense that, by paying attention to the clean and bright places in the mirror of one's own mind and making an effort to clear away any dirt, the mind will become ever more bright and shiny. Another point of the simile is that the motivation to clean a mirror comes from having looked at it. Similarly, looking at one's own morality by way of recollection can go a long way in strengthening one's motivation to keep improving the ethical foundation of one's life and practice.

EXERCISE

By way of putting into practice the aspects of recollection of morality described above, I would recommend monitoring our own conduct carefully in order to see for ourselves how it affects the condition of our mind. Such careful monitoring can bring to light the degree to which the ethical dimension of our

19 The translated passage is based on MĀ 202 at T I 772a1 to 772a4, parallel to AN 3.70 at AN I 210,1.

behaviour directly impacts on what happens in the mind. The task with such monitoring is not only to focus on unwholesome conduct and transgressions, but also to be aware of whatever wholesome conduct we may be able to identify. Every single instance of wholesome conduct or at least refraining from what is unwholesome, however small it may be, can be used to arouse a sense of compassion and joyful inspiration – compassion in the sense of realizing that we are doing to others what we would wish others do to us; inspiration in the sense that, by acting in this way, we share the beauty of virtuous conduct with arahants. Whenever we successfully refrain from an unwholesome action, this can become a source of joy by recollecting that this is what the Buddha would have encouraged us to do.

III

OBSTACLES TO CONCENTRATION

In this chapter I take up passages related to the future Buddha's overcoming of mental obstructions to the attainment of absorption. The indispensable foundation for such overcoming is of course a clear recognition of those conditions of the mind that are obstructive. Unless one recognizes obstructions for what they are, one will hardly be able to overcome them.

The basic insight that informs such recognition comes to the fore in the *Dvedhāvitakka-sutta* and its *Madhyama-āgama* parallel. According to the first part of the relevant passage, which I already translated in my *Perspectives on Satipaṭṭhāna*,[1] during the time before his awakening the Buddha had decided to divide his thoughts into two types. One of these two types covers thoughts of sensuality, ill will, and harming; the other type corresponds to their absence. The *Dvedhāvitakka-sutta* and its *Madhyama-āgama* parallel agree in reporting that, whenever the bodhisattva experienced any thought of the first type, he understood that such thought is harmful to oneself and others, that it destroys wisdom and does not lead to Nirvāṇa. On realizing this, he was able to abandon it.

Besides throwing into relief the basic ethical distinction between what is wholesome and what is unwholesome, as well as the underlying reason for this distinction, the passage is also significant as it shows that, before reaching awakening, even

1 Anālayo 2013b: 146f.

the Buddha himself had to deal with unwholesome thoughts. It can be helpful to remind oneself that the Buddha-to-be had to face the same difficulties and the disconcerting realization that unwholesomeness is in the mind, just as most of us do. In this way, by clearly recognizing that one's present mental condition belongs to the first of these two types, and that to continue dwelling in this condition is harmful and contrary to progress on the path, one follows in the footsteps of the Buddha, however distant he may seem. It is precisely such following in his footsteps that will bring one gradually closer to the total liberation from defilements that he had realized.

The same basic distinction between what is wholesome and what is unwholesome is in fact a characteristic of the teachings of a Buddha or Tathāgata. This is highlighted in the *Itivuttaka* and its Chinese parallel, which proceeds as follows:[2]

> The modes of teaching the Dharma by all Tathāgatas, arahants, rightly and fully awakened ones, are of two types. What are the two? The first is that one should rightly understand what is detrimental; the second is that one should become thoroughly disgusted by and turn away from what is detrimental.

Of the unwholesome thoughts mentioned earlier, in accounts of the Buddha's pre-awakening period the theme of sensuality is fairly prominent. According to the passage translated in the first chapter of this book, in his youth the bodhisattva would spend the whole summer season in the company of women whose task was to entertain him.[3] The same type of depiction can also be found in the *Māgandiya-sutta*, although in this case the *Madhyama-āgama* parallel does not have such a description.[4] The two discourses agree, however, that the Buddha explicitly acknowledged that during the time before his awakening he engaged in the pursuit and enjoyment of sensual pleasures. The Chinese version of the passage in question proceeds as follows:[5]

---

2 The translated passage is taken from T 765 at T XVII 676c24 to 676c26, parallel to It 39 at It 33,10 (translated Ireland 1991: 28), which speaks of the Tathāgata in the singular, instead of mentioning all Tathāgatas.

3 See above p. 5.

4 MN 75 at MN I 504,24 (translated Ñāṇamoli 1995/2005: 609f); for a comparative study see Anālayo 2011: 409.

5 The translated passage is based on MĀ 153 at T I 671a24 to 671a28.

> When I had not yet gone forth to train in the path, I obtained the five cords of sensual pleasure, obtaining easily and without difficulty what is longed for and pleases the mind, what is likeable and conjoined with sensual pleasure. Subsequently I gave up the five cords of sensual pleasure, shaved off my hair and beard, put on the monastic robes, and left the household life out of faith and became homeless to train in the path. Seeing as it really is the arising and ceasing of the five cords of sensual pleasure, their gratification, their disadvantage, and the escape from them, I dwelt with a mind that is at peace within.

In the *Māgandiya-sutta* and its parallel the Buddha continues by describing how, being with a mind inwardly at peace in this way, he did not envy others who enjoy sensual pleasures. Both discourses make it clear that, from the viewpoint of one who has gained freedom from sensual desire, those who indulge in sensual pleasures can seem similar to a leper who cauterizes his wounds over a fire. Although this action brings about temporary relief, it causes a gradual deterioration of the leper's affliction. Just as a leper who has been healed would vigorously resist being brought close to the fire he previously so eagerly sought to cauterize his wounds, similarly one who has gained the inner health of being free from sensual desire will want to avoid the fiery pit of sensuality.

A discourse in the *Saṃyutta-nikāya* and its *Saṃyukta-āgama* parallel take up the same theme of the Buddha's pre-awakening pursuit of sensual pleasures, followed in a subsequent passage by a hint regarding what it means to have a mind that is truly at peace within. Here is the first part of the relevant passage from the *Saṃyukta-āgama* version:[6]

> Formerly, when I had not yet attained full awakening, I was meditating alone in a quiet place and thought: "I should examine: what direction does my own mind often incline towards?"
>
> My own mind often pursued the five cords of sense pleasure of the past, it seldom pursues the five strands of sense pleasure

6 The translated passage is taken from SĀ 211 at T II 53a27 to 53b4 (translated Anālayo 2016c: 33), parallel to SN 35.117 at SN IV 97,18 (translated Bodhi 2000: 1190f).

> of the present, and it very seldom keeps revolving in those of the future.[7]
>
> When I had contemplated that my mind often pursued the ⟨five⟩ sense pleasures of the past,[8] I thoroughly aroused energy and effort to guard myself so that I would not again follow after the five strands of sense pleasure of the past. Because of this diligent self-protection, I gradually drew closer to supreme and right awakening.

This confirms that during his quest for awakening the Buddha had to make an effort to guard his mind against the attraction of sensual pleasures. The same is also evident in a discourse in the *Aṅguttara-nikāya*, of which no parallel is known. According to this discourse, before his awakening the Buddha found that his mind did not fully incline towards renunciation and solitude because he had not thoroughly seen the disadvantage in sensuality.[9] Nevertheless, he was strongly determined to emerge from the attraction of sensual pleasures. According to the *Pabbajā-sutta* and a parallel in the *Mahāvastu*, after going forth the future Buddha was so intent on pursuing the path to awakening that he could not be tempted to return to lay life even with lavish offers made by a contemporary king.[10]

The *Saṃyukta-āgama* discourse translated above and its *Saṃyutta-nikāya* parallel continue with an injunction by the Buddha to the monastics listening to the discourse that they should also go beyond the attraction of sensual pleasures. Next comes a passage which points to what leads beyond concern with sensuality (corresponding to what in the terms of the *Māgandiya-sutta* and its parallel is the "escape" from sensual pleasures) and what results in "dwelling with a mind at peace". The relevant part in the *Saṃyukta-āgama* reads as follows:[11]

7 In SN 35.117 at SN IV 97,20 past and present sense pleasures hold similar attraction and only those of the future are qualified to do so to a lesser degree.

8 The translation "five" is based on an emendation; the original reads "right".

9 AN 9.41 at AN IV 439,23 (translated Bodhi 2012: 1310).

10 Sn 424 (translated Bodhi 2017: 225) and Senart 1890: 199,17 (translated Jones 1952/1976: 190).

11 The translation is based on SĀ 211 at T II 53b12 to 53b14, parallel to SN 35.117 at SN IV 98,3.

> Therefore, monastics, you should realize that sphere wherein the eye ceases and which then is apart from perception of forms, wherein the ear *ceases and which then is apart from perception of sounds, wherein* the nose *ceases and which then is apart from perception of odours, wherein* the tongue *ceases and which then is apart from perception of flavours, wherein* the body *ceases and which then is apart from perception of tangibles, wherein* the mind ceases and which then is apart from perception of mental objects.

According to both versions, the monastics in the audience failed to understand the full significance of what the Buddha had said. They went to get further elucidation from Ānanda, who explained that the Buddha had spoken in reference to the "cessation of the six sense-spheres" – in other words, Nirvāṇa. The experience of Nirvāṇa puts into perspective any concern with the type of pleasure that can be experienced through the sense-doors.

In the case of the Buddha's own quest for Nirvāṇa, the removal of sensuality formed an important condition for progress on the path. This finds expression in the *Mahāsaccaka-sutta* and its Sanskrit fragment parallel in a set of three similes that involve a piece of wood and the attempt to make a fire. The first part of the simile in the Sanskrit version proceeds in this way:[12]

> It is just as if a wet and sappy piece of wood were to be thrown into water close by the shore and a person were to come in quest of fire, searching fire.

One would not be able to make fire with wood that is wet and still in the water. In the same way, it is not possible to progress to awakening when one is still indulging in sensual pleasures.

The *Mahāsaccaka-sutta* and its Sanskrit fragment parallel take the same imagery further, pointing out that it is not only necessary to abstain from actual indulgence in sensual pleasures, but one even has to wean one's mind from being obsessed with

---

12 The translated passage is found in fragment 335v7f, Liu 2010: 208, parallel to MN 36 at MN I 240,30 (translated Ñāṇamoli 1995/2005: 335); for a comparative study see Anālayo 2011: 235f. The point of the simile in both versions is to drive home that this applies independently of whether one engages in ascetic practices or not, a topic to which I return in Chapters 6 to 8.

them. The situation of one who, having left behind a life of sensual enjoyment, is still mentally obsessed with sensuality finds illustration in a wet piece of wood that has been taken out of the water. Even though the wood is no longer in the water, it is nonetheless wet and therefore still not useable to kindle a fire. Once the wood has become dry, however, it can function as fuel for a fire, just as, once the mind has at least temporarily reached aloofness from sensual desires, it will be possible to realize awakening.

A wholesome condition of the mind, which in terms of the above simile corresponds to dry wood, is described in the *Dvedhāvitakka-sutta* and its *Madhyama-āgama* parallel, mentioned at the outset of this chapter in relation to the basic distinction between unwholesome and wholesome thoughts. According to the *Madhyama-āgama* parallel to the *Dvedhāvitakka-sutta*, the Buddha's pre-awakening practice took the following form in relation to wholesome thoughts:[13]

> Practising like this, staying in a remote and secluded place, cultivating diligently a mind free from negligence, a thought without sensual desire arose in me. I realized that a thought without sensual desire had arisen. [I realized that] this is not harmful to myself, not harmful to others, and not harmful in both respects, that it [leads to] developing wisdom without difficulty and to attaining Nirvāṇa. On realizing that it is not harmful to myself, not harmful to others, and not harmful in both respects, and that it [leads to] developing wisdom without difficulty and to attaining Nirvāṇa, I in turn swiftly developed it and made much of it.
>
> Again, *practising like this, staying in a remote and secluded place, cultivating diligently a mind free from negligence,* a thought without ill will arose in me. I realized that a thought without ill will had arisen. [I realized that] this is not harmful to myself, not harmful to others, and not harmful in both respects, that it [leads to] developing wisdom without difficulty and to attaining Nirvāṇa. On realizing that it is not harmful to myself, not harmful to others,

13 The translation is based on MĀ 102 at T I 589b11 to 589b23, parallel to MN 19 at MN I 116,1 (translated Ñāṇamoli 1995/2005: 208f); for a comparative study see Anālayo 2011: 139.

and not harmful in both respects, and that it [leads to] developing wisdom without difficulty and to attaining Nirvāṇa, I in turn swiftly developed it and made much of it.

Again, *practising like this, staying in a remote and secluded place, cultivating diligently a mind free from negligence*, a thought without harming *arose in me. I realized that a* thought without harming *had arisen. I realized that this is not harmful to myself, not harmful to others, and not harmful in both respects, that it leads to developing wisdom without difficulty and to attaining Nirvāṇa. On realizing that it is not harmful to myself, not harmful to others, and not harmful in both respects, and that it leads to developing wisdom without difficulty and to attaining Nirvāṇa, I in turn swiftly developed it and made much of it.*

[When] a thought without sensual desire arose in me, I thought of it much. [When] a thought without ill will *arose in me, I thought of it much*. [When] a thought without harming arose *in me*, I thought of it much.

Again I thought: "The bodily composure and joy of one who thinks much will be lost and the mind will in turn be strained. Let me rather keep my mind in check within, constantly dwelling with inner tranquillity and mental unification in the attainment of concentration, so that my mind will not be strained."

Subsequently I in turn kept my mind in check within, constantly dwelling with inner tranquillity and mental unification in the attainment of concentration; and my mind was not strained.

The otherwise similar presentation in the *Dvedhāvitakka-sutta* adds that the bodhisattva saw nothing fearful in thinking such wholesome thoughts even for a whole day and night. The reason is that, as noted in both versions, the tendencies of one's mind are influenced by the type of thought one thinks. In other words, to keep thinking in wholesome ways will strengthen the tendency of the mind towards what is wholesome. The *Madhyama-āgama* version describes this tendency in the case of wholesome thoughts in this manner:[14]

In accordance with what one intends, in accordance with what one thinks, the mind in turn delights in that. If a monastic thinks

14 The translated passage is taken from MĀ 102 at T I 589c5 to 589c9, parallel to MN 19 at MN I 116,27.

> many thoughts without sensual desire and abandons thoughts with sensual desire, because of thinking many thoughts without sensual desire, the mind in turn delights in that.
>
> If a monastic thinks many thoughts without ill will and abandons thoughts with ill will, because of thinking many thoughts without ill will, the mind in turn delights in that.
>
> *If a monastic thinks many* thoughts without harming *and abandons* thoughts with harming, *because of thinking many* thoughts without harming, *the mind in turn delights in that.*

Nevertheless, as pointed out in both versions, excessive thinking is not conducive to concentration. Although training the mind in wholesome thought habits goes a long way in preparing entry into deeper experiences of concentration, excessive thinking will eventually prevent further progress. To the need to fine-tune the mind so as to lead it into absorption attainment I will turn in the next chapter.

EXERCISE

Probably the most important feature to be taken away from this chapter is the fundamental distinction between wholesome and unwholesome types of thought, and I would suggest making this also the theme of practical exploration. Such exploration can be based on the same basic distinction that the *Satipaṭṭhāna-sutta* and its parallels introduce with the first states of mind they list for contemplation, where the task is to recognize whether the mind is in the mode of sensual lust or not, for example, or else whether it is operating under the influence of anger or its opposite, etc.[15] In this way, we monitor with mindfulness the condition of our own mind, based on the twofold distinction that according to the *Dvedhāvitakka-sutta* and its parallels was such an integral part of the Buddha's pre-awakening progress to liberation.

Sustained practice in this way will eventually lead to realizing for ourselves the truth of the indication in the same discourse that whatever we think much of will in turn become an inclination of the mind. In a way, the famous statement by Descartes "I

15 See in more detail Anālayo 2013b: 142–8.

think, therefore I am" could be adapted to become: "(Because of what) I think, therefore I am (who I am)." Or else, to put the same more succinctly: "I become what I think."

This sets the background for appreciating that even just conceptual reflection based on the *brahmavihāras*, for example, will have an effect on our mind, which can be considerably strengthened by engaging in their meditative cultivation.[16] Every moment we are with an attitude of *mettā*, compassion, sympathetic joy, or equanimity will leave its impact not only on others, but also on our own mental household.

The realization that what we think influences our own mind not only draws attention to the perils of letting our thoughts run their course unchecked. It at the same time also opens the vista to personal transformation through the simple method of cultivating wholesome thinking instead of letting the mind dwell on what is unwholesome, be this of its own accord or due to being influenced by negative input from the outside through conversations, news, the internet, etc. Throughout, we do our best to stay with what is wholesome and keep away from what is unwholesome. As simple as this may seem, it is a way of walking in the footsteps of the Buddha.

16 On the meditative cultivation of the *brahmavihāras* see in more detail Anālayo 2015a: 151–62.

IV

ABSORPTION

The present chapter relates closely to the preceding one, in which I took up the future Buddha's overcoming of obstructions to the cultivation of deeper levels of concentration. This topic receives a more detailed exposition in the *Upakkilesa-sutta* and its *Madhyama-āgama* parallel, in which the Buddha describes his own struggle to gain absorption to a group of monastics, headed by Anuruddha, to help them deepen their concentration. Here is the first section of the relevant part from the *Madhyama-āgama* version:[1]

> I practised diligently, without negligence, my body was tranquil and settled, I had right mindfulness and right comprehension, I was without confusion, and I attained concentration and mental unification. [I thought]: "What in the world does not exist,[2] can I see, can I know that?" This affliction by doubt arose in my mind. Because of this affliction by doubt, my concentration in turn was lost and my [inner] eye disappeared. With the disappearance of my [inner] eye, the bright light and the vision of forms I had

1 The translated passage is taken from MĀ 72 at T I 536c26 to 537a1, parallel to MN 128 at MN III 157,29 (translated Ñāṇamoli 1995/2005: 1012); for a comparative study see Anālayo 2011: 736–8.

2 The translation is based on adopting the variant "is" instead of "path". This adoption follows versions of this passage found in the *Abhidharmakośabhāṣya*, Pradhan 1967: 300,12: *yat tat loka nāsti*, and in the Tibetan parallel, D 4094 *ju* 276a6 or Q 5595 *thu* 20a8: *gang yang 'jig rten na med pa*.

earlier attained, that vision of forms and bright light quickly disappeared again.

In what precedes this passage in the *Upakkilesa-sutta* and its parallel, Anuruddha and his companions had told the Buddha that they had experienced bright light and vision of forms, which then had disappeared. In the *Upakkilesa-sutta* Anuruddha states that they failed to penetrate or apprehend the "sign", *nimitta*, responsible for this.[3] In the *Madhyama-āgama* version it is the Buddha himself who points out that they had not penetrated the "sign".[4]

The expression "sign" in the present context is open to different interpretations.[5] The term *nimitta* can have just a plain causal sense. On following this causal sense, the idea behind the need to penetrate the *nimitta* would be that Anuruddha and his companions needed to discover the "cause" for the disappearance of their meditative visions. This way of understanding fits the context well, since in both versions the Buddha continued by describing a set of mental obstructions that were the cause of the disappearance of their meditative visions.[6]

Another and related meaning of the same term *nimitta* is a "mark", in the sense of the characteristics of phenomena by which perception recognizes an object. This meaning preserves the causal nuance, since it is due to the *nimitta* that recognition takes place. In a more specific sense, such a "sign" also plays a role in relation to the practice of meditation, in the sense of the characteristic or mark that, on being given attention, will become the condition for entry into deep concentration. The use of *nimitta* in the sense of a meditative "sign" as a causal factor in the gaining of absorption attainment comes to the fore particularly in the commentaries, where it regularly stands for the meditative object used for entering into deeper levels of

---

3 MN 128 at MN III 157,27; a partial Tibetan parallel in D 4094 *ju* 276a3 or Q 5595 *thu* 20a3 employs the corresponding *rgyu mtshan*.

4 MĀ 72 at T I 536c18: "you have not penetrated that sign, that is, the sign for attaining bright light and visions of forms."

5 For a survey of different senses of *nimitta* see Anālayo 2003b.

6 The Pāli commentary on the present passage, Ps IV 207,13, in fact takes *nimitta* in a causal sense.

mental tranquillity. Nevertheless, already the early discourses employ the term *nimitta* in contexts related to the development of concentration.[7] These two uses are clearly not identical. Nevertheless, the canonical use does to some degree provide a precedent for the commentaries in this respect.

This sense of *nimitta* as a mental "sign" or object used for the development of concentration would also fit the present context. At a later point of its exposition, the *Upakkilesa-sutta* in fact explicitly uses the term *nimitta* in order to refer to the vision of light and forms that Anuruddha and his companions had been unable to stabilize, a usage where *nimitta* clearly stands for a mental sign, for something that is perceived.

The same sense also appears to be relevant to a specification in the extract from the *Madhyama-āgama* translated above, which is not found in the *Upakkilesa-sutta*. According to this specification, doubt arose when the bodhisattva reflected whether he could see and know what does not exist in the world. It is precisely the shift from the commonly experienced world of the senses to mental visions and signs during the progress towards deeper stages of concentration that can easily cause the arising of uncertainty. This shift is from the known world of sensory experience to an unknown terrain consisting of purely mental visions and experiences, something that from the perspective of normal experience does not really seem to exist.[8]

Whatever may be the final word on the significance of the "sign" in the *Upakkilesa-sutta* and its parallel, the two versions agree in providing a long list of mental obstructions which the Buddha recognized one by one and overcame in his attempt to deepen concentration. Judging from the context, this must have taken place after having already left behind the first two hindrances of sensual desire and aversion.

---

7 Examples are the "sign of tranquillity", *samathanimitta*, and the "sign of concentration", *samādhinimitta*; for a survey of occurrences see Anālayo 2012a: 242. Cousins 1973: 119, in the context of examining the commentarial usage of *nimitta* as a mental sign that leads to deeper concentration, argues that "the most striking evidence for the antiquity of the concept is to be found in the *Upakkilesa-sutta*."

8 Brahm 2006: 93 explains that "after your first experience of a nimitta you think, 'what on earth was that?'"

Leaving aside two variations, the parallel versions agree in listing the following nine obstructions:[9]

- doubt,
- lack of attention,
- sloth-and-torpor,
- fear,
- elation,
- inertia,
- excess of energy,
- lack of energy,
- perception of diversity.

Most of these seem to reflect the need to balance the mind, so that it becomes neither too tense nor too lax. Moreover, perception of diversity needs to be left behind in order to experience mental unification. As soon as unification of the mind becomes even slightly unsteady, the natural tendency of the mind to seek out distraction and entertainment may step in and seize the opportunity to reach out for some diversity, eventually resulting in fully fledged distraction of the mind. Once inner balance and unification of the mind have been secured against falling into these various pitfalls, according to the *Upakkilesa-sutta* and its parallel absorption attainment comes within reach. The *Madhyama-āgama* describes the future Buddha's cultivation of absorption in this way:[10]

> I in turn cultivated three [levels of] concentration. I cultivated concentration with [directed] awareness and [sustained] contemplation, I cultivated concentration without [directed] awareness and with only [sustained] contemplation, and I cultivated concentration without [directed] awareness or [sustained] contemplation.
>
> When I cultivated concentration with [directed] awareness and [sustained] contemplation, my mind in turn inclined towards

9 Two of the eleven obstructions in the parallel versions differ, where MN 128 mentions "longing" and "excessive meditation on forms", but MĀ 72 instead speaks of "conceit" and "not contemplating forms"; see also the table in Anālayo 2011: 738. The count of altogether eleven mental obstructions recurs in the *Yogācārabhūmi*, T 1579 at T XXX 338c10, in apparent reference to a version of the present discourse.

10 The translated passage is taken from MĀ 72 at T I 538c5 to 538c10.

> concentration without [directed] awareness and with only [sustained] contemplation. In this way I was sure that I did not lose that knowledge and vision.
>
> In this way, Anuruddha, having understood it in this way, for a whole day, for a whole night, and for a whole day and night I cultivated concentration with [directed] awareness and [sustained] contemplation. Anuruddha, my practice at that time was this practice of dwelling in tranquillity.

The *Madhyama-āgama* discourse continues describing further modes of practice related to these three levels of concentration. The description in the *Upakkilesa-sutta* only mentions these three levels of concentration at the end of its exposition.

This distinction into three levels of concentration concerns the presence or absence of *vitakka* and *vicāra*, which I prefer to translate as "application" and "sustaining", on the understanding that in the context of absorption attainment the term *vitakka* does not imply the presence of conceptual thought.[11] This accords with the understanding of the translators into Chinese in the passage above, as, instead of using a Chinese character that expresses the meaning of "thought", the counterpart to *vitakka* is rather "awareness".

The threefold distinction introduced in this way comprises levels of concentration where both mental application and sustaining are present, where only sustaining is required, and where neither is required any longer. When correlated with the more familiar scheme of the four absorptions, the first two levels in the threefold distinction correspond to the first absorption, the third level to the higher absorptions.

It is perhaps significant that this passage, which describes the Buddha's pre-awakening cultivation of absorption, employs this threefold mode of presentation. As far as the early discourses allow us to judge, absorption attainment itself was already known in the ancient Indian setting before the advent of the Buddha.[12] This leaves open the possibility, however, that the

---

11 See in more detail Anālayo 2003a: 75–8 and 2017b: 123–8.

12 For a survey of passages indicative of absorption practices being already known in the pre-Buddhist Indian setting see Anālayo 2017b: 163–71.

analysis of absorption attainment into such distinct levels could have been considered an original contribution of the Buddha. In other words, the distinct perspective introduced in this way would be to divest such experiences from any metaphysical or ontological associations and instead approach them from the viewpoint of their conditionality: with the arising of such and such mental factors, such and such an experience of absorption can take place.

This analytical approach might at first have been by way of the threefold distinction mentioned in the present passage, followed later by the four-absorption model found much more frequently elsewhere in the discourses. In other words, during the Buddha's own gradual progress in absorption meditation, after having successfully overcome the various mental obstructions listed in the *Upakkilesa-sutta* and its parallel, he might at first have cultivated absorption with a particular emphasis on the presence and absence of application and sustaining.

This would be a natural result of the gradual refining of the mind evident in the type of obstructions mentioned earlier, most of which revolve around the need to balance the mind, avoiding too strong a focus just as too lax an attitude. The same theme is of relevance for progressing through the three levels of concentration mentioned in the *Upakkilesa-sutta* and its parallel. At first some subtle degree of mental effort continues and finds expression in the presence of application and sustaining. As concentration deepens, the need to apply the mind no longer arises, as it only needs to be sustained in its absorbed condition. With further progress, even that much is no longer necessary and the mind rests in a deeply concentrated state without a need for either application or its sustaining.

The more common description of absorption attainment by way of four levels instead focuses on what type of happiness is experienced. This proceeds from the joy and happiness of seclusion in the first absorption, via the joy and happiness of concentration in the second absorption and the happiness devoid of joy in the third absorption, to a culmination point in the deep equanimity of the fourth absorption. The importance accorded to happiness in this way broaches a topic to which I will return in more detail after having surveyed the bodhisattva's ascetic practices.[13] As far as the two modes of analysing the absorptions are concerned, perhaps the more commonly used mode reflects the crucial realization of the importance to be given to happiness, which formed the turning point in the bodhisattva's quest and the basis for his giving up of asceticism. This would make it meaningful to give emphasis to this particular mode of analysis when teaching others, instead of the threefold one that apparently informed the bodhisattva's own practice as described in the *Upakkilesa-sutta* and its parallel.

Be that as it may, the *Upakkilesa-sutta* and its parallel agree that the bodhisattva cultivated concentration, resulting in perceiving light or else seeing forms and in experiencing either limited or else immeasurable concentration, for a whole day, a whole night, or a whole day and night.[14] A discourse found in the two *Saṃyukta-āgama*s reports a similar qualification made by the Buddha concerning his ability to attain absorption.[15] In this case the corresponding *Saṃyutta-nikāya* discourse does not explicitly speak of an entire day or night, instead of which it reports that the Buddha would dwell in each absorption to whatever extent he wished. In spite of employing a different formulation, the implication appears to be the same.

The specification found similarly in the *Upakkilesa-sutta* and its parallel that each of these concentrative experiences of the bodhisattva took place for a whole day, a whole night, or a whole day and night is of further significance. It puts into perspective the suggestion in the Pāli commentary that the entire development of concentration described in the *Upakkilesa-sutta* took place during the night of the Buddha's awakening.[16] This suggestion does not tally with the discourse. Instead, the cultivation of the mind described in the *Upakkilesa-sutta* and its parallel must have taken much more time than just a single night and therefore needs to be positioned at a time considerably earlier than the night of the Buddha's breakthrough to liberation.

---

13 See below p. 78.

14 MN 128 at MN III 161,4 and MĀ 72 at T I 539a6.

15 SĀ 1142 at T II 302a18 and SĀ[2] 117 at T II 416c24, parallel to SN 16.9 at SN II 210,25 (translated Bodhi 2000: 671). The context is a comparison of the Buddha's ability in this respect with that of Mahākassapa.

16 Ps IV 209,26.

In fact, without previous development of the ability to attain absorption, it would be difficult to understand how the Buddha could have reached the immaterial attainments taught by his teachers Āḷāra Kālāma and Uddaka Rāmaputta, attainments which I will take up in the next chapter.

Before coming to that topic, however, I would like to return to the reference in the *Upakkilesa-sutta* and its *Madhyama-āgama* parallel to the vision of light and forms experienced during deepening concentration. The next discourse in the *Madhyama-āgama*, which has a parallel in the *Aṅguttara-nikāya*, takes up the same issue from a different, but probably complementary, perspective. The relevant passage proceeds as follows:[17]

> By staying in a remote and secluded place and because of cultivating diligently a mind free from negligence, I attained bright light and in turn visions of shapes and forms. However, I did not meet with those devas, did not exchange greetings with them, did not converse with them, and did not receive a response from them.

In agreement with its *Aṅguttara-nikāya* parallel, the *Madhyama-āgama* discourse continues from the ability to converse with those *deva*s to various other levels of knowledge regarding their celestial condition. The two discourses also agree in presenting the cultivation of such knowledge as an integral aspect of the Buddha's pre-awakening experiences; in fact the terminology used in both versions points to a close relationship with the *Upakkilesa-sutta* and its parallel. This thereby provides an additional perspective on the significance of the description of the meditative experiences in this discourse, in that seeing forms and light is at the same time related to seeing celestial beings.

Now in early Buddhist thought the external world outside and the internal world of one's own mind are seen as intrinsically interrelated; so much so that a tour through early Buddhist cosmology is at the same time a tour through various types of mental experiences.[18] When considered from this perspective,

17 The translated passage is taken from MĀ 73 at T I 539b26 to 539b29, parallel to AN 8.64 at AN IV 302,13 (translated Bodhi 2012: 1207).

18 On this close relationship see Gethin 1997 and for an application of this principle Anālayo 2016b: 128f.

the question is not so much one of having to believe in the existence of celestial beings, but one of employing the imagery of *deva*s as a way of broadening one's perspective on experiences during meditative practice.

The traditional recollection of *deva*s concerns the understanding that those celestial beings have come to their divine living condition through cultivating qualities like confidence, virtue, learning, generosity, and wisdom, and that these are qualities that one possesses oneself as well.[19] In other words, recollection of *deva*s is precisely recollecting qualities which practitioners can see within themselves, qualities that are considered in the ancient Indian setting to be the pathway to heaven.

The same applies all the more to the concentrated mental conditions described in the *Upakkilesa-sutta* and its parallel, which from the viewpoint of early Buddhist cosmology lead not just to rebirth in any heaven, but rather to those more elevated celestial spheres of the Brahmā world that correspond to absorption attainment. This in turn could be taken as an invitation to pay attention to this divine dimension of the development of concentration as a way of empowering one's own practice.

EXERCISE

As a form of practice, I suggest training in working with the opposites of too much and too little effort in the meditative cultivation of concentration, with the aim of arriving at a mental condition that is finely balanced and progressively more unified. In order to further such gradual deepening of concentration, and as a way of following the Buddha's example, we might at times recollect the divine condition of the mind that is at least temporarily removed from the hindrances. This relates to the standard forms of recollection of *deva*s, which takes as its object the qualities that have enabled others to be reborn in heaven. Independent of whether we believe in the actual existence of *deva*s and heavens or only consider such references to be metaphorical, a concentrated and balanced mind, "secluded

19 AN 6.10 at AN III 287,25 (translated Bodhi 2012: 865) and its parallels SĀ 931 at T II 238a23 and SĀ[2] 156 at T II 433a24.

from sensuality and from unwholesome states", is in a way a glimpse of heaven on earth. Recollecting this divine dimension of our own concentrated mind, even to the extent of seeing it as involving an ascending or else a being elevated or uplifted to a higher plane of experience, will strengthen our ability to withstand the downward pull of sensual distractions.

V

THE IMMATERIAL ATTAINMENTS

In this chapter I turn to the future Buddha's period of training under two teachers, Āḷāra Kālāma and Uddaka Rāmaputta. My main source for this episode is the *Ariyapariyesanā-sutta* and its *Madhyama-āgama* parallel, which I took up in the first chapter in relation to the bodhisattva's motivation to go forth. The account given in the *Ariyapariyesanā-sutta* of this period of apprenticeship recurs in other discourses in the *Majjhima-nikāya* in abbreviated form, and in one of these cases, the *Mahāsaccaka-sutta*,[1] a Sanskrit fragment parallel has preserved this description in full. This Sanskrit fragment version is therefore a third parallel to be taken into account in what follows. The part of the *Madhyama-āgama* parallel to the *Ariyapariyesanā-sutta* that is relevant to my present topic proceeds in this way:[2]

> Having become accomplished in this aggregate of morality, aspiring and searching for the supreme peace of Nirvāṇa, which is free from disease, *the supreme peace of Nirvāṇa, which is* free from old age, *the supreme peace of Nirvāṇa, which is* free from death, *the supreme peace of Nirvāṇa, which is* free from worry and sadness,

1 MN 36 at MN I 240,26 (translated Ñāṇamoli 1995/2005: 335) abbreviates, referring back to the full text given in MN 26.

2 The translated passage is taken from MĀ 204 at T I 776b5 to 776c5 (translated Anālayo 2012b: 26–8), parallel to MN 26 at MN I 163,31 (translated Ñāṇamoli 1995/2005: 256) and fragment 331r7 to 332r1, Liu 2010: 145–56; for a comparative study of this part of MN 26 see Anālayo 2011: 174–7.

the supreme peace of Nirvāṇa, which is free from defilement, I approached Āḷāra Kālāma and asked him: "Āḷāra, I wish to practise the holy life in your teaching, will you permit this?"

Āḷāra replied to me: "Venerable one, I certainly permit it. You may practise as you wish to practise."

Again I asked: "Āḷāra, this teaching of yours, did you know this teaching yourself, awaken to it yourself, realize it yourself?"

Āḷāra replied to me: "Venerable one, completely transcending the sphere of [boundless] consciousness I have attained dwelling in the sphere of nothingness. Therefore I myself have known this teaching of mine, awakened to it myself, realized it myself."

Again I thought: "Not only Āḷāra alone has such confidence, I too have such confidence, not only Āḷāra alone has such energy, I too have such energy, not only Āḷāra alone has such wisdom, I too have such wisdom, [whereby] Āḷāra has known this teaching himself, awakened to it himself, realized it himself."

Because I wished to realize this teaching, I thereupon went to stay alone and in seclusion, in an empty, quiet, and tranquil place, and I diligently cultivated a mind free from negligence. Having stayed alone and in seclusion, in an empty, quiet, and tranquil place, and diligently cultivated a mind free from negligence, not long afterwards I gained realization of that teaching.

Having realized that teaching, I again approached Āḷāra Kālāma and asked him: "Āḷāra, is this the teaching you have known yourself, awakened to yourself, realized yourself, namely, by completely transcending the sphere of boundless consciousness to attain dwelling in the sphere of nothingness?"

Āḷāra Kālāma replied to me: "Venerable one, this is [indeed] the teaching that I have known myself, awakened to myself, realized myself, namely, by [completely] transcending the sphere of boundless consciousness to attain dwelling in the sphere of nothingness."

Āḷāra Kālāma further said to me: "Venerable one, just as I realized this teaching, so too have you; just as you realized this teaching, so too have I. Venerable one, come and share the leadership of this group."

Thus Āḷāra Kālāma, being the teacher, placed me on an equal level, thereby giving me supreme respect, supreme support, and [expressing] his supreme delight.

> Again I thought: "This teaching does not lead to knowledge, does not lead to awakening, does not lead to Nirvāṇa. I would rather leave this teaching and continue searching for the supreme peace of Nirvāṇa, which is free from disease, *the supreme peace of Nirvāṇa, which is* free from old age, *the supreme peace of Nirvāṇa, which is* free from death, *the supreme peace of Nirvāṇa, which is* free from worry and sadness, the supreme peace of Nirvāṇa, which is free from defilement."
>
> I left this teaching and continued searching for the supreme peace of Nirvāṇa, which is free from disease, *the supreme peace of Nirvāṇa, which is* free from old age, *the supreme peace of Nirvāṇa, which is* free from death, *the supreme peace of Nirvāṇa, which is* free from worry and sadness, the supreme peace of Nirvāṇa, which is free from defilement.

The *Ariyapariyesanā-sutta* reports that the bodhisattva at first learned the doctrine of Āḷāra Kālāma,[3] whereas in the passage translated above and in the Sanskrit fragment version Āḷāra straightaway informed the future Buddha about the attainment of the sphere of nothingness, additionally specified in the *Madhyama-āgama* version translated above as reached by "completely transcending the sphere of [boundless] consciousness". Even though this is not explicitly mentioned in the *Ariyapariyesanā-sutta*, the same would be implicit. In fact the whole preceding series of meditative attainments, through the four absorptions and the two lower immaterial attainments, would be required in order to attain the sphere of nothingness. The same holds for the explicit indication that the bodhisattva practised diligently, mentioned in the *Madhyama-āgama* passage translated above as well as in the Sanskrit fragment, but not in the *Ariyapariyesanā-sutta*.[4] Obviously the same is implied, since without diligent practice he would hardly have been able to reach the same attainment as his teacher.

These two minor variations alert one to the need to approach descriptions of meditation practice in this and other early

3 MN 26 at MN I 164,2. Perhaps worthy of note is that this is the only Pāli discourse passage to employ the term *theravāda*; see in more detail Anālayo 2016a: 497–500.

4 The Sanskrit fragment 331v3, Liu 2010: 15, agrees in this respect with MĀ 204 at T I 776b18.

discourses with the understanding that these reflect different concerns from those in later exegetical literature, which is often characterized by a drive for the construction of complete maps of meditation techniques and experiences. In instances like the present one, however, often only the most salient features relevant to a particular context are mentioned, and knowledge of the overall picture of meditative cultivation as described in the entire corpus of the early discourses is required to fill out the details that have not been explicitly mentioned.[5] In other words, a proper appreciation of early Buddhist thought requires a systematic reading.[6] A systematic reading obliges one to read any particular passage by contextualizing it within the remainder of the textual corpus to which it belongs, rather than considering it in isolation.

This does not mean, however, that at times parts of a presentation could not have been lost in transmission. The passage above in fact provides an example, as it only mentions confidence, energy, and wisdom as qualities that the bodhisattva and his teacher had in common. Given the context of high meditative attainment, the entire set of five faculties would fit the context. In particular the two missing faculties of mindfulness and concentration are indispensable for reaching even the first absorption, let alone any of the immaterial spheres. In fact the *Ariyapariyesanā-sutta* and the Sanskrit fragment mention all five faculties.[7] This makes it fairly safe to conclude that at some

5 On this topic see also Anālayo 2017b: 149f.

6 Park 2012: 74 and 78 explains that a systematic reading is "one which provides a consistent understanding of the text, consistent not merely within itself but within a wider textual context ... [out of] an honest effort to understand the whole context of a text or its doctrinal system, proscribing minority ... from appropriating the true voice of the whole text."

7 MN 26 at MN I 164,16 and the Sanskrit fragment 331v1f, Liu 2010: 149 list all of the five faculties of confidence, energy, mindfulness, concentration, and wisdom. The same is also the case for records of the future Buddha's apprenticeship under Kālāma in the *Saṅghabhedavastu*, Gnoli 1977: 97,10. Although the *Lalitavistara* differs for the first quality, which here is will (*chanda*) instead of confidence, it does mention energy, mindfulness, concentration, and wisdom; see Lefmann 1902: 239,1. The Dharmaguptaka *Vinaya*, however, mentions only three faculties, similarly to the case of MĀ 204; see T 1428 at T XXII 780b11. This reference in its present form is clearly the outcome of textual corruption, as already noted by Bareau 1963: 18, since the Dharmaguptaka *Vinaya* actually states that Kālāma is *bereft* of confidence, energy, and wisdom.

point in the transmission of this episode a reference to the two faculties of mindfulness and concentration would have been lost in some reciter traditions.

In relation to the reflection of the bodhisattva that he has the same mental faculties as his teacher, which served to inspire him to set out to reach the same attainment, another aspect worthy of comment is the first of these five. This is *saddhā*, usually translated as "faith", although I prefer the rendering "confidence". The appropriateness of understanding the term *saddhā* to convey a sense of confidence is quite evident in the present context, since it is precisely confidence in the possibility of reaching the same accomplishment as his teacher that underlies the bodhisattva's entire reflection.[8] This thereby points to an important dimension of *saddhā* in early Buddhist thought, which is substantially different from mere blind faith. Although I will take up this topic in more detail in my conclusion to this book,[9] it might be worth noting already now that a chief ingredient in such type of *saddhā* is precisely the confidence that it is possible to liberate one's mind from hindrances and defilements. Such confidence is indispensable for embarking on the practices that lead to deep concentration experiences or else to awakening, a condition of complete and permanent mental freedom.

When such confidence had led the bodhisattva to the attainment of the sphere of nothingness, according to the *Ariyapariyesanā-sutta* he explicitly stated that the Dharma taught by his teacher, which now he had also realized, only leads to re-arising in the sphere of nothingness.[10] This makes it clear that the issue at stake is the fully fledged attainment of the sphere of nothingness. The same is implicit in the fact that, in the *Madhyama-āgama* discourse and the Sanskrit fragment version, Āḷāra Kālāma states that he has himself realized dwelling in the sphere of nothingness.[11]

---

8 Dutt 1940: 639 explains that the reference to *saddhā* in the present context stands for "confidence in his abilities to develop the powers necessary to achieve his object".

9 See below p. 225.

10 MN 26 at MN 165,12.

11 Sanskrit fragment 331v5, Liu 2010: 152.

This confirms the suggestion I made above and also in the previous chapter, in that the bodhisattva must have developed mastery of the absorptions before being able to equal the attainment reached by Āḷāra Kālāma. Without the ability to enter the lower absorptions, the future Buddha and his teacher Āḷāra Kālāma would hardly have been able to attain this immaterial sphere, such that rebirth in the corresponding immaterial realm can be expected of them.

According to the *Mahāvastu* and the *Divyāvadāna*, as well as the Pāli commentarial tradition, the bodhisattva had in fact trained under a seer before joining Āḷāra Kālāma.[12] The *Saṅghabhedavastu* of the Mūlasarvāstivāda *Vinaya* adds that he had been well established in the absorption meditation that was being practised at the place of this seer.[13] These texts confirm the impression that the bodhisattva would have already cultivated absorption before meeting Āḷāra Kālāma, who then taught him how to progress further to the attainment of the third immaterial sphere. The *Ariyapariyesanā-sutta* and its parallels in fact report that the bodhisattva was *soon* able to reach the attainments described by his teacher.[14] For the future Buddha to be able to attain swiftly what his teacher found so impressive an accomplishment that he was willing to elevate his student to his own rank of leadership makes it patently clear that the bodhisattva must have already been quite proficient in the cultivation of deep states of concentration. This contrasts with the situation described in the *Upakkilesa-sutta* and its parallel, taken up in the previous chapter, which show him having had to struggle with various obstructions to absorption attainment. Clearly, the events described in the *Upakkilesa-sutta* and its parallel need to be placed before the period of apprenticeship under Āḷāra Kālāma and Uddaka Rāmaputta.

The *Ariyapariyesanā-sutta* and its parallels continue by reporting that the same sequence of events repeated itself with the second teacher Uddaka Rāmaputta. In this case, however, the

---

12 Cowell and Neil 1886: 391,27, Senart 1890: 195,12 (translated Jones 1952/1976: 186), and Thī-a 2,17 (translated Pruitt 1998/1999: 4).

13 Gnoli 1977: 96,18.

14 MN 26 at MN I 164,25, fragment 331v3, Liu 2010: 150, and MĀ 204 at T I 776b20.

bodhisattva attained the sphere of neither-perception-nor-non-perception, which Uddaka apparently had not reached himself, as only his father Rāma had mastered this immaterial sphere.[15] In keeping with the circumstance that the bodhisattva had reached a higher realization than himself, in the *Ariyapariyesanā-sutta* Uddaka Rāmaputta invited his student to be the sole teacher of his group.[16] In the *Madhyama-āgama* version and the Sanskrit fragment, however, he only offered the same as Āḷāra had earlier, namely sharing his teacher's position with the future Buddha.[17] Due to the repetitiveness of the two accounts of the bodhisattva's apprenticeship under Āḷāra and Uddaka, it could easily have happened that the offer of sharing leadership appropriate for the case of Āḷāra influenced the wording of the offer recorded to have been made by Uddaka. If the future Buddha had surpassed Uddaka, the presentation in the *Ariyapariyesanā-sutta* would fit the narrative context better, in that Uddaka would have placed the bodhisattva at a level above himself.

Be that as it may, the main message that emerges from this part of the Buddha's pre-awakening experience is that even the refined concentrative experiences of the third and fourth immaterial spheres fall short of being the final goal. On their own they do not result in the supreme peace of Nirvāṇa the bodhisattva was aspiring to.

Nevertheless, the very fact that the future Buddha placed himself under the guidance of these two teachers conveys the impression that their mode of practice did at first sight seem to him to hold the promise of leading to the final goal. In other words, the attainments of nothingness and of neither-perception-nor-non-perception must at least to some extent point in the direction in which the bodhisattva wished to go.

This suggestion finds confirmation in a presentation in the *Cūḷasuññata-sutta* and its parallels extant in the *Madhyama-āgama* and in Tibetan translation. The three versions begin with a statement by the Buddha that he dwelled much in emptiness.[18] The body of the discourse then offers detailed

---

15 See the discussion in Skilling 1981 and Wynne 2007: 14–16.

16 MN 26 at MN I 166,26.

17 Fragment 332r8, Liu 2010: 163, and MĀ 204 at T I 776c27.

18 MN 121 at MN III 104,13 (translated Ñāṇamoli 1995/2005: 965), MĀ 190 at T I 737a7, and the Tibetan version in Skilling 1994: 150,1; see also

meditation instructions on how a gradual meditative descent into emptiness can be cultivated. This proceeds by gradually emptying one's perceptions until at one stage the perception of the sphere of nothingness comes into play. The formulation used gives the impression that the instructions are concerned with cultivating the "perception" of nothingness, not necessarily the fully fledged attainment of the corresponding immaterial sphere.[19] This differs from the *Ariyapariyesanā-sutta*, where the issue at stake is the actual attainment.

The notion of nothingness itself could have been what attracted the bodhisattva to Āḷāra Kālāma. Reaching the actual attainment then motivated him to leave Āḷāra and continue in his quest by approaching a teacher who taught what went beyond the attainment of nothingness. Against this background, it seems as if the *Cūḷasuññata-sutta* and its parallels in a way incorporate what is most beneficial from the teaching and practice of Āḷāra Kālāma by turning it into a step in a gradual descent into emptiness. Needless to say, in the *Cūḷasuññata-sutta* and its parallels the perception of nothingness is merely a stepping stone which leads on to signlessness,[20] and this in turn provides the launching pad for entry into true emptiness, the realization of the supreme peace of Nirvāṇa. This is what true emptiness amounts to, namely totally emptying the mind of all bondage and defilements.

Before coming to that, however, the future Buddha took a detour by engaging in ascetic practices, a topic that will occupy me during the next three chapters. The evident dissatisfaction with the two highest immaterial attainments, described quite vividly in the passage translated above for the case of the attainment of nothingness, appears to have been so strong that the bodhisattva decided to try a completely different approach to progress to awakening. Alongside the adoption of a different approach, a continuity that underpins the entire trajectory from going forth to his eventual gaining of awakening is his unswerving quest for reaching total liberation from old age,

---

Skilling 1997: 345–7 and Anālayo 2011: 683.

19 See Anālayo 2015a: 91.

20 For a discussion of the somewhat different progression in MN 121 and its parallels after nothingness see Anālayo 2015a: 134–6.

disease, and death, total freedom from *dukkha*.

EXERCISE

As a practical exercise, I would like to suggest cultivating meditation on emptiness in formal meditation as well as in everyday life. In brief, this can take place by attending to whatever happens or manifests as empty, during formal sitting or any activity, in the sense that there is nothing whatsoever to it that could be taken as a self or as belonging to a self, nothing whatsoever that we can truly own or completely control.[21] Everything, without any exception, is thoroughly empty in this way. Whatever problem we might encounter in life can become food for emptiness through this simple yet profound act of discerning its empty nature, ideally combined with the inner confidence (*saddhā*) that with sustained practice we will be able to emulate the Buddha's insight into emptiness. Every single act of such discerning is a step forwards towards the profound realization that underlies the Buddha's awakening and which has found expression time and again in his discourses and teachings, namely that neither a self nor something belonging to a self can be found at all, at any time, anywhere.

21 For more detailed practical instructions see Anālayo 2015a: 162–9.

VI

FORCEFUL CONTROL OF THE MIND

With the present chapter I begin to study the ascetic practices of the bodhisattva, a topic that will occupy me also in the next two chapters. The main themes to be covered in this respect are his attempt to control the mind through sheer force (present chapter), his practice of breath control (Chapter 7), and his undertaking of fasting (Chapter 8). Before turning to the first of these three topics, however, I need to discuss the ascetic practices described in the *Mahāsīhanāda-sutta* and its parallel.

The *Mahāsīhanāda-sutta*, which has a Chinese parallel found apart from the Chinese *Āgamas*, is a rather long discourse which takes as its point of departure an occasion when the Buddha had been disparaged by one of his former monastics. Being informed by Sāriputta of this disparagement, according to the *Mahāsīhanāda-sutta* and its parallel the Buddha described in detail his various qualities and powers of which the former monastic evidently had not been fully aware. This description also covers, among others, the "ten powers of a Tathāgata", which concern the Buddha's exceptional meditative endowments and abilities, and his "four intrepidities", four aspects in regard to which he need not feel any trepidation.

The ten powers comprise the Buddha's penetrative insights into what is possible and impossible, karma, ways to (rebirth) destinations, the elements in the world, the different inclinations of beings, the faculties of beings, and concentrative attainments. These come together with the three higher knowledges, namely recollection of past lives, the divine eye, and the destruction of the influxes. Together with the afore-mentioned seven, these three complete the count of ten powers. I will return to these three in my discussion of the Buddha's awakening in Chapters 11 to 13.

The four intrepidities are the Buddha's certainty of having indeed gained full awakening, having indeed eradicated the influxes (*āsava*, a term whose implications I will explore in Chapter 13), knowing indeed what are obstructions to the path, and teaching others what indeed leads to freedom from *dukkha*.

In the early discourses these ten powers and four intrepidities are a recurrent way of throwing into relief the extraordinary nature of the Buddha. The main themes that underlie this presentation would be the profound insight and comprehensive understanding the Buddha had gained through his awakening, together with his compassionate willingness to share with others what he had discovered.

Besides highlighting these powers and abilities, another topic taken up in the *Mahāsīhanāda-sutta* and its parallel is the Buddha's former practice of asceticism.[1] The two versions agree that he had undertaken various austerities in vogue among ancient Indian ascetics, such as accepting food only under specific circumstances and at specific intervals, not cleaning the body, living in extreme seclusion, and exposing the body to the vicissitudes of the climate.

A closer look at this description in the way it has come down in the *Mahāsīhanāda-sutta* brings to light some aspects that at first sight seem to involve inconsistencies, at least as long as all of these practices are considered to be part of the ascetic period subsequent to his period of training under Āḷāra Kālāma and Uddaka Rāmaputta and prior to his awakening.[2] The *Mahāsīhanāda-sutta* depicts the future Buddha undertaking ritual bathing in water three times a day, but also describes that over the years dust and dirt had accumulated on his body to the extent that it was falling off in pieces. These two practices are not

1 MN 12 at MN I 77,28 (translated Ñāṇamoli 1995/2005: 173f) and its parallel T 757 at T XVII 597a13; for a comparative study see Anālayo 2011: 115f.

2 These have already been pointed out by Dutoit 1905: 49ff and Freiberger 2006: 238f.

easily reconciled with each other, since if he undertook regular bathing the dirt on his body would have been washed away and not stood a chance of accumulating over the years. Again, the *Mahāsīhanāda-sutta* reports that he practised nakedness as well as that he wore different types of ascetic garments. Such practices are also to some extent mutually exclusive. The various ascetic practices described in this discourse do not fit easily into the period of a few years that the bodhisattva is reported to have engaged in asceticism. Moreover, during the period of his asceticism he was in the company of five men who later became his first disciples, yet according to the *Mahāsīhanāda-sutta* he dwelled in such total seclusion that he would hide as soon as he saw a human from afar.

The solution to this apparent paradox can be found in a *Jātaka* tale, according to which the Buddha had undertaken such ascetic practices ninety-one aeons ago during a former life as a naked ascetic.[3] The introductory section to this *Jātaka* in fact refers back to the same event of disparagement that also forms the place of departure of the *Mahāsīhanāda-sutta*.

The title of this tale is the *Lomahaṃsa-jātaka*, which employs the qualification "hair-raising", presumably to qualify the ascetic practices described. The same qualification recurs in the reconstructed title of a parallel to the *Mahāsīhanāda-sutta* in the Sanskrit *Dīrgha-āgama* as the *Romaharṣaṇa-sūtra*.[4] The same holds for the title of the Chinese parallel to the *Mahāsīhanāda-sutta*, which also considers the discourse to be "hair-raising". Again, the *Milindapañha* refers to the *Mahāsīhanāda-sutta* as "hair-raising", a qualification also employed in two Pāli commentaries to refer to this discourse.[5] These instances point to a close relationship between the *Lomahaṃsa-jātaka* and the *Mahāsīhanāda-sutta*, which in turn makes it safe to follow the *Jātaka*'s allocation of the ascetic practices, depicted in both, to a life of the Buddha in the distant past.

---

3 Jā 94 at Jā I 390,16 (translated Cowell 1895/2000: 229); the relevance of this tale for appreciating the description in MN 12 has already been pointed out by Hecker 1972: 54.

4 The title has been reconstructed from an *uddāna* by Hartmann 1991: 237 (§133–5).

5 Mil 396,2, Sv I 179,3, and It-a I 109,1.

During a whole life of asceticism it would indeed be possible to spend a period of time in ritual bathing and another period without washing at all until so much dirt accumulates that it flakes off, or else to practise nudity for some time and then wear different ascetic garments at other times. Thus the ascetic practices described in the *Mahāsīhanāda-sutta* and its parallel appear to belong to the same category as various other events and stories the Buddha narrates in this same discourse about his experiences in past lives. This in turn means that these ascetic practices are not part of the account of his struggle to reach awakening during his last life. For this reason they fall outside of the scope of my exploration here. Relevant to the present life of the Buddha, in particular to his practice after having mastered the immaterial attainments and before his gaining of awakening, are only three types of asceticism. These are forceful mind control, breath control, and fasting.

The future Buddha's undertaking of these three ascetic practices is the theme of the *Mahāsaccaka-sutta*, which has a parallel preserved in Sanskrit fragments. A discourse in the *Ekottarika-āgama* also reports his ascetic practices, although otherwise this discourse is not a parallel to the *Mahāsaccaka-sutta*.

Whereas the *Mahāsīhanāda-sutta*, mentioned above, begins with the challenge posed by a former monastic's disparagement, the *Mahāsaccaka-sutta* has as its point of departure a challenge posed by the debater Saccaka, who appears to have favoured asceticism of the type practised by Jains. The account of the Buddha's ascetic practices comes as part of a reply to a distinction made by Saccaka between development of the body, *kāyabhāvanā*, and development of the mind, *cittabhāvanā*. In fact the Sanskrit fragment version has the title Discourse on the Development of the Body, *Kāyabhāvanā-sūtra*, reflecting the importance of this topic to the whole text.

The contrast between development of the body and of the mind is quite relevant at the present juncture in the pre-awakening progress of the future Buddha. After having taken the meditative practice of concentration all the way up to the highest of the four immaterial attainments, he had now come to the conclusion that this was not the way to awakening. As a result, he had to find a different approach to proceed on his quest. The fact that he opted for asceticism implies that he had decided to give more importance to the physical dimension of his practice, compared to the immaterial attainments cultivated previously.

According to the *Mahāsaccaka-sutta* and its Sanskrit fragment parallel, the Buddha began his exposition by depicting a worldling who is overwhelmed by pleasant and painful feelings. In contrast, a noble disciple is not overwhelmed by pleasant and painful feelings. The relevant part in the Sanskrit fragment version proceeds as follows:[6]

> A learned noble disciple, being touched by bodily feelings that are painful, severe, sharp, piercing, disagreeable, and threatening to life, does not sorrow, does not become weary, does not lament, does not beat the breast, does not cry, and does not become distraught.
>
> With the cessation of that painful feeling, pleasant feeling arises. Being touched by pleasant feeling, [the learned noble disciple] does not lust for pleasure and does not experience lust for pleasure.
>
> Not lusting for pleasure and not experiencing lust for pleasure, arisen painful bodily feelings do not remain obsessing the mind [of the learned noble disciple], arisen pleasant bodily feelings *do not remain obsessing the mind*, arisen painful mental feelings *do not remain obsessing the mind*, arisen pleasant mental feelings do not remain obsessing the mind.

The *Mahāsaccaka-sutta* does not distinguish between bodily and mental feelings at this juncture.[7] Otherwise the two versions agree in describing how to avoid that one's mind be overwhelmed by feelings. To achieve this requires an interrelated attitude in relation to pleasure and pain. Establishing a non-reactive stance with one helps to maintain such a non-reactive

---

6 The translated passage is based on fragment 330v4 to 330v7, Liu 2010: 140f (here and elsewhere I adopt corrections, supplementations, and emendations by the editor without explicitly noting these as such), parallel to MN 36 at MN I 239,27 (translated Ñāṇamoli 1995/2005: 334); for a comparative study see Anālayo 2011: 233.

7 Another difference manifests in the ensuing part, where MN 36 relates pleasant feelings to the development of the body and painful feelings to the development of the mind. Judging from the Sanskrit fragment this could be a transmission error; see also Anālayo 2011: 233f.

stance with the other. When one does not get upset about pain and elated about pleasure, the impact feelings in general have on the mind diminishes; they no longer have the same ability as earlier to remain obsessing one's mind.

Having received this clarification, Saccaka brings up the topic of the Buddha's own ability in this respect, couched in terms of the Buddha's development of body and mind. In reply, the Buddha affirms that he has indeed developed body and mind, which forms the starting point for relating his pre-awakening practices. After covering his apprenticeship under Āḷāra Kālāma and Uddaka Rāmaputta, the Buddha turns next to his ascetic practices. Here is the relevant part from the Sanskrit fragment version, which sets in right after the Buddha has described that he left the way of practice taught by Uddaka Rāmaputta:[8]

> I went to the village of Senāyana at Uruvelā, south of Gayā. There I saw a delightful spot of land, a lovely forest thicket by the delightful river Nerañjarā, cool, flowing, with gravel, good access, green grass, expansive banks, and adorned with various trees.[9] Having seen it, I thought:
>
> "This is indeed a delightful spot of land, a lovely forest thicket by the delightful river Nerañjarā, cool, flowing, with gravel, good access, green grass, [expansive banks], and adorned with various trees. It is indeed suitable that a son of a good family, who is intent on striving, should undertake striving based on [such] a forest thicket. I am intent on striving. Let me now undertake striving based on this forest thicket."
>
> Thus I entered that forest thicket and sat at the root of a certain tree with legs folded crosswise, keeping the body erect,

8 The translated passage is based on fragment 332v2 to 333r2, Liu 2010: 164–70, parallel to MN 36 at MN I 242,23. In MN 36 this is preceded by three similes that involve a piece of wood and the attempt to make a fire, which I discussed above p. 27–8. In the Sanskrit fragment version these similes instead come later, which seems a preferable placing as they imply that progress to awakening does not depend on asceticism. Such an insight would have a more natural placing after the bodhisattva had tried asceticism, instead of before he had engaged in it; see also Anālayo 2011: 235f.

9 This first part is only given in abbreviation in MN 36, to be supplemented from MN 26 at MN I 166,36, which shows some minor differences in the description.

> and with mindfulness established in front. With teeth clenched and tongue pressed against the roof of the mouth I dominated, constrained, and overpowered mind with mind. [When] with teeth clenched and tongue pressed against the roof of the mouth I was dominating, constraining, and overpowering mind with mind, [at that time] sweat poured forth from all my pores.
>
> It was just as if a strong man, having grabbed hold of a weak man by both arms, were to hold him down and constrain him, and sweat were to pour forth from all his pores. In the same way when, with teeth clenched and tongue pressed against the roof of the mouth, I was dominating, constraining, and overpowering mind with mind, at that time sweat poured forth from all my pores. Tireless energy was produced in me, the body was calm and not agitated, mindfulness was established without confusion, and the mind was concentrated and unified.

The *Mahāsaccaka-sutta* does not describe the sitting posture adopted by the bodhisattva for this practice. Moreover, according to its presentation the body was not calm, but overwrought by the painful striving. The two versions agree that the Buddha concluded his description with a reference to the feelings experienced. In the Sanskrit fragment version this statement proceeds in this way:[10]

> Feeling such feelings that are painful, severe, sharp, piercing, disagreeable [and threatening to life] did not remain obsessing the mind, in so far as I had developed the body.

A difference here is that the *Mahāsaccaka-sutta* does not explicitly provide a relation between the ability to experience such painful feelings without being overwhelmed and the development of the body. Nevertheless, the key point that emerges from this passage in both versions, which forms a continuous theme throughout the future Buddha's ascetic practices, is his ability to avoid being overwhelmed by painful feelings. This is a feature to be kept in mind.

In relation to the above description of the bodhisattva's attempt to overpower mind with mind, it is worth noting that the same mode of practice recurs in the *Vitakkasaṇṭhāna-sutta* and

10 The translated passage is based on fragment 333r2, Liu 2010: 170.

its parallel.[11] The decisive difference is that here this forms a last resort after a whole series of alternative modes for overcoming unwholesome thought have turned out to be unsuccessful.

If the parallelism should hold for the Buddha's own progress to awakening, the implication would be that, after having had personal experience of the immaterial spheres, he found that these were not sufficient to remove unwholesome thought from his mind. This would explain why he came to the conclusion that even such sublime meditative experiences "do not lead to Nirvāṇa" and why he felt he needed to continue for "the supreme peace of Nirvāṇa, which is free from defilements". From this viewpoint, it would indeed be natural for him to try next to remove defilements from the mind by sheer force, as described in the passage above. In other words, after attempts to leave defilements behind through the cultivation of deep concentration had not been successful, he now opted for a direct confrontation in an attempt to force defilements out of the mind.

This method does indeed stop unwholesome thoughts in the mind, which explains why it features in the *Vitakkasaṇṭhāna-sutta* and its parallel as a last resort when one is hopelessly overwhelmed by unwholesome thoughts and perhaps on the brink of expressing these in unwholesome words or actions. This has only a temporary effect, however. Due to the conditioned and not-self nature of the mind, it is not possible to control it completely by sheer willpower. Instead, a gradual process of mental cultivation is required to change the habit patterns of the mind step by step.

Since an attempt to force the mind to be free from unwholesomeness can only have a short-term effect, it is in this respect comparable to the temporary aloofness from unwholesome mental conditions reached with an immaterial attainment. Both do not last. The bodhisattva must soon enough have realized this, which would have spurred him on to attempt to gain control over the mind in other ways. I will survey these other ways in the next two chapters.

---

11 MN 20 at MN I 120,35 (translated Ñāṇamoli 1995/2005: 213) and MĀ 101 at T I 588c17; see also Anālayo 2011: 142.

EXERCISE

Although the central aspect of practice that emerges from this chapter is forceful mind control, I recommend not making this a regular practice, unless we are really close to engaging in a seriously unwholesome action. An emergency brake has its place to avoid an accident, but using it too often will simply not be conducive to progress. Instead of employing mere forceful control of the mind as soon as unwholesomeness manifests, the other methods described in the *Vitakkasaṇṭhāna-sutta* could be explored one after the other in order to counter a frequently occurring unwholesome thought we might experience during daily life or in meditation. The basic procedure, once just becoming aware of the situation has not sufficed for the thought to go naturally into abeyance, is to try out one of the five methods listed in this discourse. If that has not been successful, we try out the next. In this way we adopt a gradual procedure instead of resorting to sheer force, in line with the Buddha's own discovery that just trying to overpower the mind offers only temporary relief and does not result in truly liberating it from defilements.

Listed in brief, the five methods appropriate when we experience recurrent unwholesome thoughts are:[12]

- turn to something wholesome instead;
- realize the danger of what is going on;
- set aside the issue at hand;
- gradually relax the motivational force behind it;
- use forceful suppression as an emergency brake.

12 For a more detailed survey of these methods see Anālayo 2013b: 149–54.

VII

BREATH CONTROL

In this chapter I continue to study the ascetic practices of the future Buddha. After having tried to control his mind by sheer force, according to the *Mahāsaccaka-sutta* and its Sanskrit fragment parallel he engaged in breath control, a practice also reported in an otherwise unrelated discourse in the *Ekottarika-āgama*. The Sanskrit fragment parallel describes his practice in this way:[1]

> Then I thought: "Suppose I were to meditate on ⟨breathless⟩ meditation."[2] I stopped inhalations and exhalations through the mouth and nose. Having stopped inhalations and exhalations through the mouth and nose, all the winds struck my head and there was an excessive headache in my head.
>
> It was as if a strong man were to strike the head of a weak man with the tip of a sharp iron sword and there were to be an excessive headache in his head. In the same way, having stopped inhalations and exhalations through the mouth and nose, all the winds struck my head and there was an excessive headache in my head.
>
> Tireless energy was produced in me, the body was calm and not agitated, mindfulness was established without confusion, the mind was concentrated and unified.

---

1 The translated passage is based on fragment 333r2 to 333r6, Liu 2010: 171–3, parallel to MN 36 at MN I 243,4 (translated Ñāṇamoli 1995/2005: 337) and EĀ 31.8 at T II 671a12 (translated Bronkhorst 1993/2000: 13); see also Anālayo 2011: 237.

2 The translation "breathless" is based on emending *adhyātmaka*, "internal", to *aprāṇaka*.

Similar to the case of the ascetic practice of forceful mind control, discussed in the previous chapters, here, too, the *Mahāsaccaka-sutta* differs in describing that the body was not calm, but overwrought by the painful striving. It agrees with the Sanskrit fragment version that the painful feelings experienced at this time did not remain obsessing the mind of the bodhisattva.

The continuity of the present ascetic practices with the previously undertaken attempt at subduing the mind by sheer force lies not only in the ability to experience even strong painful feelings without being overwhelmed by them. In addition, the attempt to practise "breathless meditation" seems to spring also from the same basic attitude of trying to exert forceful control. Given that even overpowering mind with mind, "with teeth clenched and tongue pressed against the roof of the mouth", had not led the bodhisattva to the goal of his quest, it is natural that he would try out other means to enforce control. In fact, if one just tries for a moment to clench one's teeth and press the tongue against the roof of the mouth, one will come to appreciate that the next step taken in the same direction would naturally be to practise retention of the breath.

The *Mahāsaccaka-sutta*, the Sanskrit fragment version, and a parallel in the *Ekottarika-āgama* agree in reporting several modes of practising breathless meditation. The simile of the headache caused by being struck with the tip of a sword on the head, which in the passage translated above serves to illustrate the first mode of breath control, occurs in the *Mahāsaccaka-sutta* in relation to the second such mode.[3] The first simile in the *Mahāsaccaka-sutta*, which describes a smith's bellows, in turn illustrates the second mode of breath retention in the Sanskrit fragment version. The third mode of this type of practice compares with a strong man who tightens a leather band around the head of a weak man, and the fourth mode of breath retention finds illustration in a butcher carving up a cow's belly.[4] These two images are standard descriptions of painful experiences in the early discourses. The same holds for a fifth mode of breath

3 MN 36 at MN I 243,37; see also EĀ 31.8 at T II 671a21, which has a related simile.

4 In EĀ 31.8 at T II 671a25 the simile of the butcher illustrates what here is the last of three modes of breathless meditation.

control, which leads to pain comparable to what a weak man would experience on being roasted over a pit of hot coals by two strong men.

After having described these different modes of breath retention, the *Mahāsaccaka-sutta* reports that *deva*s witnessing the bodhisattva's striving commented on his condition, wondering whether he was either already dead or else about to pass away.[5] Such a comment is not found in the Sanskrit fragment version, and in the *Ekottarika-āgama* discourse it rather occurs after the bodhisattva had undertaken fasting.[6]

The *Mahāvastu* reports that men sent by the bodhisattva's father to observe his condition were under the impression that he must be dead, because his breathing had stopped.[7] An *Udāna* collection extant in Chinese translation narrates that, on seeing that he no longer breathed, some *deva*s had come to the conclusion that the bodhisattva was dead.[8] In this way, the presentation in the *Mahāsaccaka-sutta*, according to which the bodhisattva undertook breath retention to such a degree that others thought he might be dead or on the verge of death, receives support from other accounts of the future Buddha's ascetic practices. In fact, even just the bare description of these modes of "breathless" meditation and the accompanying similes make it clear that he must have engaged in this practice with considerable fervour.

This is of interest not only because it shows the future Buddha's strong determination to pursue what at that time appeared to him to be a potential pathway to awakening. It also seems to reflect an apparent interest in the process of breathing. In line with the perspective mentioned in the previous chapter, according to which the various ascetic practices described in the *Mahāsīhanāda-sutta* and its parallel pertain to a past life of the Buddha, his present-life asceticism comprises only the exercises described in the *Mahāsaccaka-sutta* and its parallels, which are forceful mind

5 MN 36 at MN I 245,1.

6 EĀ 31.8 at T II 671a7. The sequence of events in this account is not without problems, however, as here the practice of breath retention comes only after fasting. Yet, a body weakened due to prolonged fasting would probably not be strong enough to undertake the physically demanding practice of the "breathless" meditations described in the parallel versions.

7 Senart 1890: 208,4 (translated Jones 1952/1976: 198).

8 T 212 at T IV 644b13.

control, breath retention, and fasting. Whereas the first and the last are presented only in one modality, the parallel versions agree in describing several different modes of engaging in breath retention. The *Ekottarika-āgama* discourse presents three such modes, and the *Mahāsaccaka-sutta* and its Sanskrit fragment parallel five modes. This gives the impression that the "breathless" meditation should be considered to have had a particularly prominent place in the bodhisattva's ascetic striving. Thus he tried out different modalities of breath retention before giving it up as not conducive to the goal of his aspiration, realizing that to withhold the breath was as unsuccessful as forceful control of the mind in removing the roots of defilements within.

Such apparent prominence finds a complement in the report that, after having reached awakening, the Buddha appears to have had a predilection for mindfulness of breathing. In fact he spent a solitary retreat entirely dedicated to this practice.

Similar to the case of forceful mind control, which still found a place as a last resort in the set of five ways for overcoming unwholesome thoughts in the *Vitakkasaṇṭhāna-sutta* and its parallel, meditation related to the breath continued to be of practical relevance to the Buddha after his awakening. However, the mode of practice changes substantially. Instead of breath retention, the task becomes just to be aware of the breath as it naturally flows in and out.

In order to explore this topic further, in what follows I turn to a discourse that describes the Buddha going on retreat and undertaking mindfulness of breathing. In an appendix to my study of *Mindfully Facing Disease and Death*, I already translated a version of this discourse found in the Mūlasarvāstivāda *Vinaya*. By way of complementing this and my other translations of various versions of the instructions on mindfulness of breathing in sixteen steps, here is the first part of the *Saṃyukta-āgama* discourse on the Buddha's retreat practice of mindfulness of breathing:[9]

9 The translated discourse is SĀ 807 at T II 207a8 to 207a21, parallel to SN 54.11 at SN V 325,19 (translated Bodhi 2000: 1778) and T 1448 at T XXIV 32c2 (translated Anālayo 2016b: 245). The actual exposition of the sixteen steps is given in abbreviated form in the original, which therefore needs to be supplemented based on the full instructions found previously in the *Saṃyukta-āgama* collection, namely in SĀ 803 at T II 206a27 (translated Anālayo 2013b: 228f).

Thus have I heard. At one time the Buddha was dwelling in the Icchānaṅgala forest. At that time the Blessed One said to the monastics:

"I wish to sit in meditation for two months.[10] All monastics should no longer come, except only for the monastic who brings me food and for the time of the observance day."[11]

At that time, having said this, the Blessed One sat in meditation for two months. Not a single monastic dared to come, except only for bringing him food and for the time of the observance day.

At that time, having completed the two months of sitting in meditation and coming out of meditation, the Blessed One sat in front of the community of monastics and said to the monastics:

"If outside wanderers come and ask you: 'In what meditation has the recluse Gotama been sitting during these two months?', you should reply: 'The Tathāgata has been dwelling by giving attention to mindfulness of breathing during the two months of sitting in meditation.' Why is that?

"In these two months I dwelled giving much attention to mindfulness of breathing. When breathing in I was mindfully breathing in, understanding it as it really is;[12] when breathing out, I was mindfully breathing out, understanding it as it really is.

"When *breathing in* long *I was mindfully breathing in long, understanding it as it really is; when breathing out long I was mindfully breathing out long, understanding it as it really is.* When *breathing in* short *I was mindfully breathing in short, understanding it as it really is; when breathing out short I was mindfully breathing out short, understanding it as it really is.*

"I was mindfully experiencing the whole body when breathing in, understanding it as it really is; I was mindfully experiencing the whole body when breathing out, understanding it as it really is. I was mindfully calming bodily activity when breathing in, understanding it as it really is; *I was mindfully calming bodily activity when breathing out, understanding it as it really is.*

10 SN 54.11 at SN V 326,1 speaks instead of a retreat of three months.

11 SN 54.11 does not refer to the *uposatha*, the fortnightly meeting of monastics to recite the code of rules.

12 The recurrent reference to "understanding as it really is" is without a counterpart in SN 54.11, although the same can safely be assumed to be implicit.

"I was mindfully experiencing joy when breathing in, understanding it as it really is; I was mindfully experiencing joy when breathing out, understanding it as it really is. I was mindfully experiencing happiness when breathing in, understanding it as it really is; I was mindfully experiencing happiness when breathing out, understanding it as it really is.

"I was mindfully experiencing mental activity when breathing in, understanding it as it really is; I was mindfully experiencing mental activity when breathing out, understanding it as it really is. I was mindfully calming mental activity when breathing in, understanding it as it really is; I was mindfully calming mental activity when breathing out, understanding it as it really is.

"I was mindfully experiencing the mind when breathing in, understanding it as it really is; I was mindfully experiencing the mind when breathing out, understanding it as it really is. I was mindfully gladdening the mind when breathing in, understanding it as it really is; I was mindfully gladdening the mind when breathing out, understanding it as it really is.

"I was mindfully concentrating the mind when breathing in, understanding it as it really is; I was mindfully concentrating the mind when breathing out, understanding it as it really is. I was mindfully liberating the mind when breathing in, understanding it as it really is; I was mindfully liberating the mind when breathing out, understanding it as it really is.

"I was mindfully contemplating impermanence when breathing in, understanding it as it really is; I was mindfully contemplating impermanence when breathing out, understanding it as it really is. I was mindfully contemplating eradication when breathing in, understanding it as it really is; I was mindfully contemplating eradication when breathing out, understanding it as it really is.

"I was mindfully contemplating dispassion when breathing in, understanding it as it really is; I was mindfully contemplating dispassion when breathing out, understanding it as it really is. I was mindfully contemplating cessation when breathing in, understanding it as it really is; I was mindfully *contemplating* cessation when breathing out, understanding it as it really is."

The sequence of the three insight contemplations after impermanence in the passage translated above reflects a recurrent difference compared to expositions of the sixteen steps of mindfulness of breathing in Pāli texts, where the three final steps are rather dispassion, cessation, and letting go.[13] The final tetrad thus involves the three topics of impermanence, dispassion, and cessation in all versions. The difference between accounts of mindfulness of breathing in sixteen steps is that in one type of description, found regularly in Pāli texts, dispassion and cessation lead to letting go; in the other type of description, however, dispassion and cessation do not lead on to something else and are instead preceded by eradication.[14]

After describing the sixteen steps of mindfulness of breathing, the *Saṃyukta-āgama* discourse continues with a description that is not found in its *Saṃyutta-nikāya* parallel. A comparable passage occurs in the Mūlasarvāstivāda *Vinaya*.[15] Both state that the Buddha stilled gross activities and entered a still more subtle dwelling, which led *deva*s witnessing his practice to make comments similar to those reported above in relation to the bodhisattva's period of breathless meditation, thinking that the Buddha was dead or that he was about to pass away.

This passage further supports the close relationship between the Buddha's undertaking of breathless meditation during the period of his ascetic practices and his cultivation of mindfulness of breathing after his awakening. The decisive difference is that, by progressing through the sixteen steps, a condition of not needing breath to the extent of appearing dead to observers is not reached through forceful control, but through a gradual procedure of calming the body and mind based on mindful observation.

In agreement with its *Saṃyutta-nikāya* parallel, the *Saṃyukta-āgama* discourse and the Mūlasarvāstivāda *Vinaya* conclude with the Buddha speaking in praise of mindfulness of breathing as a noble dwelling, a divine dwelling, and a dwelling of

---

13 See in more detail Anālayo 2013b: 232f and 2016b: 234f.

14 The implications of this step could be fleshed out with the help of the *Girimānanda-sutta*, which in agreement with its Tibetan counterpart stipulates the removal of thoughts related to sensuality, ill will, and harming, as well as to any other unwholesome quality, as constituting the perception of eradication or abandoning; see in more detail Anālayo 2016b: 102f and 223–6.

15 T 1448 at T XXIV 32c21.

the Tathāgata.[16] This confirms the overall impression that mindfulness of breathing in sixteen steps was a meditation practice held in special esteem by the Buddha.

EXERCISE

As a practical exercise, I would like to recommend cultivating the sixteen steps of mindfulness of breathing in the awareness that this is the noble and divine dwelling of the Tathāgata, a meditation practice the Buddha often recommended and regularly undertook himself. By engaging in this practice, we enact for ourselves what reflects a decisive shift of understanding that led the Buddha to realize awakening. This shift of understanding involves the realization that to force our way through to liberation does not work, instead of which the key to freedom lies in mindful observation. Applied to the breath, instead of interfering with, or even trying to stop, the natural flow of breathing, this shift in understanding finds its expression in being just mindful of natural breathing. Such being mindful can rely on the following scheme of sixteen steps, each being undertaken while remaining aware of the continuously changing process of naturally breathing in and breathing out.

- know breaths to be long
- know breaths to be short
- experience the whole body
- calm bodily activity

- experience joy
- experience happiness
- experience mental activity
- calm mental activity

- experience the mind
- gladden the mind
- concentrate the mind
- free the mind

16 SĀ 807 at T II 207a29 and T 1448 at T XXIV 32c28, which have several additional epithets not found in the Pāli version.

- contemplate impermanence
- contemplate dispassion/eradication
- contemplate cessation/dispassion
- contemplate letting go/cessation

One possible way of implementing this scheme could begin by becoming aware of the breath and its length (in terms of either long or short breath). Next we broaden the field of our awareness from the breath to the whole body in the sitting posture, and then relax both breath and body, allowing them to become calm.

Awareness can proceed from the joy that naturally arises due to the calming down of bodily processes to the calmer experience of happiness. Having become aware of any other mental activity that might be taking place can then lead to a calming of any such mental activity.

At this juncture awareness can be turned back to that which knows, the mind itself. The naturally arisen gladness that results from such turning back can lead on to collecting the mind in concentration and allowing it to rest freely in the condition of inner freedom from distraction, clinging, and identification.

Throughout the preceding steps, awareness of the inhalations and exhalations served as a continuous reminder of impermanence. This fact of impermanence could now be brought to the forefront of attention and become the foundation for arousing dispassion, next proceeding to cessation in the sense of attending to the ending of impermanent phenomena, and finally letting go in the most comprehensive manner possible. Alternatively, on following the *Saṃyukta-āgama* version translated above, insight into impermanence could lead over to eradication and then to dispassion and cessation.[17]

---

17 For more detailed practical suggestions on how to implement the sixteen steps of mindfulness of breathing see Anālayo 2016b: 229–36 and forthcoming.

VIII

FASTING

This is the last of three chapters on the topic of the future Buddha's ascetic practices. Having engaged in mind control and various modes of breath retention, his next and final attempt to reach awakening through asceticism involved fasting. Just as it seems natural to proceed from having tried to control the mind (by pressing the tongue against the palate and clenching the teeth) to attempting to stop the breath, similarly it seems natural that trying to control one's intake of oxygen leads to trying to control one's intake of food.

The *Mahāsaccaka-sutta* and its parallels agree that at first the Buddha thought of going on a complete fast; the same is also recorded in the *Saṅghabhedavastu* of the Mūlasarvāstivāda *Vinaya*. Having become aware of his intention to stop eating altogether, some *deva*s approached the bodhisattva and announced that they would infuse divine essence through his pores to nourish him.[1] This narration relates to a notion held in ancient India, according to which an accomplished saint no longer partakes of ordinary food and subsists solely on divine nourishment. According to the *Mahāsaccaka-sutta* and its parallels, the bodhisattva rejected this option and decided that, instead of completely stopping to take food, he would just take very small quantities of it.

1 MN 36 at MN I 245,8 (translated Ñāṇamoli 1995/2005: 339), fragment 334v2, Liu 2010: 189, EĀ 31.8 at T II 670c19 (translated Bronkhorst 1993/2000: 12), and Gnoli 1977: 102,4.

The *Mahāsaccaka-sutta* and its parallels describe the results of the Buddha's fasting in similar ways. The bodhisattva's limbs became emaciated and his buttocks took on the appearance of a camel's hoof. His eyes sunk into their sockets and his scalp shrivelled up. The Sanskrit fragment version depicts the pitiable condition of his body as follows:[2]

> [Thinking] at one time: "I will get up", I fell on my face. [Thinking]: "I will sit down", I fell on my back. Taking hold of the lower part of the body I encountered its upper parts; taking hold of the upper parts of the body I encountered its lower parts. Just rubbing and chafing this body with both hands to ease it, the bodily hair, whose roots had rotted, fell off to the ground.

Instead of speaking of the upper and lower parts of the body, the *Mahāsaccaka-sutta* and the *Ekottarika-āgama* discourse describe how touching the belly he would reach the backbone and vice versa.[3] This makes more sense and suggests that this part of the Sanskrit fragment suffered from some error during its transmission. The *Mahāsaccaka-sutta* also reports that the bodhisattva would fall over when trying to urinate and defecate. The parallel versions agree that, as with the earlier ascetic practices, the painful feelings experienced did not overwhelm his mind.

Having reduced his own body to such a condition eventually made it clear to the future Buddha that the attempt to reach liberation through self-inflicted pain was not the right path. The Sanskrit fragment version reports his reflection in this way:[4]

> "Whatever recluses and brahmins dwelled devoted to the practice of painful striving, none of them went further and beyond this." I thought: "This path is also inadequate for knowledge, inadequate for vision, and inadequate for supreme and right awakening."

---

2 The translated passage is based on fragment 335v3 to 335v5, Liu 2010: 204.

3 MN 36 at MN I 246,3 and EĀ 31.8 at T II 671a2. Regarding the appalling condition to which the bodhisattva had reduced his body, it is perhaps worthy of note that, according to Karetzky 1992: 100, "the starving Bodhisattva image was unacceptable in most of Asia ... during the thousands of years of Indian artistic tradition, such subjects were totally avoided. Only during the Kushan period were images of the starving ... Buddha created."

4 The translated passage is based on fragment 336v4 to 336v5, Liu 2010: 220.

The *Mahāsaccaka-sutta* reports the same conclusion with the minor difference that not only recluses and brahmins of the past but also those of the future and the present will not go beyond what the bodhisattva had experienced.

The change of attitude the Buddha-to-be underwent with respect to the value of fasting can also be seen in the *Mahāsakuludāyi-sutta* and its *Madhyama-āgama* parallel. According to both versions the Buddha highlighted the contrast between the abundant food he would at times take and the meagre amount of food taken by some of his disciples.[5] The example serves to convey to the audience of the discourse that there is no point in honouring the Buddha for eating little, as on giving importance to such a type of conduct one should rather honour some of his disciples who excelled him in this respect. In other words, as a teacher the Buddha did not accord overarching importance to austerities related to food intake and felt quite free to lag behind in this respect compared to some of his more ascetically inclined disciples, evidently because he had realized the limitations of asceticism as such.

This does not mean, however, that food was no longer an issue from his perspective. A discourse in the *Saṃyutta-nikāya* and its *Saṃyukta-āgama* parallel highlight the importance of developing a penetrative understanding of food. The *Saṃyukta-āgama* version puts the matter like this:[6]

> Having penetrative understanding of edible food, one abandons lustful craving for the five strands of sensual pleasure. Of one who removes lustful craving for the five strands of sensual pleasure, I do not see a single fetter, in respect to the five strands of sensual pleasure, that underlies such a learned noble disciple and that has not been removed, [such that would lead to] returning to be born in this world because of being bound by that single fetter.

The commentary on the corresponding passage in the *Saṃyutta-nikāya* explains that the teaching in this passage refers to

---

5 MN 77 at MN II 6,31 (translated Ñāṇamoli 1995/2005: 633) and its parallel MĀ 207 at T I 783a4 (the passage seems to have suffered from an error in transmission; see Anālayo 2011: 421f note 154).

6 The translation is based on SĀ 373 at T II 102c3 to 102c6, parallel to SN 12.63 at SN II 99,8 (translated Bodhi 2000: 598).

progress up to the third level of awakening, non-return.[7] This implies that finding the proper way of handling food and cultivating insight into one's eating habits and patterns can have a remarkable potential. In other words, even such a rather mundane activity as eating can have quite an impact on one's meditative development, for good or for worse.

The relationship drawn in this way between food and sensuality might also explain the rationale behind the bodhisattva's undertaking to fast. Once the attempt to enforce control over the mind and breath retention had not worked, the idea could have been that by fasting the tendency to sensuality in the mind can be weakened and overcome. Yet, in the end only the body was weakened, but the tendency to sensuality was not overcome. This requires, as the passage above clarifies, "penetrative understanding" of food, rather than mere abstention from it.

The degree of inner independence from attachment to food that can be reached through such penetrative understanding finds its expression in an episode reported in a discourse in the *Saṃyutta-nikāya* and its parallels. The Buddha had gone to beg for food without receiving anything. Being accosted by Māra, according to a *Saṃyukta-āgama* version of this episode the Buddha expresses his mental independence in the following way:[8]

> Even if I do not have anything,
> I delight in being self-sufficient.
> Just as the radiant devas,
> I will keep feeding on joy.
>
> Even if I do not have anything,
> I delight in being self-sufficient.
> I will keep feeding on joy,
> That does not depend on having a body.

The *Saṃyutta-nikāya* version similarly speaks of feeding on joy, comparable to the radiant *deva*s (although it has this description as a single verse). According to early Buddhist cosmology, these *deva*s dwell in a celestial realm corresponding to the second absorption.

7 Spk II 111,9.
8 The translation is based on SĀ 1095 at T II 288a23 to 288a26, parallel to SN 4.18 at SN I 114,22 (translated Bodhi 2000: 207f); another parallel, EĀ 45.4 at T II 772b4, instead reports a reply in prose.

In other words, the main point of the poem would be to highlight the joy of deep concentration as what one can "feed on", instead of requiring a continuous supply of tasty food and other material conveniences in order to be able to experience joy.

In recognition of the potential of the proper attitude to food and its relation to some degree of restraint, although not to the extent of imposing on oneself prolonged periods of fasting, the discourses report the Buddha laying down successive regulations to restrict the food intake of his monastic disciples. In the *Laṭukikopama-sutta* and its *Madhyama-āgama* parallel, a monastic reports the reaction caused when the Buddha promulgated a rule that his ordained disciples should not eat in the evening. In the Chinese version the monastic relates what happened in this way:[9]

> Formerly the Blessed One told the monastics: "Abandon eating at night." Blessed One, having heard this we could not stand it, we could not endure it, we did not want it, and we did not like it. Of the two meals [in a day], this is the superior one, the most excellent one, the most superb one, the most attractive one, and the Blessed One was now instructing us to abandon it, the Well-gone One was instructing us to cut it off. We even said: "The Great Recluse cannot [just] do away with our food!"[10]

In agreement with the Pāli parallel, the *Madhyama-āgama* discourse continues with the monastic stating that, in spite of their initial reaction to this ruling by the Buddha, out of their deep respect for their teacher the monastics followed his injunction. Not all monastics were obedient in this way, however, and the Buddha's ruling that they should take only a single meal even met with open resistance. This can be seen in the *Bhaddāli-sutta* and its parallels. Here is the relevant part from the *Ekottarika-āgama*:[11]

---

9 The translated passage is taken from MĀ 192 at T I 741a19 to 741a23, parallel to MN 66 at MN I 448,16 (translated Ñāṇamoli 1995/2005: 552); for a comparative study see Anālayo 2011: 363. In this discourse, this is the second restriction on food promulgated by the Buddha.

10 The last statement has no counterpart in MN 66.

11 The translation is based on EĀ 49.7 at T II 800b28 to 800c3 (translated Anālayo 2016a: 90), parallel to MN 65 at MN I 437,15 (translated Ñāṇamoli 1995/2005: 542) and MĀ 194 at T I 746b20; for a comparative study see Anālayo 2011: 358f.

> At that time the Blessed One told the monastics: "I always take my meal in a single sitting [per day] and my body is at ease, strong, and thriving. Monastics, you should also take a single meal [per day] and your body will be at ease, strong, and thriving, enabling you to cultivate the holy life."
>
> Then Bhaddāli said to the Blessed One: "I cannot endure a single meal. The reason is that my strength will become feeble."

The parallel versions report that Bhaddāli kept refusing to follow the Buddha's injunction even when presented with alternative options on how to implement the rule and still ensure he would get his fill. Besides this act of disobedience by Bhaddāli, another noteworthy aspect is the emphasis the Buddha places on feeling at ease and strong when taking a single meal. This marks the difference from the fasting he did before his awakening, which resulted in weakening the body. Drawing out the implications, any restraint one might wish to implement in regard to one's eating habits should not be applied in a way that leads to an actual weakening of health and thereby becomes an obstruction to the practice.

Bhaddāli was not the only one to resist the injunction to eat only a single meal. When the news of this rule reached another group of monastics, according to the *Kīṭāgiri-sutta* and its *Madhyama-āgama* parallel these monastics reasoned that they felt quite at ease and strong eating throughout the day, hence they saw no reason for changing their eating habits. This in a way puts the suggestion I made in the previous paragraph into perspective, in that the point is not to use health as an excuse for indulgence.

The Buddha then explained to these monastics the rationale behind his giving such instructions, which can be taken as a guideline for finding the proper point of balance between self-indulgence and self-torment. The *Madhyama-āgama* parallel reports this as follows:[12]

> Since I understood as it really is, saw, comprehended, achieved, rightly and fully realized that with some pleasant feelings evil and

12 The translated portion is taken from MĀ 195 at T I 751a8 to 751a21, parallel to MN 70 at MN I 475,34 (translated Ñāṇamoli 1995/2005: 579); for a comparative study see Anālayo 2011: 377f.

unwholesome states increase and wholesome states decrease, for this reason I tell you to abandon such pleasant feelings.

Since I understood as it really is, saw, comprehended, achieved, rightly and fully realized that with some pleasant feelings evil and unwholesome states decrease and wholesome states increase, for this reason I tell you to cultivate such pleasant feelings.

Since I understood as it really is, saw, comprehended, achieved, rightly and fully realized that with some painful feelings evil and unwholesome states increase and wholesome states decrease, for this reason I tell you to abandon such painful feelings.

Since I understood as it really is, saw, comprehended, achieved, rightly and fully realized that with some painful feelings evil and unwholesome states decrease and wholesome states increase, for this reason I tell you to cultivate such painful feelings.

Why is that? I do not tell you to cultivate all bodily pleasure and I also do not tell you not to cultivate all bodily pleasure. I do not tell you to cultivate all bodily pain and I also do not tell you not to cultivate all bodily pain.

I do not tell you to cultivate all mental pleasure and I also do not tell you not to cultivate all mental pleasure. I do not tell you to cultivate all mental pain and I also do not tell you not to cultivate all mental pain.

Although the *Kīṭāgiri-sutta* does not bring in the distinction between bodily and mental pleasure or pain, the gist of its presentation is similar. The fundamental insight described in both versions would reflect the Buddha's own experiments with asceticism. His post-awakening attitude towards food can be seen as a reasonable middle-way approach of recommending some restraint with food intake to the extent to which this will not interfere with the health of the body. Based on this behavioural framework, the task is to leave behind feelings of a worldly type, which stimulate the growth of defilements, and instead cultivate feelings of an unworldly type, which lead to liberation.

Behind all this stands the crucial shift of perspective from reacting to feelings based on their affective trigger to giving importance instead to their wholesome or unwholesome repercussions. The natural tendency of the untrained mind is to pursue pleasure and avoid pain. Asceticism attempts to counter this by doing the opposite, advocating the pursuit of self-inflicted pain and the avoidance of pleasure. The future Buddha had personal experience of both: the tendency of the untrained mind to find pleasure in sensual indulgence, as he had done himself in his youth, and the tendency of ascetic attitudes to believe that as long as it is painful it must be effecting purification. Now he knew better. Leaving behind both extremes, the Buddha found the middle path in relation to feelings by giving emphasis to their overall repercussions instead of to their affective tone, be it by craving for pleasure instead of pain or by advocating pain over pleasure.

It appears to be the same basic shift in perspective which the *Satipaṭṭhāna-sutta* and its parallels inculcate in their instructions for contemplation of feeling.[13] Such contemplation proceeds through two stages. The first is bare recognition of the affective tone of feeling as being pleasant, painful, or neutral. This type of mindfulness practice weans the mind from the ingrained tendency to react to feeling on the spot, a topic to which I return in Chapter 10.

Once that much has been established, the second stage comes into play, where each type of feeling is further distinguished into worldly and unworldly types. This seems to be concerned with the same basic distinction that also underlies the above passage from the *Kīṭāgiri-sutta* and its parallel, namely the relation of feelings to progress to liberation. Whatever their affective tone, the crucial question is whether the experience of such feeling has wholesome or unwholesome results, whether it is connected to worldliness or to its opposite, not whether it is pleasant or unpleasant in the moment of being experienced. Such awareness is similar to the basic distinction of thoughts into two types in the *Dvedhāvitakka-sutta* and its *Madhyama-āgama* parallel, discussed in Chapter 3.[14]

EXERCISE

As a practical exercise, I would like to recommend cultivating the inner joy of contentment and generosity as a way of going

13 See Anālayo 2013b: 117–23.
14 See above p. 23.

beyond the attractions of material pleasures. In relation to food in particular, this could take the form of mindful eating as a way of reducing excessive intake of food, as well as sharing particularly delectable food with others. In more general terms, the task would be to find joy in giving away things rather than hoarding them, in sharing rather than keeping for ourselves. Such joy can be encouraged by intentionally recollecting our own generosity and rejoicing in it, which is one of the standard forms of recollection.

Beyond the gift of material things, another dimension of generosity can also be the gift of time and attention, especially when others are suffering and in bodily or mental pain. All such occasions can later become occasions for recollecting our own generosity and thereby strengthening the tendency of the mind to seek the type of joy that does not depend on what is material. Strengthening this tendency can take inspiration from the verse translated above, according to which the Buddha "will keep feeding on joy" when no food is available.

Happiness is mental after all. Searching for it via sense experiences is therefore a detour. Searching for happiness within, by establishing a wholesome condition of the mind, is more straightforward and more meaningful than trying to do so through sensual gratification.

IX

FINDING THE PATH

In this chapter I examine the future Buddha's discovery of the path to awakening. This has its place after he had reviewed his ascetic practices and realized that, even though he had undertaken them in a manner that could hardly be surpassed, they had not led him to awakening. Apparently as part of a review of what he had tried out so far, the bodhisattva remembered an experience of the first absorption from his youth.[1] The relevant part of the Sanskrit fragment parallel to the *Mahāsaccaka-sutta* describes his remembrance in this way:[2]

> Then I thought: "I remember that accompanying my father, the Sakyan Suddhodana, at his work and while being seated in the shadow of a rose-apple tree, I dwelled secluded from sensuality and secluded from evil and unwholesome states, with application and its sustaining, with joy and happiness born of seclusion, having attained the first absorption. This may be the path, the way adequate for knowledge, adequate for vision, and adequate for supreme and right awakening."

The *Mahāsaccaka-sutta* reports a similar memory, which led the bodhisattva to come to the definite conclusion that this was the path to awakening.[3] In other words, the reasoning underlying

1 For a version of this episode see above p. 6.

2 The translated passage is based on fragment 336v5 to 336v7, Liu 2010: 222f, parallel to MN 36 at MN I 246,30 (translated Ñāṇamoli 1995/2005: 340).

3 In an account of the present episode in the Dharmaguptaka *Vinaya*, T 1428 at T XXII 781a7 (translated Bareau 1963: 48), the insight is that

his adoption of the path of ascetic practices had turned out to be mistaken, in particular the belief that happiness needs to be avoided at all costs and that progress to liberation requires inflicting pain on oneself.

The mistaken notion that happiness needs to be avoided at all costs comes to the fore in a passage found next in the *Mahāsaccaka-sutta*, according to which the future Buddha thought to himself: "Why am I afraid of that happiness which is a happiness apart from sensuality and unwholesome states?"[4] This implies that earlier he had indeed been afraid of happiness, even of the type of happiness that is not related to sensuality or other unwholesome states.

The type of reasoning behind such apprehensions recurs in a discussion with Jain ascetics, reported in the *Cūḷadukkhakkhandha-sutta* and its parallels. In the course of this discussion, the Jains assert that happiness cannot be gained through happiness, but instead requires going through pain.[5] The belief that happiness is to be gained through pain comes up again as an opinion voiced by a prince in the *Bodhirājakumāra-sutta* and its Sanskrit fragment parallel, in reply to which the Buddha then relates his own pre-awakening quest.[6] In the Pāli version, the Buddha leads over to this account of his former practices with the following statement:[7]

> Before my awakening, when still being an unawakened bodhisattva, I thought as well: "Happiness is not to be reached through happiness; happiness is to be reached through pain!"

---

liberation can be attained "on following this path".

4 The translation is based on MN 36 at MN I 246,37 to 247,2, which has no equivalent in the Sanskrit fragment version. Nakamura 2000: 183 notes that "Gotama thus makes the bold declaration that there is no need to be afraid of happiness."

5 MN 14 at MN I 93,36 (translated Ñāṇamoli 1995/2005: 188), with parallels in MĀ 100 at T I 587b28 and EĀ 41.1 at T II 744b9; see also T 55 at T I 850c17 for what might be a translation based on another version of such a statement, and for a comparative study that also covers yet another parallel, T 54, Anālayo 2011: 123.

6 MN 85 at MN II 93,13 (translated Ñāṇamoli 1995/2005: 706), which has a parallel in fragment 342r4, Silverlock 2009: 77; for a comparative study see Anālayo 2011: 481.

7 The translated part is found in MN 85 at MN II 93,15 to 93,18.

The passage translated above, found only in the Pāli version, appears to be concerned in particular with the bodhisattva's period of asceticism. It must have been the belief that happiness is to be reached through (self-inflicted) pain that motivated the future Buddha during the time of his ascetic practices. Having been unable to reach liberation in this way, he was ready to relinquish this belief. This also appears to be the chief implication of the recollection of his former experience of an absorption.

The sources that report this previous absorption experience vary regarding his age and also the depth of concentration he reached at that time. The presentation in the *Mahāsaccaka-sutta* and its Sanskrit fragment parallel, according to which he had attained the first absorption, receives support from the *Madhyama-āgama*, the *Divyāvadāna*, the *Buddhacarita*, and several other biographies of the Buddha preserved in Chinese.[8] According to a discourse in the *Ekottarika-āgama* and the *Lalitavistara*, however, he attained not only the first but all four absorptions.[9] The same position is also taken by the *Milindapañha* and some biographies of the Buddha preserved in Chinese.[10]

In view of the struggle the bodhisattva went through before mastering absorption, reported in the *Upakkilesa-sutta* and its parallel, it seems improbable that during what appears to be an earlier time he had already experienced the fourth absorption. Perhaps the presentation in the *Ekottarika-āgama* and the *Lalitavistara*, as well as in the *Milindapañha* and in some Chinese biographies of the Buddha, results from an attempt to improve on the marvellous quality of this former experience by increasing the depth of concentration attained.[11]

---

8 MĀ 32 at T I 470c18 (and MĀ 117 at T I 608a2, translated above p. 6), Cowell and Neal 1886: 391,16, Johnston 1936/1995: 46 (§5.10, see also T 192 at T IV 8c16), T 184 at T III 467b23, T 186 at T III 499b9, and T 190 at T III 706a20.

9 EĀ 31.8 at T II 671b11 and Lefmann 1902: 263,17 (see also T 187 at T III 560b17); see also Waldschmidt 1929/1982: 10.

10 Mil 290,1, T 189 at T III 629a27, and T 193 at T IV 66b18; see also Bu ston's *History of Buddhism*, Obermiller 1932/1986: 15.

11 Foucher 1949: 93 deems the presentation in the *Lalitavistara* to be part of a general tendency to exaggeration, and Horsch 1964: 117 considers the description in the *Milindapañha* to be a departure from the original. Durt 1982: 116 even qualifies the reference to the attainment of the fourth absorption as an absurd exaggeration.

Regarding the bodhisattva's age at the time of this former absorption experience, according to the Pāli commentary he was still rather young. The commentary mentions that his father had carried him along and that the wet-nurses had left him alone under the rose-apple tree.[12] This gives the impression that he was just a small child.[13] An absorption attained at a fairly young age would then have been during a period of his life before he indulged in sensual pleasures. Recollecting that would in turn have made it clear to the Buddha-to-be that such happiness and pleasure has no relation whatsoever to sensuality, even indirectly, a distinction that would not have been as evident with any absorption experienced after he had gone forth. Although absorption attainment is of course aloof from sensuality, the very fact of seeking such pleasure could still be suspected to foster the general quest of the mind for pleasure, even of a sensual type. Such is in fact the reasoning underlying the avoidance of anything pleasurable by those pursuing ascetic practices.

The *Mahāvastu*, however, reports that he had taken a stroll together with his father before sitting down under the rose-apple tree.[14] Moreover, according to the *Mahāvastu* this meditative experience made his father anxious that his son might want to go forth. In order to distract him, the father sent women to entertain his son with song and dance.[15] From the viewpoint of the *Mahāvastu*, he must have been considerably older than an infant and would no longer have been at an age where sensuality was of no influence on his mind. The *Saṅghabhedavastu* of the Mūlasarvāstivāda *Vinaya* and the *Buddhacarita* locate the experience of the first absorption after his legendary four encounters with someone suffering from old age, someone sick, a dead person, and finally a monastic.[16] In these versions he appears to have already been a young man at that time.

An individual Chinese translation that parallels this part of the *Mahāsaccaka-sutta* even places the original experience soon

12 Ps II 290,25.

13 Mil 289,26 in fact takes the position that he was only one month old. This seems too young for him to be able to sit in meditation and attain absorption.

14 Senart 1890: 45,4 (translated Jones 1952/1976: 42).

15 Senart 1890: 144,6 (translated Jones 1952/1976: 138f).

16 Gnoli 1977: 76,24 and Johnston 1936/1995: 46 (§5.10).

after his going forth. The relevant part, which describes his recollection after the realization that asceticism is not the path to awakening, proceeds as follows:[17]

> Then I further thought: "Just after going forth I had gone to a Sakyan grove to sit in tranquillity under a rose-apple tree whose shadow did not move, it being shady and cool. At that time, secluded from being defiled by any sensuality and unwholesome states, with application and sustaining, with joy and happiness born of seclusion, I had realized the first concentrative absorption. This is the right path for awakening as it really is."

The suggestion that he had this absorption experience soon after going forth would imply that the description in the *Upakkilesa-sutta* and its parallel concerns the bodhisattva's attempts to replicate this experience and gradually gain mastery of absorption. In fact both versions start their account by reporting that he had attained concentration but then lost it again.

If his absorption experience should instead be placed in his early childhood, however, then this presentation could be read in the light of research on children who remember past lives. Cases of this type tend to involve children who at an age of about two years or even earlier start to exhibit informational and behavioural memories from what they experience as one or more past lives.[18] Some years later, as they grow up, such memories and related behaviours tend to become weaker or even be lost completely. An illustrative case involves a Thai girl who at the age of two was taken for the first time to the monastery in which according to her memories she had lived in a former life. She reportedly not only executed the traditional forms of worship and offerings correctly, but also went on her own to sit down cross-legged in meditation posture for half an hour, without having been told by anyone to do so or having earlier witnessed this done at her home by others.[19]

On adopting such a reading of the present episode, an absorption experienced in early youth by the bodhisattva could

---

17 The translation is based on T 757 at T XVII 599a14 to 599a18.

18 For a survey of different aspects of such behavioural memories see Stevenson 1987/2001: 115–20.

19 Stevenson 1983: 40.

then be considered a behavioural continuity with a past life. This would presumably be from a more distant life given that, according to the *Acchariyabbhutadhamma-sutta* and its *Madhyama-āgama* parallel, he had spent his last life before the present one in the Tusita Heaven.[20] In early Buddhist cosmology the Tusita Heaven is inferior to the heavenly realms in which those who have mastery of absorption are reborn. Thus he could not have passed away as one who had mastered absorption in his last two lives before becoming the Buddha, otherwise he would not have been reborn in Tusita or after that as a human.

Be that as it may, what remains common ground among the texts reporting this episode is that he recollected an experience of absorption from the time before he had set out to cultivate the two modes of practice he later found insufficient to lead him to his goal: the immaterial attainments and asceticism. Recalling what he had experienced earlier, well before he had engaged in the practices that in the end had not led him to awakening, helped the bodhisattva to change perspective. The resultant change of perspective is based on the realization that wholesome types of happiness need not be shunned, as they can support progress to awakening. This is precisely the insight that comes to the fore in the *Kīṭāgiri-sutta* and its *Madhyama-āgama* parallel, taken up in the previous chapter, which report the Buddha clarifying his own realization that some types of pleasure are obstructive, but others are not. The decisive criterion is therefore not the affective nature of a particular experience, but its wholesome or unwholesome repercussions.

The basic shift of understanding that led the Buddha to finding the path to awakening recurs in a discourse in the *Saṃyutta-nikāya*, in which Māra challenges the Buddha for having given up his ascetic practices. In what follows I translate the *Saṃyukta-āgama* parallel:[21]

> At one time the Buddha was dwelling at the location of Uruvelā by the side of the river Nerañjarā, below the Bodhi tree, having

20 MN 123 at MN III 119,35 (translated Ñāṇamoli 1995/2005: 980) and its parallel MĀ 32 at T I 470a14 (translated Bingenheimer et al. 2013: 248); for a comparative study see Anālayo 2011: 702.

21 The translated discourse is SĀ 1094 at T II 287c21 to 288a8, parallel to SN 4.1 at SN I 103,1 (translated Bodhi 2000: 195f).

just reached full awakening. At that time the Blessed One, being alone in a quiet place and with his mind collected in meditative reflection, thought like this:

"I am now liberated from ascetic practice. It is well. I am now well liberated from ascetic practice. Previously I cultivated right aspiration, now it has already born fruit and I gained unsurpassed awakening."

Then Māra, the Evil One, thought: "Now the recluse Gotama is dwelling at the location of Uruvelā by the side of the river Nerañjarā, below the Bodhi tree, having just reached awakening. I will now approach him to give him trouble." He transformed himself into a youth, stood in front of the Buddha, and said in verse:

"The abode of extensively cultivating ascetic practices
Brings about the attainment of purity.
Now that you have turned back and given them up,
What are you searching for here?
You wish to search for purity here,
Yet there is no way for you to attain purity."

Then the Blessed One thought: "This is Māra, the Evil One, who wants to disturb me", and he said in verse:

"I understood that the cultivation of all ascetic practices,
Is altogether pointless.
In the end one does not gain benefit,
Comparable to a bow that only makes sound.[22]

"Morality, concentration, learning, and wisdom are the path,
All of which I have already cultivated.
I have attained the foremost purity,
A purity that is unsurpassable."

The *Saṃyutta-nikāya* version differs in so far as, according to its report, Māra had actually read the mind of the Buddha and thereby come to know what he was thinking. Another difference is that, instead of illustrating the futility of asceticism with a bow (without arrows), the simile in the *Saṃyutta-nikāya* describes oars and rudders on dry land. Moreover, the qualities the Buddha proclaimed he had cultivated are only morality,

22 The translation is based on adopting a variant reading.

concentration, and wisdom. In fact the reference to "learning" in the discourse translated above seems less suited to the context.

Alongside such differences, however, the two versions agree in throwing into relief the Buddha's realization of the futility of ascetic practices. They also serve to contextualize the memory of his absorption experience by mentioning, in addition to the cultivation of concentration, also the need for morality and wisdom. These are the three trainings that form the foundation for the Buddhist path to awakening and also underlie the noble eightfold path. This confirms what would already have become evident from the foregoing discussion, in that the path found by the Buddha was not just absorption attainment on its own.

In fact, as mentioned in Chapter 4,[23] as far as the early discourses allow us to judge, absorption attainment was already known in the ancient Indian setting before the advent of the Buddha. Such ability would indeed have been required for Āḷāra Kālāma and Uddaka's father Rāma to reach the third and fourth immaterial spheres.

The present episode, instead of equating the whole path to awakening with the attainment of the first absorption, seems to imply that recollecting the former absorption experience led the bodhisattva to the realization that wholesome types of happiness need not be shunned. This enabled him to progress to awakening, a progress that requires all three trainings and thus a combining of concentration with the cultivation of morality and wisdom.

EXERCISE

By way of putting into practice a realization that appears to have been pivotal in the Buddha's discovery of the path to awakening, I would suggest making a conscious effort to cultivate wholesome types of joy. For this purpose, I recommend contemplation of the mind as described in the *Satipaṭṭhāna-sutta* and already broached in Chapter 3 as well as awareness of the absence of the hindrances mentioned in Chapter 4. Whereas in Chapter 3 the task was to cultivate clear recognition of the presence or absence of lust, anger, etc., building on this recognition we could now

23 See above p. 36.

give special attention to all those moments in daily life when our own mind is not overwhelmed by strong defilements. This much is reason enough to rejoice. Cultivating such wholesome joy can become a way of honouring the Buddha through walking the path he discovered by encouraging wholesome types of happiness and leaving behind unwholesome ones.

In support of this suggestion I would like to note that it is an integral aspect of contemplation of the mind in the *satipaṭṭhāna* scheme to be aware of the absence of defilements, even if only temporarily. The instructions are to recognize not only the presence of, for example, lust and anger in our mind, but also their absence. Such absence can be made an occasion for the arousing of joy. Such rejoicing need not be confined to the absence of the hindrances during formal meditation, but can have its place any time during daily life, as soon as we have a moment of time to inspect the condition of our mind.

Needless to say, my recommendation here is not meant to encourage turning a blind eye to our own defilements. The point is only to make a conscious effort to proceed from attention given to our faults to giving similar attention to our positive sides and employ these as a source for arousing joy. The cultivation of such joy will go a long way in strengthening the ability of the mind to remain free from succumbing to defilements on the next possible occasion.

X

DETERMINATION

From the Buddha's discovery of the path to awakening, taken up in the preceding chapter, I now proceed to his strong determination to follow this path through to its final goal. This strong determination finds expression in a passage in the *Mahāgosiṅga-sutta* and its parallels. The discourse features several eminent monastics who engaged in what appears to be a playful competition. In the course of this, each eulogized a particular quality of an accomplished practitioner that could match the beauty of the moonlit grove where they were meeting, a quality in which the respective speaker was particularly accomplished. When the monastics approached the Buddha to receive his verdict regarding which of them had spoken well, he endorsed all of their statements by replying that they had all spoken well. Then he added yet another quality, which the context suggests was the one the Buddha considered to be characteristic of himself. In the *Madhyama-āgama* parallel to the *Mahāgosiṅga-sutta*, this characteristic is as follows:[1]

> Suppose when the night is over, at dawn, in compliance with dwelling in dependence on a town or village, a monastic puts on the robes and takes the bowl to enter the village to beg for food, with the body well guarded, all the faculties well collected,

---

1 The translation is based on MĀ 184 at T I 729b16 to 729b23, parallel to MN 32 at MN I 219,28 (translated Ñāṇamoli 1995/2005: 312), EĀ 37.3 at T II 711c16, and T 154.16 at T III 82b8; see also Anālayo 2011: 215f.

> and mindfulness well established. Having begged for food, after midday, having put away robes and bowl as well as washed hands and feet, with a sitting mat placed over the shoulder [the monastic] approaches a forest, the foot of a tree, or an empty quiet place. Spreading out the sitting mat, [the monastic] sits down cross-legged [with the determination]: "I will not release the cross-legged sitting until the influxes are eradicated." [The monastic] in turn does not release the cross-legged sitting until the influxes are eradicated.

The *Mahāgosiṅga-sutta* gives fewer details regarding what needs to be done previous to the sitting and does not explicitly state that the strong determination (not to break posture until liberation from the influxes has been attained) is indeed carried out to its successful completion. The same appears nevertheless to be implicit in its presentation.

Two other discourses in the *Madhyama-āgama* associate this strong determination with the occasion when the bodhisattva approached the seat of awakening.[2] The *Lalitavistara* and the *Saṅghabhedavastu* of the Mūlasarvāstivāda *Vinaya*, as well as the introductory narration to the *Jātaka* collection, confirm that this was indeed the bodhisattva's determined attitude when sitting down for the meditation session that resulted in his awakening.[3] This episode appears to be the nucleus out of which the hagiographic account developed that depicts the Buddha seated under the tree of awakening and assailed by Māra and his host who are unable to displace him from his seat.

When evaluating the implications of the above strong determination, it needs to be kept in mind that for the Buddha to sit for long stretches of time was not necessarily a challenge. This comes to the fore in a discussion between the Buddha and Jain ascetics, reported in the *Cūḷadukkhakkhandha-sutta* and its parallels and already mentioned in the previous chapter. In the course of this discussion, the Jains assert that happiness cannot be gained through happiness, but instead requires going through pain. This affirmation finds its illustration in the contrast provided by King

---

2 MĀ 157 at T I 679c11 and MĀ 204 at T I 777a12; see also T 212 at T IV 644c14.

3 Lefmann 1902: 262,3, Gnoli 1977: 113,23, and Jā I 71,24.

Bimbisāra, presumably brought in by the Jains as an example of someone who has free access to sensual pleasure. In other words, if the true happiness of liberation did not depend on experiencing pain, then even someone who lives in luxury and surrounded by sensual pleasures like the king of the country would at the same time be making progress to liberation.

In reply to the Jains (referred to as Nigaṇṭhas), in the *Cūḷadukkhakkhandha-sutta* the Buddha conveys his shift of perspective by comparing the happiness of a king to the happiness of absorption. The relevant passage in the *Madhyama-āgama* parallel to the *Cūḷadukkhakkhandha-sutta* proceeds as follows:[4]

> I asked them again: "Nigaṇṭhas, am I able, as I wish, to experience delightful joy and deep happiness for one day and one night by remaining in silence and without speaking?" The Nigaṇṭhas replied: "Indeed, Gotama."
>
> *I asked them again: "Nigaṇṭhas, am I able, as I wish,* to experience delightful joy and deep happiness for two, for three, for four, for five, for six, [even] for seven days and seven nights *by remaining in silence without speaking?"* The Nigaṇṭhas replied: "Indeed, Gotama."
>
> I asked them again: "Nigaṇṭhas, what do you think, whose happiness is superior, that of King Bimbisāra or mine?" The Nigaṇṭhas replied: "Gotama, as we came to understand what the recluse Gotama has said, the happiness of Gotama is superior, that of King Bimbisāra does not match it."

The *Cūḷadukkhakkhandha-sutta* differs in so far as here the Buddha just affirms that he is able to experience happiness for up to seven days and nights, rather than asking the Jains for confirmation. Another difference is that in the *Cūḷadukkhakkhandha-sutta* the Buddha specifies that such experience of continuous happiness takes place "without moving the body", a specification also

4 The translated passage is taken from MĀ 100 at T I 587c15 to 587c22, parallel to MN 14 at MN I 94,29 (translated Ñāṇamoli 1995/2005: 189), T 54 at T I 849a28, T 55 at T I 851a3, and EĀ 41.1 at T II 744b14 (here the reference is to the king's inability to do so, as the description of the Buddha's ability appears to be abbreviated and no longer mentions the time span); for a comparative study see Anālayo 2011: 123.

found in a parallel in the *Ekottarika-āgama*. The same would be implicit in the other versions, whose description must be referring to the same type of deep happiness experienced during absorption attainment.

The ability to sit for up to seven days and nights experiencing the bliss of deep concentration provides a helpful background to the passage from the *Mahāgosiṅga-sutta* and its parallels regarding the strong determination not to break posture until awakening is reached. Although this indubitably depicts an unswerving determination, it does not imply that the future Buddha was sitting through excruciating pain or with a forceful mental attitude. In fact the pointlessness of trying to force the mind to do what one wants, just as the futility of suffering through self-inflicted pain, had become patently clear to the bodhisattva well before the present juncture of events, leading to his abandoning of asceticism.

In this way the passage translated at the outset of this chapter is probably best understood as conveying the building up of the basic motivation discussed in the first chapter of this book, namely the bodhisattva's quest to find the supreme peace of Nirvāṇa which is free from old age, disease, and death. This motivation forms a continuous theme throughout the whole trajectory of his experiences from going forth up to the present moment. It is this unswerving motivation that made him give up the sublime meditative experiences reached under the tuition of Āḷāra Kālāma and Uddaka Rāmaputta and also made him let go of the pursuit of asceticism. Throughout apparent failures his determination seems to have become stronger rather than lessened, until it reaches the present final peak.

This provides a powerful example of the potential and importance of keeping one's own motivation clearly in mind as a guiding force for meditation practice. Repeated recollection of one's aim to progress towards liberation will form an inclination of the mind, as is the case with any thought one recurrently engages in (according to the *Dvedhāvitakka-sutta* and its parallels, which I took up in Chapter 3). Such an inclination of the mind can become a major force for sustaining progress until one indeed has realized the goal of one's aspiration.

In a way this mirrors the role of right view in relation to the remainder of the noble eightfold path. According to the *Mahācattārīsaka-sutta* and its parallels, the eight factors build on each other with right view as their foundation.[5] The *Mahācattārīsaka-sutta* and its parallels agree that the task of right view is to recognize whether other path factors like intention, speech, action, and livelihood are leading in the right direction. In the case of intentions, this requires implementing the basic distinction of thoughts into wholesome and unwholesome types that according to the *Dvedhāvitakka-sutta* and its *Madhyama-āgama* parallel formed a central dimension of the bodhisattva's own practice. Unwholesome thoughts and intention are harmful for oneself and others, they do not lead to Nirvāṇa. Wholesome thoughts and intentions are not harmful and do form part of the conduct that leads to Nirvāṇa. The same holds for unwholesome versus wholesome speech, action, and livelihood. In this way the *Mahācattārīsaka-sutta* and its parallels can be taken as fleshing out the repercussions of the attitude enshrined in right view, which in turn mirrors the basic motivation of the future Buddha to set out in quest of Nirvāṇa.

The *Mahāsaccaka-sutta* and its Sanskrit parallel offer further details on the sitting with determination that was to lead the bodhisattva to the breakthrough to Nirvāṇa. They report that, after having nourished his body to regain his strength, he next cultivated the four absorptions. The relevant part in the Sanskrit fragment version proceeds like this:[6]

> Secluded from sensuality *and secluded from evil and unwholesome states, with application and its sustaining, with joy and happiness born of seclusion*, I dwelled having attained the first absorption.

The Sanskrit fragment continues by reporting that his experience of this attainment took place in the presence of the same qualities that he had relied on earlier during his ascetic practices:

---

5 MN 117 at MN III 76,1 (translated Ñāṇamoli 1995/2005: 938f) and its parallels MĀ 189 at T I 735c8 (translated Anālayo 2012b: 295) and D 4094 *nyu* 46b2 or Q 5595 *thu* 86a6. For a comparative study see Anālayo 2011: 658.

6 The translated passage is based on fragment 337r4 to 337r6, Liu 2010: 228, parallel to MN 36 at MN I 247,18 (translated Ñāṇamoli 1995/2005: 340f).

> Tireless energy was produced in me, the body was calm and not agitated, mindfulness was established without confusion, the mind was concentrated and unified.

Another continuity with the earlier asceticism is the bodhisattva's report that the feelings arisen did not overwhelm his mind. This forms a continuous theme for the painful feelings of his various ascetic practices, but with the present experience of the pleasure of absorption it takes a different form, as follows:

> Feeling such wholly peaceful and sublime feelings did not remain obsessing the mind, as I had thus developed the body and developed the mind.

The *Mahāsaccaka-sutta* differs in so far as it states that the feelings that did not remain overwhelming his mind were of the pleasant type, in contrast to the qualification of these feelings as peaceful and sublime in the Sanskrit fragment version. Both versions continue with the same presentation for the other three absorptions. In the case of the fourth absorption, the *Mahāsaccaka-sutta* still specifies that such pleasant feelings did not remain overwhelming the mind of the bodhisattva. This shows that in this respect the Sanskrit fragment version has a preferable formulation, since to speak of peaceful and sublime feelings works for all four absorptions, whereas to refer to pleasant feelings, *sukhā vedanā*, does not suit the fourth absorption too well,[7] because it is a precondition for its attainment that pleasant feelings have been left behind.

Alongside this minor variation in formulation, however, the two versions agree that monitoring the impact of feelings on the mind forms a basic continuity from the onset of the bodhisattva's ascetic practices to his gaining of the fourth absorption on the eve of his awakening. They also agree that neither intensely painful nor intensely pleasant feelings had been able to overwhelm the mind of the bodhisattva. Needless to say, at the time of going through these experiences he was not yet awakened, making it clear that to cultivate the ability to keep the mind from being overwhelmed by feeling is not the sole domain of awakened ones.

---

7 This has already been pointed out by Vetter 1996: 62.

According to a discourse in the *Saṃyutta-nikāya* and its *Saṃyukta-āgama* parallel, insight into feeling became a dimension of the Buddha's awakening.[8] This confirms the importance of insightful contemplation of feeling for the Buddha's progress to, and eventual attainment of, the goal of his aspiration.

The importance given to the experience of feeling in this way could explain why the scheme of *satipaṭṭhāna* meditation has allotted a distinct place to its contemplation. To direct mindfulness to body and mind, as is the case with the first and the third *satipaṭṭhāna*, is in a way natural, but to carve out an additional place for feeling by way of the second *satipaṭṭhāna* seems less obvious at first sight. Perhaps it is precisely the bodhisattva's own experience during his quest for awakening that made plain to him the need to give special importance to feeling, together with the importance of mindfully monitoring what one is doing and in what way this affects the condition of one's mind.[9]

It is such mindful monitoring that led him to the realization that the two paths he had tried were not capable of leading him to his goal. The same mindful monitoring during his actual striving enabled him to experience pain and pleasure without being overwhelmed by them. This is precisely the task that underlies contemplation of feeling. As mentioned briefly in Chapter 8, contemplation of feeling requires being aware of feeling as pleasant, painful, or neutral. The chief challenge here is neither to ignore the feeling tone of present experience nor to react to it immediately. Instead, one just remains aware and thereby learns to experience fully the affective push that comes usually so closely intertwined with the experience of feeling as to lead to instant reactions by way of desire and aversion. Here

---

8 SN 36.24 at SN IV 233,12 (translated Bodhi 2000: 1281f, who has divided the text into two separate discourses) and its parallel SĀ 475 at T II 121c12 (the exposition is abbreviated).

9 Carrithers 1983: 51 reasons that during his period of asceticism "the Buddha had repeatedly disciplined himself to ignore those sensations and impulses which ordinarily issue in action or reaction ... he had ignored the calls of hunger and thirst which accompanied his fast, as he ignored those pains of the body ... the effect of such long-standing discipline ... [is] to break long-standing, automatic and unconscious habits" of reacting to feeling.

the bodhisattva's own practice furnishes an inspiring example. Even with the excruciating pain of asceticism carried to the extreme of bringing him to the brink of death, just as with the sublime pleasures of deep absorption, he was able to maintain the mindful vantage point of being aware without reacting, thereby preventing his mind from being overwhelmed by the experience of any of these feelings.

EXERCISE

By way of following the example set by the Buddha's pre-awakening ability to remain unaffected by painful and pleasant feelings, discussed in the present chapter, contemplation of feeling seems an obvious choice. In addition to the basic task of just being aware of feeling and recognizing its affective tone, an additional dimension could be developed based on the idea of sitting with determination. This should certainly not be taken to the extreme point of suffering through agonizing pain – in fact to do so can have consequences on our health that will be detrimental to progress on the path. However, it is possible to employ the situation of being seated in meditation as a way of exploring with mindful investigation how painful feelings affect the mind. Such can be done by simply remaining aware for a moment of any itch or discomfort, rather than immediately relieving it. Only after having clearly noticed the painful sensation, and the push in the mind to take action, do we indeed change posture or scratch ourselves.

Training in this way can in the course of time make us become more aware of the pervasiveness of subtle painful feelings throughout a range of physical activities. Putting on or taking off clothes to avoid the unpleasant feeling of being too cold or too hot, eating and drinking to avoid the pangs of hunger and thirst, defecating and urinating to avoid the affliction of congestion ... there is no end to the activities to be done continually in order to counter the body's inherent tendency to give rise to painful feeling. Just directing awareness to this dimension of bodily experience can have a remarkable transformative potential on our attitudes and priorities.

Besides exploring painful feelings in the way described above, and as a way to balance out such practice, another usually unnoticed feeling could be made the object of our attention. This is the rather subtle pleasant feeling in the mind that results from just being in the present moment. Comparable to the case of the pain inherent in having a body, noticing the joy of being fully in the here and now takes time and effort. Its recognition also has considerable potential, in particular by way of helping the mind to remain anchored in the only period of time in which we can truly live, which is neither the past nor the future, but solely the present moment. Coming back to the joy of the present moment can also be of considerable assistance in emerging from mental negativity, be this caused by our own inner tendencies or by some external event. A moment of joyful respite from negativity, facilitated by just attending to the present moment as it is, can go a long way in preparing us to deal effectively with whatever problem has manifested and thereby ensuring that the mind stays on course in the realm of what is wholesome.

Another practice I would like to suggest is taking inspiration from the example of the Buddha's unswerving motivation. We could make the motivation that informs our practice, in the form this has emerged from the reflections suggested in Chapter 1, a part of our formal meditation practice. This could be done by just briefly attending mentally to that motivation when starting a sitting, so as to give meaning and context to what we are about to do and thereby ensure that the natural unfolding of our meditative cultivation has an orientation point in what we have chosen as the main direction for our life and practice.

XI

RECOLLECTION OF PAST LIVES

With the present chapter my exploration moves to the night of the Buddha's awakening. Based on the refined degree of mental imperturbability reached through attainment of the fourth absorption, the events during the night of awakening unfold with the Buddha's cultivation of the three higher knowledges (*tevijjā*), which I take up in this and the next two chapters respectively.

The first of these three higher knowledges is the ability to recollect one's own past lives. This stands in natural continuity with the future Buddha's recollection of previous events from the present life, taken up in Chapter 9, in the course of which he had recalled an absorption experienced at an earlier point of his life. This memory triggered in him the crucial insight concerning the role of wholesome joy for progress on the path to awakening. From this viewpoint it is only natural that he would extend the same mode of recollection further back to past lives.

Notably, the awakening of the previous Buddha Vipassin is not preceded by any recollection of past lives.[1] This difference, when considered in the light of the many similarities in the descriptions of the qualities and activities of the Buddhas Vipassin and Gotama, makes it fair to conclude that the recollection of past lives should be considered a specific aspect

1 DN 14 at DN II 35,22 (translated Walshe 1987: 213), with parallels in Sanskrit fragments, Waldschmidt 1956: 147 (§9d4), DĀ 1 at T I 7c7, and T 3 at T I 156b21.

of the Buddha Gotama's individual approach to awakening, namely as a natural extension of his having recollected events from earlier periods of his present life.

The *Ekottarika-āgama* parallel to the *Bhayabherava-sutta* reports his cultivation of this first of the three higher knowledges in the following way:[2]

> Then, while dwelling in seclusion and being in possession of these four higher states of mind (i.e. the four absorptions), relying on this concentrated mind, flawlessly pure, free from fettering tendencies, having obtained fearlessness, I cognized my own past lives during countless aeons.
>
> At that time I recollected my past-life experiences: one birth, two births, three births, four births, five births, ten births, twenty births, thirty births, forty births, fifty births, a hundred births, a thousand births, aeons of arising and dissolution, in all their details, [recollecting that] "I formerly was born there, with such a given name, such a family name, eating food like this, experiencing pleasure and pain like this, passing away from there I was reborn here, dying here I was reborn there"; from beginning to end I completely understood its causes and conditions.

A minor difference is that the *Bhayabherava-sutta* does not speak of "causes and conditions"; instead it describes recollecting the "aspects and particulars" of those past lives. The description given in common in the two versions highlights central aspects of one's sense of identity in each of the past lives recollected. First and foremost is one's name, and the name of the family or clan to which one belongs. Then comes the food one eats, which represents the kind of lifestyle one has. Another aspect recalled is the pleasure and pain experienced.

In any one of these lives, a particular name would have been "me", the family name would have been "my" family, and the food as well as the pleasure and pain would have been "my" lifestyle and experiences. Yet, on passing away from there and being reborn here, quite a different name would now be "me", a different family "my family", and a different type of food as well

---

2 The translated passage is taken from EĀ 31.1 at T II 666b22 to 666b29 (translated Anālayo 2016a: 20f), parallel to MN 4 at MN I 22,9 (translated Ñāṇamoli 1995/2005: 105); see also Anālayo 2011: 41.

as pleasure and pain "my" lifestyle and experiences. In this way, becoming aware of the different "aspects and particulars" of those past lives is at the same time a way of becoming aware of the "causes and conditions" responsible for the sense of identity associated with each.

In other words, perhaps the recollection of past lives helped the bodhisattva to gain insight into the constructed nature of the sense of identity, a product of a particular set of conditions that in the round of rebirths keeps changing from life to life. Insight into the lack of a substantial self behind the process of rebirth would in turn inevitably put a spotlight on the "causes and conditions" that ensure continuity. In short, it would have opened the vista towards a gradually deepening insight into dependent arising (*paṭicca samuppāda*), in particular regarding the role of craving.

Craving is indeed the "housebuilder" of one's sense of self through the round of rebirths, mentioned in a verse in the *Dhammapada* and its parallel in the *Udānavarga*. The latter reads:[3]

> Housebuilder, you have been seen,
> You will not build a house again.
> All your rafters are broken,
> The [roof] ridge is destroyed.
> The mind has reached the unconstructed
> And attained the end right here.

The commentary on the corresponding verse in the *Dhammapada* understands the motif of building a house in this verse to refer to the construction of one's sense of self, *attabhāva*.[4] Recollecting his previous lives in their various details would have revealed to the bodhisattva the incessant constructing activities of the housebuilder, together with the futility of all building efforts, which just result in *dukkha* again and again.

Besides highlighting the details recollected of individual past lives, the *Bhayabherava-sutta* and its *Ekottarika-āgama* parallel also draw attention to the degree to which the bodhisattva extended

---

3 The translation is based on verses 31.6f, Bernhard 1965: 409f, parallel to Dhp 153f (translated Norman 1997/2004: 22).

4 Dhp-a III 128,7. Coomaraswamy 1916: 35 note 3 comments that "the house is, of course, the house – or rather the prison – of individual existence; the builder of the house is desire (*taṇhā*) – the will to enjoy and possess."

his review to lives in the distant past, even aeons ago. In early Buddhist cosmology, an aeon stands for a very long time span, explained to be longer than the time period it would take to wear away a huge stone mountain if once every hundred years it were to be stroked with a piece of cloth.[5] A discourse in the *Saṃyutta-nikāya* and its parallel report that the Buddha eventually recollected ninety-one such aeons.[6] In spite of having recollected lives from thus far back in the past, however, he could not discover a beginning point of his faring onwards in *saṃsāra*. As stated elsewhere, such a beginning point simply cannot be discerned.[7]

According to the *Mahāsīhanāda-sutta* and its Chinese parallel, it would be hard to find a type of rebirth the Buddha had not already experienced, except for being reborn in the Pure Abodes.[8] In early Buddhist cosmology, the Pure Abodes are heavenly realms in which only non-returners are reborn, those who have attained the third level of awakening. For one in this realm there is no coming back to earthly existence. Had the bodhisattva ever gained rebirth in this realm, after that it would have been impossible for him to be born as a human again.

In this way, through the ability to recollect his past lives the Buddha would have gained an all-round perspective on *saṃsāra* (except for the Pure Abodes), enabling him to ascertain that he had experienced all possible kinds of lives during an exceedingly long period reaching back far into the past, but without an identifiable beginning point.

The *Pāsādika-sutta* and its *Dīrgha-āgama* parallel proceed from the Buddha's recollection of past lives to his knowledge of the

5 SN 15.5 at SN II 181,24 (translated Bodhi 2000: 654) and its parallels SĀ 949 at T II 242c7, SĀ² 342 at T II 487c26, and EĀ 52.4 at T II 825c12.

6 SN 42.9 at SN IV 324,18 (translated Bodhi 2000: 1346) and its parallels SĀ 914 at T II 230c1, SĀ² 129 at T II 423c11, and D 4094 *ju* 250a6 or Q 5595 *tu* 285b1.

7 See, e.g., SN 15.3 at SN II 179,23 (translated Bodhi 2000: 652) and its parallels SĀ 938 at T II 240c26 and SĀ² 331 at T II 486a19; part of a corresponding statement has been preserved in Sanskrit fragment SHT I 167 R3, Waldschmidt et al. 1965: 95. Another parallel, EĀ 51.1 at T II 814a28, has no counterpart to this introductory statement, although the rest of the discourse makes it clear that the same basic principle holds.

8 MN 12 at MN I 82,1 (translated Ñāṇamoli 1995/2005: 176) and its parallels EĀ 31.8 at T II 672a18 and T 757 at T XVII 596b19.

future,[9] stating that the Buddha had unimpeded knowledge of the past. In regard to the future he had the knowledge born of awakening, which the *Pāsādika-sutta* explains to be the knowledge that he will not be born again. This is in fact the most important type of knowledge in early Buddhist thought, namely bringing to an end the round of rebirths through full awakening.

The early discourses do not present the ability to remember one's past lives as something specifically Buddhist. Probably the decisive difference in the case of the Buddha's cultivation of this ability would have been that such recollection formed part of his overall examination of his past deeds, starting off with his asceticism and moving gradually further into the past, all reviewed from the perspective of what leads onwards to awakening. In fact the point made in the *Mahāsīhanāda-sutta* and its Chinese parallel is precisely that purification is not to be gained by just undergoing the round of rebirths.

The quest for liberation can safely be assumed to have been at the forefront of the bodhisattva's attention when recollecting his various past lives, and it would be this particular perspective that turned such recollection into another step in the arousing of insight that eventually culminated in his awakening.

Another aspect of the cultivation of recollection of past lives I would like to take up is the relationship of such remembrance to mindfulness. Elsewhere I have argued that in early Buddhist thought mindfulness and memory are closely interrelated, yet not identical.[10] In fact *satipaṭṭhāna* practice requires being in the present moment, rather than remembering something from the past. Thus the relationship to memory can be found in the fact that, when one is mindful in the present moment, it will be easier later to recall what one did. Moreover, the openly receptive attitude that can be cultivated through mindfulness is helpful for actual recall.

The same quality of mindfulness would also provide a perspective on the Buddha's progress to awakening and his later teaching of the four *satipaṭṭhāna*s. Mindfulness of the body

9 DN 29 at DN III 134,9 (translated Walshe 1987: 436) and DĀ 17 at T I 75b28.

10 Anālayo 2003a: 47f, 2013b: 30–8, and 2017b: 26–34.

combined with awareness of the arising of fear in the mind came up in Chapter 2 in relation to the *Bhayabherava-sutta* and its parallel. The continuity of mindful observation of the mind can be seen in the bodhisattva's clear distinction between wholesome and unwholesome thoughts, discussed in Chapter 3 in relation to the *Dvedhāvitakka-sutta* and its parallel. Mindfulness of feeling came to the fore with the ascetic practices, taken up in Chapters 6 to 8, where the Buddha-to-be was able to remain mindful of the pain he experienced without being overwhelmed by it. He then maintained the same mindful composure with the pleasant feelings of absorption. The topic of mindful recognition of a hindrance to deeper meditation practice relates to his monitoring the mind while overcoming various obstructions to the attainment of absorption, taken up in Chapter 4 based on the *Upakkilesa-sutta* and its parallel. Finally his insight into the importance of wholesome joy, taken up in Chapter 9, opened the way for allocating to joy the place it deserves among the awakening factors. Mindful recognition of the presence of an awakening factor and its cultivation are a central dimension of contemplation of dharmas.[11] In this way, selected aspects of the four *satipaṭṭhāna*s relate to different episodes of the Buddha's quest for awakening.[12]

After his continuous monitoring of his own practice with mindfulness had led him to the realization that his asceticism was fruitless, the same process of mindful monitoring then fed into mindful recollection of his present and past lives. Recollecting experiences from the present life, in particular those related to his quest, yielded the much needed insight regarding what constitutes the path to awakening. An extension of recollection of past experiences to former lives led to the equally crucial insight into the predicament of *saṃsāra*, based on

---

11 Anālayo 2013b: 176.

12 Carrithers 1983: 50 comments on the Buddha's pre-awakening practice that this "required not only a power of concentration, but also a kind of mindfulness and self-possession through which the Buddha could in fact see what was going on in his mind and body. Indeed it was just these qualities, mindfulness and self-possession (*sati-samapajañña*), which were to be taught throughout the Buddha's mature discourses ... the ability to witness here and now with full lucidity the inner and outer strata of oneself (and, by extension, the analogous experiences of others)."

his own experiences, probably together with a dawning insight into the constructed nature of the sense of self.

A discourse in the *Saṃyutta-nikāya* and its parallels in the different *Saṃyukta-āgamas* place the Buddha's reflection that the four *satipaṭṭhānas* constitute the direct path to awakening at the time right after he had gained the final goal, thereby giving the impression that this particular aspect of the teachings should be seen as a direct outcome of his quest for awakening. Here is the relevant part from the so-called "other" *Saṃyukta-āgama* (T 100):[13]

> At one time the Buddha was at the village of Uruvelā, by the side of the river Nerañjarā, below the Bodhi tree, having just accomplished Buddhahood. Seated alone below the tree in meditative reflection, the Buddha thought:
>
> "There is only one path capable of purifying living beings, make them become free from pain and vexation, enabling them to get rid of and to terminate unwholesome and evil deeds, to obtain the benefit of the right Dharma on being taught the Dharma, namely the four satipaṭṭhānas.
>
> "What are referred to as the four satipaṭṭhānas? [They are] the satipaṭṭhāna of contemplating the body, the satipaṭṭhāna of contemplating feelings, the satipaṭṭhāna of contemplating the mind, and the satipaṭṭhāna of contemplating dharmas.
>
> "If a person does not cultivate the four satipaṭṭhānas, [such a] one is far away from the Dharma of noble ones, far away from the path of noble ones. If one is separated from the path of noble ones, one is far away from the deathless. If one is far away from the deathless, then one does not escape from birth, old age, disease, death, worry, sorrow, pain, and vexation. I say that a person like this will certainly be unable to gain separation from all dukkha.
>
> "If one cultivates the four satipaṭṭhānas, then one is close to the Dharma of noble ones. If one is close to the Dharma of noble ones, then one is close to the path of noble ones. If one is close to the path of noble ones, then one is close to the principle of deathlessness. If one is close to the principle of deathlessness, then

13 The translation is based on SĀ² 102 at T II 410b10 to 410b23, with parallels in SN 47.18 at SN V 167,4 (translated Bodhi 2000: 1647), SĀ 1189 at T II 322a28, and SĀ³ 4 at T II 494a18.

one is able to gain an escape from birth, old age, disease, death, worry, sorrow, pain, and vexation. If one escapes from birth, old age, disease, death, worry, sorrow, pain, and vexation, I say that a person like this is separated from all dukkha."

The *Saṃyutta-nikāya* version additionally specifies that the four *satipaṭṭhāna*s are undertaken diligently, clearly comprehending, and mindful, staying free from desire and discontent with regard to the world. The Pāli discourse does not explicitly refer to escaping from birth, old age, and death, although the same is implicit in its relating the practice of the four *satipaṭṭhāna*s to the realization of Nirvāṇa.

The parallel versions agree that at this juncture Brahmā intervened and confirmed the appropriateness of the Buddha's reflection. The location and the trope of celestial approval make it safe to conclude that the passage is meant to portray the Buddha's teaching of the four *satipaṭṭhāna*s as an outcome of his realization, and by implication as a final result of the experiences that led him to awakening.

Now according to the *Acchariyabbhutadhamma-sutta* the bodhisattva was already in possession of mindfulness on descending into his mother's womb.[14] The *Madhyama-āgama* parallel qualifies him to have done so "knowingly" which, even though it does not use the word mindfulness, would imply a similar mental condition of being aware. The depiction common to both versions would imply that he was held to have been acquainted with the basic quality of mindful knowing already at that time.

The teaching of the four *satipaṭṭhāna*s would then build on the basic quality of mindfulness, with which the bodhisattva was apparently familiar before his awakening. As an outcome of the Buddha's awakening, the scheme of four *satipaṭṭhāna*s could then be seen to mirror his own pre-awakening experiences, which would have shown to him the liberating potential of cultivating mindfulness in relation to these four domains of experience and for this reason perhaps motivating him to pour mindfulness into the mould of the four *satipaṭṭhāna*s.

---

14 See above p. 83 note 20 and the discussion of this type of description in both versions in Anālayo 2010: 28–46.

EXERCISE

As a practical exercise, I recommend the cultivation of the four *satipaṭṭhāna*s. This could be done by first becoming aware of our whole *body*. Such proprioceptive awareness involves *feeling* the body, opening the vista to the affective dimension of the present moment of our experience, which in turn facilitates becoming aware of the overall condition of our *mind*. In this way, any situation, be it during formal meditation or when engaging with the outside world, can in principle be approached by trying to remain anchored in whole-body awareness and allow the mindfulness established in this way to become receptive to the affective dimension of this experience and its repercussions on the mind. Contemplation of dharmas then finds its expression in the overall orientation towards progress to liberation that we have given to our life and practice, in particular by avoiding mental states that hinder such progress and by cultivating those that facilitate it. Any situation we experience can in one way or another be related to this orientation. By remaining established in mindfulness we can bring the viewpoint of the Dharma to bear on whatever happens, thereby allowing any experience to become a means for progress to liberation.

XII

THE DIVINE EYE

In this chapter I turn to the higher knowledge of the divine eye, which stands for the ability to perceive, with the mental eye as it were, the passing away and being reborn of other living beings. According to the *Saṅghabhedavastu*, once the bodhisattva had recollected his past lives, he wanted to ascertain the underlying cause of this process, which led him to cultivate the divine eye.[1] This ties in with the observation made in the last chapter that the future Buddha would have approached the knowledge of recollecting past lives from the viewpoint of its bearing on his main quest to reach freedom from old age, disease, and death.

At the same time this progression exemplifies a basic pattern of *satipaṭṭhāna* meditation of proceeding from contemplating internally to doing so externally, which I take as implying that, having observed something within oneself, one then proceeds to an awareness of how this manifests in others.[2] The same shift from internal to external also appears to underlie the progression from the first to the second higher knowledge, which proceeds from contemplating one's own repeated passing away and being reborn to observing how others pass away and

---

1 Gnoli 1977: 118,11.

2 Anālayo 2003a: 94–102 and 2013b: 15–19; see also 2017b: 37f note 39. On the possibility of becoming aware of the mental condition of others see also Krueger 2012.

are reborn.[3] Although I am not aware of any explicit indication that the internal and external dimensions of *satipaṭṭhāna* contemplation relate to the internal and external dimensions of the two higher knowledges realized by the Buddha on the eve of his awakening, the parallelism as such seems to me striking enough to take it into consideration.

Be that as it may, the *Ekottarika-āgama* parallel to the *Bhayabherava-sutta* presents the future Buddha's realization of the second higher knowledge in this manner:[4]

> Again, relying on this concentrated mind, flawless and free from fettering tendencies, a mind that is established in concentration and has obtained fearlessness, I also came to know the being born and passing away of living beings. With the divine eye I moreover saw living beings of various types being born and passing away, of good appearances or bad appearances, in good destinies or bad destinies, attractive or ugly, in accordance with their wholesome or evil conduct. I completely distinguished all that.
>
> Whatever living beings who have undertaken evil bodily conduct, evil verbal conduct, evil mental conduct, have slandered noble ones, have constantly cherished wrong views and been associated with wrong views, with the destruction of the body at death they are reborn in hell.
>
> Whatever living beings who have undertaken wholesome bodily conduct, cultivated wholesome verbal conduct, and cultivated wholesome mental conduct, have not slandered noble ones, have constantly cultivated right view and been associated with right view, with the destruction of the body at death they are reborn in a good realm in heaven.
>
> Thus with the divine eye that is purified and flawless I saw living beings of various types being born and passing away, of

---

3 Strong 2001: 74 explains that the first knowledge "gives a temporal dimension to the Buddha's realization. It shows that there was never, until now, a time for him in which death and rebirth did not exist." The second knowledge and its resultant "vision of other beings in different realms of rebirth gives a spatial dimension to the Buddha's realization. It shows that there is no place of refuge, no state of existence in this cosmos, where one can escape death and rebirth."

4 The translation is based on EĀ 31.1 at T II 666c2 to 666c12 (translated Anālayo 2016a: 21f), parallel to MN 4 at MN I 22,27 (translated Ñāṇamoli 1995/2005: 105f); see also Anālayo 2011: 41.

good or bad appearance, in good or bad destinies, attractive or ugly, in accordance with their former conduct, I completely distinguished [all that].

A central theme that emerges from the above description is the future Buddha's insight into the working mechanism of karma, whereby he directly perceived how good and bad deeds affect the circumstances of one's rebirth.[5] The brief description given in the above passage can be fleshed out by turning to the *Mahākammavibhaṅga-sutta* and its parallels.[6] These examine mistaken conclusions drawn by other practitioners based on witnessing with the divine eye the following four instances:

- evil conduct followed by rebirth in hell,
- evil conduct followed by rebirth in heaven,
- good conduct followed by rebirth in hell,
- good conduct followed by rebirth in heaven.

This goes to show that the correlation between good conduct and heaven or bad conduct and hell does not inevitably affect the next life right away. The reason is that the conditions for the next birth do not only depend on the conduct adopted shortly before passing away, but also on conduct performed previously in the same or other former lives.

Seeing that someone who had performed an evil deed is reborn in heaven, for example, does not imply that doing evil has no painful consequences. When considered from a wider perspective of this particular person's past deeds, it becomes clear that the heavenly rebirth was due to other good deeds. Besides, the evil done will still come to fruition, but at another time.

In other words, the correlation between good conduct and heaven, or bad conduct and hell, is correct in principle, but

5 Blomfield 2011: 93 aptly sums up that the Buddha "saw how minds condition the reality they experience, and the universe of change he apprehended was deeply moral. While selfish and cruel actions lead to suffering, kind and generous ones bring happiness. That is the true meaning of karma."

6 MN 136 at MN III 209,12 (translated Ñāṇamoli 1995/2005: 1060) and its parallels MĀ 171 at T I 707a19 and D 4094 *ju* 264a4 or Q 5595 *thu* 6b8; see also Anālayo 2011: 778f.

the way this works out in actual experience is rather complex, as conditions from the distant past may override more recent conditions. This helps to appreciate the significance of the description of the Buddha's recollection of past lives as having extended far back into his own past, mentioned in the previous chapter. Due to its extensive scope, the first higher knowledge had furnished him with a comprehensive vision that put things into proper perspective.

The complexity of the working out of karma in turn fuels disenchantment with faring onwards in *saṃsāra*, as it implies that even those of good conduct sooner or later will experience the fruition of some evil done in the distant past. When considered from this perspective, rather than trying to construct an agreeable living condition for oneself in one way or another, the overall vision of the relentless passing away and re-arising of living beings points to the need to find a way out of the entire predicament of being subject to *saṃsāra*.

This perspective comes to the fore in a discourse in the *Saṃyutta-nikāya* and its parallels. Here is the *Saṃyukta-āgama* version:[7]

> When I had been recollecting my former lives, at the time when I had not yet accomplished full awakening, being alone in a quiet place with the mind collected in meditative reflection, a thought like this arose in me: "The world has entered a disaster, namely being born, growing old, becoming sick, passing away, changing, and coming to be reborn. Yet living beings do not understand as it really is on what birth, old age, disease,[8] and death depend, and what is beyond them."

The Pāli and Sanskrit fragment parallels to this passage do not explicitly relate this insight to the bodhisattva's recollection of past lives, but only state that it took place before his awakening. In agreement with its Pāli and Sanskrit parallels, the above discourse continues by depicting the future Buddha's exploration of the links of dependent arising (*paṭicca samuppāda*).

---

7 The translated passage is taken from SĀ 285 at T II 79c28 to 80a3, parallel to SN 12.10 at SN II 10,2 (translated Bodhi 2000: 537) and to Sanskrit fragments, Tripāṭhī 1962: 89f, and SHT X 3865R, Wille 2008: 200.

8 "Disease" is only mentioned in a variant reading.

The Buddha's pre-awakening insight takes the following form in an *Ekottarika-āgama* discourse:[9]

> Formerly, at the time when I was a bodhisattva and had not yet accomplished the awakening of a Buddha, I had this thought: "This world is extremely afflicted: there is birth, there is old age, there is disease, and there is death, yet one does not gain an end to the origination of these five aggregates of clinging."

Although the *Saṃyutta-nikāya* parallel does not explicitly mention the five aggregates of clinging, the *Ekottarika-āgama* discourse's relation of these to the Buddha's pre-awakening insight receives support from another *Saṃyutta-nikāya* discourse. This discourse reports that the bodhisattva investigated the gratification, disadvantage, and escape in relation to the five aggregates of clinging, and that such insight was a dimension of his awakening.[10]

The analysis into five aggregates of clinging points to those dimensions of experience with which one tends to identify. These would presumably have become evident to the bodhisattva during his recollection of past lives, which would have shown him how a sense of selfhood in one experience builds on a particular body, feelings, perceptions, volitional formations, and consciousness, only to be replaced by a different body etc., fulfilling the same role in another life. Moreover, the same recollection would also have revealed to him that, even though each of these aggregates is experienced as "me" or "mine", none of them is continuously how one would want them to be, that is, each of these aggregates is not truly under one's control.[11] In this way penetrative insight into the five aggregates of clinging

---

9 EĀ 38.4 at T II 718a14 to 718a17, parallel to SN 12.65 at SN II 104,6 (translated Bodhi 2000: 601); for other parallels see below note 13.

10 SN 22.26 at SN III 27,31 (translated Bodhi 2000: 873). The parallel SĀ 14 at T II 2c12 (translated Anālayo 2012c: 23) does not explicitly relate its corresponding exposition to the time before the Buddha's awakening. The same is implicit in its presentation, however, as both versions conclude that the Buddha claimed to have reached awakening when he fully understood these aspects of the five aggregates of clinging.

11 This is precisely the topic of the second discourse given according to tradition by the Buddha after his awakening; cf. SN 22.59 at SN III 66,27 (translated Bodhi 2000: 901) and Anālayo 2014a: 5–8 for a translation of the parallel SĀ 34 and a survey of other parallels.

and their dependent arising would have become central aspects of the liberating wisdom that led the Buddha to awakening.

Another parallel to the above *Ekottarika-āgama* discourse can be found in the *Saṃyukta-āgama*, which proceeds as follows:[12]

> When I had been recollecting my former lives, at the time when I had not yet accomplished full awakening, being alone in a quiet place with the mind collected in meditative reflection, I had this thought: "Because of the existence of what state do old age and death exist? What state is the condition for the existence of old age and death?"
>
> Then, giving right attention, full comprehension as it really is arose: "Because of the existence of birth, old age and death exist; old age and death exist because of the condition of birth."

The discourse continues with becoming, clinging, craving, feeling, contact, and the six sense-spheres, after which it turns to name-and-form as follows:

> "Because of the existence of what state does name-and-form exist? What state is the condition for the existence of name-and-form?"
>
> Then, giving right attention, full comprehension as it really is arose: "Because of the existence of consciousness, name-and-form exists, name-and-form exists because the condition of consciousness exists."
>
> Then I thought thus: "This returns from consciousness as its limit, it does not go beyond it."

Parallels in the *Saṃyutta-nikāya*, in Sanskrit fragments, and Chinese translation do not explicitly relate the above insight to the bodhisattva's recollection of past lives. Nevertheless, from the viewpoint of the pre-awakening events this seems a meaningful placing.

Several parallels also state more explicitly that, just as consciousness is the condition for name-and-form, so name-and-form is the condition for consciousness.[13] In other words,

---

12 The translations are from SĀ 287 at T II 80b25 to 80b28 and 80b29 to 80c3.

13 The parallels are SN 12.65 at SN II 104,29, Sanskrit fragments, Bongard-Levin et al. 1996: 77 (§I.12) (see also Or 15009/85r4, Nagashima 2009: 154, Or 15009/175g, Melzer 2009: 216, and Or 15009/661r1, Kudo and Shono 2015: 459), and parallels in Chinese translation, T 713 at T XVI 826c6, T 714 at T XVI 828a4, and T 715 at T XVI 829b17.

these two links stand in a relationship of reciprocal conditioning to each other.[14] This is the "limit" his investigation revealed to him at this point.

Such a mode of presentation does not conflict with the standard exposition of twelve links, which in fact come up in full when the discourse takes up the cessation mode of dependent arising.[15] Yet, in his investigation of dependent arising, the Buddha-to-be at the present juncture of events apparently first reached up to the reciprocal conditioning of consciousness and name-and-form.

This is what even the refined meditative attainment reached under Āḷāra Kālāma and Uddaka Rāmaputta had not been able to take him beyond: the conditioned nature of consciousness. Already during the time of his apprenticeship under these two teachers, the Buddha-to-be had realized that the solution to the predicament of *saṃsāra* was not to be found through the profound meditative abstraction of the immaterial spheres. At the present juncture, he would have realized why this was so: however much refined, these experiences do not go beyond the basic reciprocal conditioning between consciousness and name-and-form. Although form has been left behind and name has been greatly subdued, a remnant of name remains, sufficient for the conditioning relationship with consciousness to continue.

With ignorance acting via formations as the conditioning force, the reciprocal conditioning between consciousness and name-and-form is the hub around which the wheel of *saṃsāra* revolves. Had the Buddha realized this earlier, he would probably not have felt any need to engage in asceticism.

Regarding the standard formulation of dependent arising, several individual links appear to follow the pattern of, and thereby presumably involve an implicit criticism of, a Vedic creation myth.[16] Another instance of such employment of concepts, apparently known in the ancient Indian setting, concerns the four truths, which convey the implications of awakening with the help of a medical scheme of analysis (to

14 See in more detail Anālayo 2015a: 106–10.

15 Ñāṇananda 2015: 77 explains that "the non-understanding of the inter-relation between consciousness and name-and-form itself is *'avijjā'*."

16 See Jurewicz 2000.

be discussed in Chapters 16 and 17). In both cases, the Buddha apparently relied on already existing ideas, but decisively reformulated them in such a manner that, alongside creating a sense of familiarity and thereby facilitating understanding, these were able to convey the novelty of his discovery. Needless to say, this does not in any way diminish the importance of the Buddha's actual realization or of the doctrine of *paṭicca samuppāda*. It only means that the formulation of the whole series of twelve links probably stands in dialogue with modes of thought current in the ancient Indian setting. An appreciation of this facilitates discerning the chief points made with this formulation, without getting sidetracked by its details:

- the identification of craving as the chief culprit for being subject to *saṃsāra*,
- the insight that consciousness does not go beyond its conditioned interrelation with name-and-form,
- the realization that the solution to the predicament of *saṃsāra* requires the cessation of ignorance.

The Buddha's discovery in this respect finds illustration, in the discourse translated above, in the example of a person who chances on a forest path that leads to an ancient city that had been abandoned and forgotten. Having made this discovery, the person then informs others so that eventually the city is renovated and made use of again.

The importance of insight into dependent arising also comes to the fore in the report that the Buddha spent days after his awakening reviewing the links of *paṭicca samuppāda* in the arising and cessation mode. Here is the relevant passage from the Chinese parallel to the *Udāna* collection:[17]

> At the time of having rightly awakened and having just become a Buddha, during seven days of meditation and being in a concentrative attainment, the Tathāgata gave attention to the twelve conditions. He separately and distinctly understood their arising and understood their cessation.

17 The translated part is taken from T 212 at T IV 775c19f, which parallels Ud 1.3 at Ud 2,21 (translated Ireland 1990: 13) or Vin I 1,4 (translated Horner 1951/1982: 1); see also, e.g., the *Saṅghabhedavastu*, Gnoli 1977: 127,5.

For the Buddha to keep reviewing dependent arising and dependent cessation for quite some time after his awakening points to a meditative dimension inherent in this particular doctrine. Far from being merely a matter of intellectual reflection, it rather involves the all-important meditative realization of the cessation of ignorance through full awakening, a topic to which I return in the next chapter.

EXERCISE

By way of practice, I suggest taking up dependent arising for meditative reflection and contemplation. For this purpose I recommend using in particular the reciprocal conditioning of consciousness and name-and-form, thereby following up the mode of investigation that appears to have played such a crucial part in the Buddha's own insight into dependent arising.

To put this into practice requires first of all a clear recognition of the presence of the flow of consciousness throughout experience. This can be distinguished from the more active dimensions of the process of material phenomena and their mental processing by being contacted, felt, and perceived, by being given attention to and being reacted to in one way or another.[18] Recognition can take place by turning attention to that part of the mind which knows, that which is aware of such mental processing.

Once meditative practice has led to a recognition of these two dimensions of experience, consciousness and name-and-form, the same insight can be related to everyday situations. In any situation it is in principle possible, if mindfulness and equanimity are sufficiently established, to step back internally from active involvement for a moment and just be with the receptivity of bare knowing, and then from the vantage point of having stepped back observe the unfolding of the process of conditionality of our experience in the present moment.

---

18 According to SN 12.2 at SN II 3,34 (translated Bodhi 2000: 535) and its parallel EĀ 49.5 at T II 797b28, name stands for the following mental functions (apart from consciousness): feeling, perception, intention, contact, and attention; see in more detail Anālayo 2015a: 106ff.

With sustained practice this mode of contemplation can become a powerful support for insight practice leading to the direct realization of the cessation of the first link in the series, the cessation of ignorance. This follows the example set by the Buddha's own liberating insight into the cessation of dependent arising, where with the cessation of the first link the entire series leading up to *dukkha* is deprived of its foundation.

XIII

AWAKENING

The long trajectory surveyed in the preceding chapters comes to its culmination point with the Buddha's attainment of full awakening, discussed in the present chapter. This trajectory covered the establishing of a moral foundation, overcoming obstacles to concentration, cultivating the immaterial attainments, and the ascetic detour of forceful mind control, breath retention, and fasting. The impasse reached in this way led to the eventual discovery of the path and its cultivation by attaining the two higher knowledges of recollection of past lives and the divine eye, which would have led to insight into the constructed nature of the sense of selfhood and into the series of conditions responsible for the genesis of *dukkha*. The task still to be accomplished at the present juncture of the Buddha's progress to awakening is to reach the cessation of ignorance, with which dependent arising is fully understood and freedom from *dukkha* is realized.

According to the *Saṅghabhedavastu*, once the bodhisattva had recollected his past lives and with the help of the divine eye come to witness the impact of karma on the process of passing away and being reborn, he realized that the operating mechanism behind the round of *saṃsāra* is to be found in the three influxes (*āsava*).[1] These need to be eradicated in order to reach the final goal of full liberation. The relevant part from the

1 Gnoli 1977: 118,27.

account of the Buddha's actual attainment of awakening in the *Ekottarika-āgama* parallel to the *Bhayabherava-sutta* presents this culmination point of his quest as follows:[2]

> Again, relying on this concentrated mind, with its flawless purity and freedom from fettering tendencies, a state of mind that has attained concentration and has attained fearlessness, I attained the destruction of the influxes in the mind. I knew that "this is *dukkha*" as it really is, not falsely.
>
> Then, at that time, when I had attained this mental condition, I attained liberation of the mind from the influx of sensuality, from the influx of existence, and from the influx of ignorance.
>
> By attaining liberation, I in turn attained knowledge of liberation, knowing as it really is that birth and death have been extinguished, the holy life has been established, what had to be done has been done, there will be no more coming again to a womb.
>
> Brahmin, this is reckoned the third [higher] knowledge that I attained in the last period of the night, [being] no longer obscured.

The corresponding section in the *Bhayabherava-sutta* is more detailed overall. It describes the insight into *dukkha* with the help of the scheme of four truths, a topic I will take up in subsequent chapters. The Pāli version also states that the realization of full awakening entails the knowledge that the holy life has been lived, what had to be done has been done, and there will be no more coming to any state of being. In relation to the final statement on having attained the third higher knowledge, the *Bhayabherava-sutta* adds that ignorance was dispelled and knowledge arose, that darkness was dispelled and light arose, and that this is what happens when one dwells diligently.

The *Ekottarika-āgama* version draws out the implications of the Buddha's awakening in the following manner:[3]

> How is it, brahmin, do you have this thought: "The Tathāgata [still] has sensuality in his mind, ill will in his mind, and ignorance

---

2 The translated passage is taken from EĀ 31.1 at T II 666c14 to 666c20 (translated Anālayo 2016a: 22), parallel to MN 4 at MN I 23,11 (translated Ñāṇamoli 1995/2005: 106f).

3 The translated passage is taken from EĀ 31.1 at T II 666c20 to 666c25, parallel to MN 4 at MN I 23,29.

> in his mind, and he stays in secluded dwelling places without having eradicated these?" Brahmin, you should not see it like this. The reason is that the Tathāgata has now discarded all influxes forever, he continually delights in secluded dwellings and not in the company of humans.
>
> Because I have now seen these two benefits,[4] I delight in secluded dwellings and [solitary] places. What are the two? In addition to dwelling in secluded places being [suitable] for myself, it concurrently [serves] to deliver incalculable sentient beings [by setting an example for them].

Instead of referring to incalculable sentient beings, the *Bhayabherava-sutta* speaks of compassion for later generations. Alongside such minor variations, the two versions agree in presenting the realization of awakening in terms of the total removal of defilements, in other words, the eradication of the three influxes, *āsava*.[5]

Information on the implications of the term *āsava* from a practical perspective can be gathered from a discourse in the *Aṅguttara-nikāya* and its parallels. The discourse proceeds by taking up various key terms, such as sensuality, *dukkha*, as well as the influxes, in order to clarify what in each case is the cause of their arising, their diversity, their result, their cessation, and the path leading to such cessation. In the case of the influxes, the corresponding section in a parallel in the *Madhyama-āgama* proceeds as follows:[6]

> How does one know the influxes? There are reckoned to be three influxes: the influx of sensual desire, the influx of existence, and the influx of ignorance. This is reckoned to be "knowing the influxes".
>
> How does one know the cause for the arising of the influxes? [The cause] is reckoned to be ignorance. Because of ignorance, the influxes in turn exist. This is reckoned to be "knowing the cause for the arising of the influxes".

---

4 The translation is based on adopting a variant that adds "two".

5 For a brief survey of the three influxes see Anālayo 2016b: 88 and on the significance of the term *āsava* Anālayo 2017e: 325ff.

6 MĀ 111 at T I 599b25 to 599c9, parallel to AN 6.63 at AN III 414,8 (translated Bodhi 2012: 962f); see also T 57 at T I 851c28.

How does one know the result of the influxes? [The result] is reckoned to be the bondage of ignorance. Because of being stained by the influxes, one experiences as a result the attaining of a good realm of existence or else the attaining of a bad realm of existence. This is reckoned to be "knowing the result of the influxes".

How does one know the diversity of the influxes? [The diversity] is reckoned to be that there are influxes [leading to] rebirth in hell, or else there are influxes [leading to] rebirth among animals, or else there are influxes [leading to] rebirth among hungry ghosts, or else there are influxes [leading to] rebirth in a heaven, or else there are influxes [leading to] rebirth among human beings. This is reckoned to be "knowing the diversity of the influxes".

How does one know the cessation of the influxes? [The cessation] is reckoned to be that, ignorance being eradicated, the influxes are in turn eradicated. This is reckoned to be "knowing the cessation of the influxes".

How does one know the path to the cessation of the influxes? [The path] is reckoned to be the noble eightfold path: right view, *right intention, right speech, right action, right livelihood, right effort, right mindfulness*, and right concentration; these are the eight. This is reckoned to be "knowing the path to the cessation of the influxes".

If a monastic knows the influxes in this way, knows the cause for the arising of the influxes, knows the experiencing of the result of the influxes, knows the diversity of the influxes, knows the cessation of the influxes, and knows the path to the cessation of the influxes, then this is reckoned to be fulfilling the holy life, enabling the ending of all the influxes.

In relation to the result of the influxes, the *Aṅguttara-nikāya* parallel speaks of acquiring an individual form of existence as the result of merit or demerit,[7] which fleshes out the significance of the reference in the *Madhyama-āgama* version to the attaining of a good or bad realm of existence. Otherwise the two versions agree closely in showing that the three influxes originate from

7 AN 6.63 at AN III 414,21; another minor difference is a matter of sequence, as AN 6.63 takes up the diversity before turning to the result.

ignorance and are responsible for the continuity of being subject to *saṃsāra*. Freedom from this predicament therefore requires eradicating them, for which purpose the noble eightfold path needs to be cultivated.

Regarding how to remove the influxes, the *Sabbāsava-sutta* presents altogether seven practices. The main practical implications of these seven are:

- seeing the four noble truths instead of uselessly speculating,
- restraining the sense-doors,
- using one's requisites properly,
- enduring various hardships,
- avoiding what is dangerous and unsuitable,
- removing what is unwholesome,
- cultivating the awakening factors.

Each of these activities is explicitly related to the removal of the influxes. Here the term *āsava* clearly functions in a more general sense than in the enumeration of the three influxes in the account of the Buddha's awakening as well as in the passage on knowing the influxes, translated above. The perspective offered here discloses various dimensions of practice that will in one way or another contribute to progress to liberation from the three influxes. The *Madhyama-āgama* parallel to the *Sabbāsava-sutta* presents instructions for the last out of these seven methods in the following manner:[8]

> How are influxes removed through attention? A monastic gives attention to the first awakening factor of mindfulness in dependence on seclusion, in dependence on dispassion, in dependence on cessation, leading to liberation. *A monastic gives attention to the second awakening factor of investigation-of-*dharmas *in dependence on seclusion, in dependence on dispassion, in dependence on cessation, leading to liberation. A monastic gives attention to the third awakening factor of* energy *in dependence on seclusion, in dependence on dispassion, in dependence on cessation, leading to liberation. A monastic gives attention to the fourth awakening*

8 MĀ 10 at T I 432c16 to 432c21 (translated Bingenheimer et al. 2013: 61), parallel to MN 2 at MN I 11,21 (translated Ñāṇamoli 1995/2005: 95f).

factor of joy *in dependence on seclusion, in dependence on dispassion, in dependence on cessation, leading to liberation. A monastic gives attention to the fifth awakening factor of* tranquillity *in dependence on seclusion, in dependence on dispassion, in dependence on cessation, leading to liberation. A monastic gives attention to the sixth awakening factor of* concentration *in dependence on seclusion, in dependence on dispassion, in dependence on cessation, leading to liberation. A monastic* gives attention to the seventh awakening factor of equipoise in dependence on seclusion, in dependence on dispassion, in dependence on cessation, leading to liberation.

For one who does not give such attention, afflictions and sorrow will arise. Giving such attention, afflictions and sorrow will not arise. This is reckoned to be the removal of the influxes through attention.

Instead of "giving attention" to the awakening factors, the *Sabbāsava-sutta* speaks of their "cultivation", *bhāvanā*; both expressions can safely be assumed to convey the same basic meaning. Another difference is that the notion of leading to "liberation" has as its counterpart in the Pāli version that such practice should ripen in "letting go". In spite of terminological differences, here, too, the basic import appears to be the same.

A discourse in the *Saṃyutta-nikāya*, which has a range of parallels, highlights that instructions on the cultivation of the awakening factors are in a way an outcome of the Buddha's awakening. Just as the manifestation of a wheel-turning king's universal sovereignty comes in conjunction with the arising of seven magical treasures, in the same way the manifestation of a Buddha, a Tathāgata, comes in conjunction with the appearance of the seven awakening factors. The implication appears to be that only a Buddha, one who has reached awakening on his own, is able to identify these seven as what is required for awakening and then teach their cultivation to others.[9] The second part of this comparison between a wheel-turning

9 Whereas most of the parallel versions employ the same term to designate the appearance of the treasures and of the awakening factors, in T 38 at T I 822b4 the counterpart to the "appearance" of the treasures is the Tathāgata's "teaching" of the awakening factors.

king and a Tathāgata proceeds as follows in a parallel in the *Ekottarika-āgama*:[10]

> When a Tathāgata emerges in the world, the seven treasures of the awakening factors in turn emerge in the world. What are the seven? They are reckoned to be the mindfulness awakening factor, the [investigation-of]-dharmas awakening factor, the energy awakening factor, the joy awakening factor, the tranquillity awakening factor, the concentration awakening factor, and the equipoise awakening factor, which emerge in the world. When a Tathāgata emerges in the world, these seven treasures of the awakening factors in turn emerge in the world.
>
> Therefore, monastics, you should try to make an effort to cultivate these seven awakening factors. Monastics, you should train in this way.

A minor difference is that in the *Saṃyutta-nikāya* discourse the Buddha does not explicitly tell the monastics in his audience that they should make an effort in cultivating the awakening factors, although the same can safely be assumed to be implicit.

For such cultivation, the instructions in the *Sabbāsava-sutta* and its parallel point to a recurring mode in which these seven awakening factors should be developed in order to ripen in awakening. In my study *Perspectives on Satipaṭṭhāna* I discussed this in more detail from a practical viewpoint.[11] The account of the Buddha's progress to awakening provides further depth to these instructions, as the four aspects of seclusion, dispassion, cessation, and letting go/liberation to some extent seem to correspond to key elements of the report of what happened on the night of the Buddha's awakening.

In the case of the Buddha's progress to awakening, the precondition for the three higher knowledges was his attainment of the fourth absorption, which establishes a supremely firm degree of *seclusion*. In fact the notion of seclusion is explicitly mentioned already in the standard account of the first

---

10 EĀ 39.7 at T II 731b19 to 731b24, parallel to SN 46.42 at SN V 99,9 (translated Bodhi 2000: 1595), MĀ 58 at T I 493a16 (translated Bingenheimer et al. 2013: 359), T 38 at T I 822a29, and SĀ 721 at T II 194a19; see also Anālayo 2013b: 218.

11 Anālayo 2013b: 219–26.

absorption, which is *secluded* from sensuality and unwholesome states and results in the experience of joy and happiness born of such *seclusion*.

The first higher knowledge of recollecting his own former lives would have functioned as a catalyst for *dispassion*. Of course dispassion towards *saṃsāra* is a continuous theme throughout the Buddha's whole quest, but this trajectory could well have reached its culmination point when he recalled all his various former existences and witnessed the various ups and downs he had experienced in the past.

The second higher knowledge of the divine eye completed his direct insight into the working mechanism of karma, showing this to be a general principle applicable to living beings. This knowledge stands in close relationship to the principle of dependent arising, which is fully understood with the cessation of its links. The inclination of the Buddha-to-be towards achieving the *cessation* mode of dependent arising seems a significant implication of this part of the night of his awakening.

Such inclining would have been based on his insight into the reciprocal conditioning between consciousness and name-and-form, which he would have gained with the first and the second higher knowledge. This insight would have made it clear to him that he had to find a way of going beyond both consciousness and name-and-form, in order to achieve the *cessation* of ignorance that fuels their continuous interplay from one life to the next. In other words, he had to find a way of going beyond the whole gamut of experience in order to step out of the reciprocal conditioning relationship between consciousness and name-and-form.

Clearly, the solution could not be found by refining or subduing perception, comparable to what he had done when training under his two teachers Āḷāra Kālāma and Uddaka Rāmaputta. Any such approach does not transcend the limits of the conditionality of consciousness and name-and-form. Instead, he now had to *let go* of perception altogether, allowing it to *cease* in order to become fully *liberated*, whereby all attachments, craving, influxes, and ignorance are fully *let go of* and come to *cease* forever.

With the third knowledge, then, he reached the culmination point of his practice through completely *letting go* of all and everything in the most thorough manner possible, whereby he finally realized *liberation* and became a Buddha, a fully awakened one.

Presented in a summary manner, the correspondences I would like to suggest are as follows:

The Buddha's Progress to Awakening:	Cultivation of the Awakening Factors:
absorption attainment	establishing seclusion
recollection of past lives	arousing dispassion
divine eye	inclining towards cessation
removal of the influxes	letting go to be liberated

Identifying these correlations is not only of interest in relation to the Buddha's own progress and subsequent teaching. It also makes cultivation of the awakening factors – in dependence on seclusion, dispassion, and cessation, culminating in letting go and reaching liberation – become a way of following in the footsteps of the Buddha's own progress to awakening.

EXERCISE

As a practical exercise I suggest cultivating the awakening factors based on seclusion, dispassion, and cessation, leading up to letting go and liberation. The present suggestion stands in close relationship to the exercise to be explored in Chapter 15, which concerns balancing the awakening factors.

The mode of practice in the present chapter rests on *seclusion* from the hindrances having been achieved. Once that has been achieved, we could just remain aware of the impermanent flow of phenomena in the present moment based on well-established mindfulness. The continuity of such mindfulness can be facilitated by enlivening the practice through arousing an inquisitive or investigative mental attitude of really wanting to know what is happening right now. Such an attitude relies on and in turn engenders energy, which leads on to the subtle joy of being fully in the present moment. Combined with calmness of the body and mind this leads via concentration, in the sense of absence of any distraction, to a superb condition of mental equipoise.

Based on this condition, we could then cultivate an attitude of *dispassion*, of becoming dispassionate with what anyway is of such a fleeting nature. Dispassion in turn leads over to the willingness to allow things to come to an end, when attention turns to the *cessation* aspect in what is impermanent, to the disappearance of phenomena. Practice proceeds to ever deepening levels of *letting go* of, and becoming *liberated* from, any attachment or clinging to phenomena. Eventually, practice matures and with a supreme act of *letting go* the *liberating* experience of Nirvāṇa takes place.[12]

The additional input that the present chapter offers is the taking of inspiration for such a form of practice from the apparent similarity between these four aspects in the cultivation of the awakening factors and the trajectory of the Buddha's own practice on the night of his breakthrough to awakening.

---

12 For more detailed instructions see Anālayo 2013b: 219f and 2016b: 226f and 234f.

XIV

THE DECISION TO TEACH

Beginning with this chapter, my exploration shifts from the trajectory that led up to the Buddha's awakening to aspects of his conduct and practice afterwards, from the time right after his awakening until his meditative passing away. The main theme of the present chapter is the recently awakened Buddha's decision to teach.[1] In the *Madhyama-āgama* parallel to the *Ariyapariyesanā-sutta*, this decision occurs right after the description of the Buddha's awakening. The relevant part proceeds as follows:[2]

> Knowledge arose, vision arose, and I was concentrated on the requisites of awakening.[3] I knew as it really is that birth has been extinguished, the holy life has been established, what had to be done has been done and there will be no experiencing of a further existence.
>
> Having just awakened to the supreme, right, and complete awakening, I thought in turn: "To whom should I first teach the Dharma?" I further thought: "Should I now first teach the Dharma to Āḷāra Kālāma?"

1 For a survey of textual and artistic depictions of the Buddha's activities during the first seven weeks after his awakening see, e.g., Bopearachchi 2016.

2 The translated part is taken from MĀ 204 at T I 777a17 to 777a25, parallel to MN 26 at MN I 169,31 (translated Ñāṇamoli 1995/2005: 262); see also Anālayo 2011: 178–82 and 2012b: 31f.

3 A reference to the *bodhipakkhiyā dhammā* is not found in MN 26.

> At that time there was a deva up in the sky who told me: "Great sage, may you know that Āḷāra Kālāma passed away seven days ago." I also came to know for myself that Āḷāra Kālāma had passed away seven days ago.
>
> I further thought: "It is a great loss for Āḷāra Kālāma that he did not get to hear this Dharma. If he had heard it, he would have quickly understood the Dharma in accordance with the Dharma."

The same pattern repeats itself with Uddaka Rāmaputta, whom the Buddha thought of next as someone capable of understanding, only to find out that he also had recently passed away.[4]

The Buddha's wish to teach these two first seems to reflect not only a sense of gratitude to his former teachers, but also his assessment of their potential, in that they "would have quickly understood", as stated in the passage translated above. Since Uddaka had apparently not reached the attainment realized by his father Rāma, it is natural for the Buddha to think first of teaching Āḷāra Kālāma, who had himself mastered the third immaterial attainment and thus would presumably have been the more highly accomplished practitioner of the two teachers. In this way, even though the bodhisattva found the immaterial attainments to fall short of leading him to the final goal of full liberation he had been searching for, at the present juncture he does consider them to provide a good foundation for quickly understanding what he had realized.

Regarding what preceded the Buddha's decision concerning whom to teach first, the *Ariyapariyesanā-sutta* and its *Madhyama-āgama* parallel show a rather substantial difference. Instead of turning from the Buddha's awakening right away to his reflection regarding whom he might teach, the *Ariyapariyesanā-sutta* reports that the Buddha was at first hesitant to teach at all. Brahmā became aware of this and came down to earth to intervene and beseech the Buddha to teach. Only after this intervention did the Buddha decide to share his discovery. A

4 MN 26 at MN I 170,15 notes that he had passed away the night before, but according to MĀ 204 at T I 777a29 this had already happened two weeks earlier. A discourse in the *Ekottarika-āgama*, EĀ 24.5 at T II 618b10 (translated Bareau 1988: 79), reports that he had just passed away the night before. EĀ 24.5 thereby concords with the presentation in MN 26.

comparable description is found in a discourse in the *Ekottarika-āgama*, which reports the episode in this manner:[5]

> At that time, when the Blessed One had recently attained awakening, this thought in turn arose in him: "Now this Dharma of mine is profound, to understand it is difficult, to comprehend it is difficult, to be able to realize it is difficult, which cannot be done by [mere] reflection. It is peaceful and sublime, to be realized by the wise capable of distinguishing its meaning, of practising without becoming weary, and of gaining delight.
>
> If I were to teach this sublime Dharma to others and they would not accept it with confidence and not receive it respectfully, that would be in vain and quite wearisome, having harmful results. I should best keep silent now. Why should I have to teach the Dharma?"

According to a *Saṃyutta-nikāya* parallel to this *Ekottarika-āgama* discourse, the Buddha thought that in particular specific conditionality (*idappaccayatā*) and the realization of Nirvāṇa are difficult to see. The Pāli version does not have a rhetorical question about the necessity to teach, although the same is implicit in a verse, in which the Buddha states his decision not to teach what he had found with such difficulty, as those under the influence of defilements will not easily understand it. This would imply that his engaging in teaching was not an inevitable result of his awakening, but rather depended on the receptivity and capability of his prospective audience.

According to the *Ekottarika-āgama* account, in his timely intervention Brahmā illustrated the differing capabilities of beings with the example of different lotus flowers, some of which are completely submersed in water, some have risen just to the surface of the water, and still others have risen higher. The *Saṃyutta-nikāya* parallel attributes this simile to the Buddha himself who, after having been invited by Brahmā, surveys the world and realizes the differing capabilities of beings. In both versions the simile exemplifies that, even though some are indeed so submersed in defilements that they will not

5 The translated passage is found in EĀ 19.1 at T II 593a24 to 593b1 (translated Bareau 1988: 78), parallel to SN 6.1 at SN I 136,1 (translated Bodhi 2000: 231).

understand, others are capable of understanding, their faculties are sufficiently ripe for being led to awakening. What they require, however, is someone to show them the path. To some degree they are in a similar predicament as the Buddha had been himself when he had set out on his quest for awakening, being at that time also uncertain of which path of practice and conduct can lead him to liberation.

After Brahmā's intervention, the *Ekottarika-āgama* version proceeds as follows:[6]

> At that time the Blessed One, who had understood the thought in the mind of Brahmā, out of compassion and empathy for all living beings spoke in verse:
>
> "Now Brahmā has come to persuade
> The Tathāgata to open the doors of the Dharma.
> [Let] those who hear it obtain sincere faith,
> And distinguish the essentials of the profound Dharma."[7]

Besides this discourse in the *Ekottarika-āgama*, the *Ariyapariyesanā-sutta*'s report of Brahmā's intervention, even though not found in its *Madhyama-āgama* parallel, does receive support from other accounts of events after the Buddha's awakening in several *Vinaya*s and biographies of the Buddha,[8] and has also inspired artistic representations.[9]

The same basic difference regarding the need for an intervention to motivate a Buddha to teach recurs in relation to the former Buddha Vipassin. The *Mahāpadāna-sutta* and its *Dīrgha-āgama* parallel report an intervention by Brahmā to

---

6 The translation is based on EĀ 19.1 at T II 593b15 to 593b20.

7 EĀ 19.1 at T II 593b19 continues with a second verse, not found in SN 6.1, which describes standing on top of a high mountain and being able to see various types of living being all around as an illustration of the Buddha's vision of the Dharma.

8 Examples are the Dharmaguptaka *Vinaya*, T 1428 at T XXII 786c20 (translated Bareau 1963: 138), the Mahīśāsaka *Vinaya*, T 1421 at T XXII 103c19 (translated Bareau 1963: 137), the Mūlasarvāstivāda *Vinaya*, Gnoli 1977: 128,29 (with its Chinese and Tibetan counterparts in T 1450 at T XXIV 126b16 and Waldschmidt 1957: 111,11), the *Mahāvastu*, Senart 1897: 315,1 (translated Jones 1956/1978: 304), and the *Lalitavistara*, Lefmann 1902: 394,8.

9 For a survey see Anālayo 2011: 178 note 175.

convince the recently awakened Vipassin to teach,[10] whereas no reference to Brahmā is found in a Sanskrit fragment version and in a partial parallel preserved in Chinese translation.[11] In this way, in the case of both Vipassin and Gotama Buddha the famous episode of Brahmā's intervention is not reported in all discourse versions. This leaves open the possibilities that either it was lost in some traditions or else it might have been added in the others. In short, this particular episode is less well established in tradition than, for example, the Buddha's ensuing decision to share his discovery first with his two former teachers.

The episode itself is significant in so far as it conveys the impression that the Buddha needed prompting to start teaching. Without such prompting, presumably he might not have taught the Dharma. The need for Brahmā's timely intervention becomes particularly prominent in the *Ekottarika-āgama* passage translated above, where the Buddha reflects: "Why should I have to teach the Dharma?" In other words, is it really a must that those who have reached awakening on their own will share this discovery with others? The possibility that someone might realize awakening without the guidance of a teacher but still not teach it widely to others finds its expression in the Buddhist traditions in the figure of the Paccekabuddha. Paccekabuddhas awaken on their own, yet do not have a following of disciples whom they teach.[12]

It is only with subsequent developments that the Buddha comes to be seen as having prepared himself during numerous past lives for his task as a teacher who leads others to awakening. The early stages in the development of the bodhisattva ideal,[13] to the extent to which these can be reconstructed from the texts still at our disposal, do not yet allot compassion a prominent place. Nevertheless, the early discourses do attribute the cultivation of *mettā* to the Buddha in one of his past lives. Due to the close relationship between *mettā* and compassion, at least in early Buddhist thought, this does imply that the meditative cultivation

10 DN 14 at DN II 36,21 (translated Walshe 1987: 213) and DĀ 1 at T I 8b22.
11 Waldschmidt 1956: 148 note 2 and T 3 at T I 156c14.
12 On the Paccekabuddha in early Buddhist thought see Anālayo 2016a: 215–38 and 249–65.
13 For a more detailed study see Anālayo 2010 and 2017a.

of the opening of the heart was something the Buddha already undertook in a previous existence. Here is the *Madhyama-āgama* version of the relevant passage:[14]

> I recollect that in former times I made merit for a long time and experienced its fruit for a long time, which were delightful to be recalled in the mind. Having in former times practised mettā for seven years, for seven [aeons] of evolution and dissolution I did not come [back] to this world.

The parallels agree in attributing the sustained practice of *mettā* to the Buddha in one of his past lives. However, such *mettā* practice is not in any way related to the idea of benefiting other beings or progressing to Buddhahood. Instead, it is presented as a source of merit that led to heavenly rebirths for a very long time. In other words, the point of bringing up such former life practice of *mettā* is to emphasize the importance of making merit in order to experience happiness in the future.

A discourse in the *Saṃyutta-nikāya* and its parallels highlight that the discovery and teaching of the Dharma marks the decisive difference between a Buddha or a Tathāgata and his arahant disciples. The discourse begins by stating that a Tathāgata and an arahant have both cultivated penetrative understanding of the five aggregates of clinging and become liberated. The *Saṃyukta-āgama* version continues as follows:[15]

> A Tathāgata, who is an arahant, fully awakened, has been able to realize the Dharma himself, the Dharma that had not been heard before, to penetrate to supreme awakening. He teaches the Dharma to future generations to awaken his disciples, namely the four establishments of mindfulness, the four right efforts, the four bases for supernormal power, the five faculties, the five powers, the seven awakening [factors], and the eight[fold] path.

---

14 The translated passage occurs in MĀ 138 at T I 645c20f, parallel to AN 7.58b at AN IV 89,1 (translated Bodhi 2012: 1062, referred to as discourse 62) and It 22 at It 15,5 (translated Ireland 1991: 15), as well as to Sanskrit fragments, Tripāṭhī 1995: 168, and SHT 412.32, Sander and Waldschmidt 1980: 65.

15 The translation is based on SĀ 75 at T II 19c3 to 19c10 (translated Anālayo 2013a: 39), parallel to SN 22.58 at SN III 65,21 (translated Bodhi 2000: 901) and a Sanskrit fragment version, SHT IV 30b R, Sander and Waldschmidt 1980: 80.

> Monastics, this is called a Tathāgata, who is an arahant, fully awakened, who has attained what had not been attained, who has gained what had not been gained, who understands the path, who distinguishes the path, who teaches the path, who penetrates the path, who moreover is able to teach and admonish disciples successfully, who in this way teaches them rightly and in such a way that they joyfully delight in the good Dharma. This is reckoned to be the difference between a Tathāgata and an arahant.

The *Saṃyutta-nikāya* version presents the whole matter in a more succinct way, explaining that the Tathāgata has given rise to, brought into being, and proclaimed the path; he is the one who knows the path, has discovered it, and is skilled in it. The disciples now dwell following this path, having come to possess it afterwards. Alongside minor differences, the main point made in both versions remains that discovering *and* teaching the Dharma is the characteristic of a Buddha. In fact according to one of the intrepidities of the Buddha, mentioned in Chapter 6, he was certain of being able to teach others what indeed leads to freedom from *dukkha*.

The above does not imply, however, that arahants do not teach out of compassion. The point is only that their teaching is based on what they realized after having been taught by the Buddha, whereas the Buddha taught what he had realized on his own. Another discourse shows the Buddha encouraging his first disciples, who had just become arahants, to wander far and wide in order to benefit beings. The relevant passage in the *Saṃyukta-āgama* proceeds like this:[16]

> At that time the Blessed One said to the monastics: "I have already been liberated from human and divine bondage and you have also attained liberation from human and divine bondage. You should wander among the people, for the taking across of many, for the welfare of many, for the peace and happiness of humans and devas. You should each leave singly and not wander with a companion."

16 The translated part is taken from SĀ 1096 at T II 288b1 to 288b4, parallel to SN 4.5 at SN I 105,24 (translated Bodhi 2000: 198) and Vin I 20,36 (translated Horner 1951/1982: 28); see also the *Mahāvastu*, Senart 1897: 415,8 (translated Jones 1956/1978: 416), and the *Saṅghabhedavastu*, Gnoli 1977: 148,21.

The two versions agree that the Buddha emphatically told his disciples to go each on their own, presumably so that in this way they can be present in different parts of the region, thereby maximizing the possibility that someone ready to understand will meet one of them and receive liberating teachings. In this way, here the Buddha passes on to his disciples the task he had taken on himself and which, according to the *Ariyapariyesanā-sutta* and several parallels, he did only after Brahmā's successful intervention had clarified that there are indeed those who will understand. In this way the intervention by Brahmā, at least from the viewpoint of those sources that report this episode, had major repercussions and would in the end have to be considered responsible for the Dharma being still available nowadays.

In early Buddhist thought, becoming one among the type of celestial beings that live in the Brahmā Heavens can be achieved through the meditative cultivation of the *brahmavihāra*s. One of these *brahmavihāra*s is compassion and this is indeed the one relevant to Brahmā's timely intervention. In fact the example of the Buddha's decision to teach and his passing on the same duty to his fully awakened disciples, independent of whether this decision originally required a prompting by Brahmā or not, clearly point to compassion.[17]

EXERCISE

By way of actual practice, the cultivation of compassion recommends itself as a way of following the Buddha's example in teaching others out of this altruistic motivation. The cultivation of a compassionate attitude could begin by arousing a sense of gratitude for the benefits we have experienced due to coming into contact with the Dharma. Having aroused joyful inspiration through such a sense of gratitude offers a convenient starting point for cultivating the attitude of being ourselves willing to share the Dharma with others in whatever way possible for us.

---

17 In early Buddhist thought, compassion features in two interrelated modes. One of these is active compassion, *anukampā*, which typically takes the form of teaching the Dharma; the other is compassion as a quality of meditative practice, *karuṇā*. Needless to say, each supports the other.

For formal meditation I suggest employing whatever image or phrase we might find useful to stimulate compassion as a starting point, but then proceed from such practice to letting go of such supports and just dwell in the mental attitude of compassion. In this way, from "doing" compassion, as a starting point, we move on to just "being" in the mental condition of compassion and allow it to become boundless. The condition of boundlessness is achieved simply by not consenting to any boundary becoming a limit to our compassionate disposition.[18]

Formal meditation practice undertaken in this way will naturally assist us to react with an altruistic outlook in everyday situations. Making an intentional effort to avoid harming others to the best of our ability and to remain with a compassionate attitude even towards those who do not reciprocate builds the foundation for meditation practice in turn. Both in conjunction can gradually transform ourselves and thereby provide substantial support for the path to awakening. In this way, we re-enact the compassionate disposition that is responsible for the Buddha's decision to teach and therefore for our own ability to learn and practise the Dharma.

18 See in more detail Anālayo 2015a: 151–62.

XV

THE TWO EXTREMES

In this chapter I take up the first part of what according to tradition was the teaching with which the Buddha set in motion the wheel of Dharma. The discourse in question, addressed to the five who had been his companions during his ascetic practices, begins with the two extremes that need to be avoided in order to be able to reach awakening. Before coming to the actual delivery of this distinction, however, I first need to turn to the narration that leads up to this first discourse by the Buddha.

The *Ariyapariyesanā-sutta* and its *Madhyama-āgama* parallel report that, once the Buddha had found out that Āḷāra Kālāma and Uddaka Rāmaputta had both passed away, he decided to teach the five who had been his companions during his period of asceticism. The *Madhyama-āgama* version proceeds in this way:[1]

> Having just awakened to supreme, right, and complete awakening, I thought: "To whom should I first teach the Dharma?" I further thought: "The five monastics of former times have been of much benefit by supporting me in my efforts. When I practised asceticism, those five monastics served me. Should I now first teach the Dharma to the five monastics?"
>
> I further thought: "Where are the five monastics of former times now?" With the purified divine eye that transcends [the vision] of

1 The translated part is taken from MĀ 204 at T I 777b3 to 777b11, parallel to MN 26 at MN I 170,20 (translated Ñāṇamoli 1995/2005: 263); see also Anālayo 2011: 182 and 2012b: 32f.

> human beings I saw that the five monastics were in the Deer Park at the Dwelling-place of Seers near Benares. After staying under the tree of awakening according [to my wishes], I gathered my robes, took my bowl, and approached Benares, the city of Kāsi.

According to the Mahīśāsaka and Mūlasarvāstivāda *Vinaya*s, these five former companions had been sent by the Buddha's father to look after the bodhisattva.[2] A discourse in the *Ekottarika-āgama* reports that they had been following the bodhisattva since his birth.[3] An alternative perspective emerges with the *Lalitavistara*, according to which the five, who were formerly disciples of Uddaka Rāmaputta, had witnessed how the bodhisattva quickly achieved what they had not reached after much practice.[4] The fact that he was not satisfied with what he had achieved was what motivated them to follow him and also leave Uddaka.

Given that these five left the bodhisattva when he gave up his ascetic practices, the presentation in the *Lalitavistara* fits the narrative context well. Had these five been friends from his early youth or sent by his father to look after him, the fact that he decided to change his mode of practice would not really furnish sufficient reason for them to leave him. Such a decision makes more sense if they had followed him in the hope of benefiting from his realization. In such a case, once he had given up asceticism and thus what they considered necessary to reach realization, it would be natural if they decided to leave him and proceed on their own.

The *Ariyapariyesanā-sutta* and its *Madhyama-āgama* parallel continue by relating that, on his way to teaching the five, the Buddha met a wanderer by the name of Upaka. The *Madhyama-āgama* reports this encounter as follows:[5]

---

2 T 1421 at T XXII 104a19 and Gnoli 1977: 99,4.

3 EĀ 24.5 at T II 618b14 (translated Bareau 1988: 79).

4 Lefmann 1902: 245,17.

5 The translation is based on MĀ 204 at T I 777b11 to 777b17, which does not give precise indications as to where the meeting with Upaka took place. According to MN 26 at MN I 170,33, it took place between Gayā and the place of awakening. Similarly to MĀ 204, reports of the present episode in EĀ 24.5 at T II 618c1, T 211 at T IV 594b10, T 212 at T IV 717b18, and the *Saṅghabhedavastu*, Gnoli 1977: 131,23, do not provide further specifications regarding the location of this meeting, except for indicating that it took place en route to Benares. The *Mahāvastu*, Senart 1897: 325,11 (translated Jones 1956/1978: 316), locates the meeting near a village in the vicinity of Benares.

> At that time the heterodox practitioner Upaka saw from afar that I was coming and said to me:
>
> "Venerable friend Gotama, your faculties are clear, your appearance is very sublime, your face shines. Venerable friend Gotama, who is your teacher? Under whom do you train in the path? In whose teaching do you have confidence?"
>
> At that time I replied to Upaka in verse:
>
> "I am peerless, the supreme victor
> Without attachment to anything,
> Liberated by the destruction of all craving,
> Awakened by myself, whom should I call my teacher?"

Their exchange eventually ends with Upaka stating: "may it be so" and departing.[6] His reaction contrasts with his earlier inspiration, where on seeing the Buddha he wished to know under whose teacher and with what practice such an impressive demeanour and appearance had been accomplished. Clearly the episode sets out with someone who feels inspired and who appears almost ready for conversion. Yet the Buddha's claim to be supreme and have no teacher evidently failed to convince Upaka. Perhaps the present episode could be read as pointing to the need for the Buddha to find ways of communicating his realization that will convince others, beyond a simple claim to being the supreme victor.[7]

Unlike Upaka, who at least was quite inspired initially, the five former companions believed that the Buddha had abandoned striving, a situation that needed to be addressed skilfully in order to convince them to place trust in what the Buddha had to offer.[8] The *Madhyama-āgama* parallel to the *Ariyapariyesanā-sutta* depicts their attitude in the following way:[9]

---

6 For a comparative survey of differences among the records of the full verse exchange between Upaka and the Buddha see Anālayo 2011: 183f.

7 Blomfield 2011: 105 reasons that "Upaka's indifference to Gautama's pronouncement showed that ... he would need to do more than simply declare his realisation if he wanted to convince others."

8 On the importance of such initial arousing of confidence in the Buddha's awakening in general see also below p. 227–8.

9 The translated part is taken from MĀ 204 at T I 777c1 to 777c5.

> Then the five monastics saw from afar that I was coming. They established a firmly set agreement with each other, saying: "Venerable friends, you should know that this recluse Gotama is coming. He is of many desires and of many wants, he partakes of exquisite food and drink, fine cereals, rice, flour, ghee, and honey, and he applies sesame oil to his body. Now that he is coming back, you stay seated and take care not to rise up in greeting and do not pay homage to him. Keep a seat for him but do not invite him to sit on it."

The *Ariyapariyesanā-sutta* and a partial parallel in the *Ekottarika-āgama* report a similar agreement made among the five.[10] This episode shows that it was not going to be easy to convince them that, rather than being one who has reverted to a life of luxury, the Buddha had reached the final goal of liberation. Even though the five eventually did not keep their earlier agreement and were more welcoming to the Buddha than they had planned, when he claimed to have reached awakening they were not easily convinced. Here is the *Madhyama-āgama* version of their reply:[11]

> Friend Gotama, formerly your conduct was in such a [determined] way, your following a path was in such a [determined] way, and your ascetic practices were in such a [determined] way, yet you were unable to attain a superhuman state, a distinction in noble knowledge and noble vision. How could this be the case now, when you are of many desires and of many wants, partaking of exquisite food and drink, fine cereals, rice, flour, ghee, and honey, and when you apply sesame oil to your body?

In the *Ariyapariyesanā-sutta* they even object three times. Evidently the topic of the inefficacy of asceticism had to be tackled in order to clarify that the Buddha had given up his earlier conduct because it was not productive of awakening,

---

10 According to the *Lalitavistara*, Lefmann 1902: 408,5, one of the five, known in the Pāli tradition as Koṇḍañña, disagreed with the rest of the group on how they were to receive the Buddha, although he did not speak up. His less disdainful attitude would presumably explain why he could reach stream-entry on hearing the Buddha teach the four truths, unlike the other four.

11 The translated part is taken from MĀ 204 at T I 777c19 to 777c22.

not because he had lost the inspiration to continue his quest for liberation. At the same time, the Buddha also had to make it clear that his change of approach did not imply a reverting to sensuality and a life of luxury. In other words, he had to clarify that there is more than just these two alternatives of either asceticism or else sensual indulgence; he had to reveal to them the middle path. This fundamental clarification of the middle path, the first part of the teaching with which according to tradition the Buddha set in motion the wheel of Dharma, has been preserved as a discourse on its own in the *Ekottarika-āgama*. Here is a translation of the relevant section:[12]

> Then the Blessed One said to the [five] monastics: "There are these two modalities that one training in the path ought not to become involved with. What are the two modalities? That is, they are the state of being attached to sensual pleasures and their enjoyment, which is lowly and the state of the commoner, and the assemblage of these [self-inflicted] pains with their manifold vexations. These are reckoned to be the two modalities that one training in the path ought not to become involved with.
>
> "Having left behind these two modalities in this way, I have myself reached the essential path that leads to the attainment of full awakening, to the arising of vision, to the arising of knowledge, [whereby] the mind attains appeasement, attains the penetrative knowledges, accomplishes the fruits of recluseship, and reaches Nirvāṇa.
>
> "What is the essential path that leads to the attainment of full awakening, that arouses vision, arouses knowledge, [whereby] the mind attains appeasement, attains the penetrative knowledges, accomplishes the fruits of recluseship, and reaches Nirvāṇa? That is, it is this noble eightfold path, namely right view, right thought, right speech, right action, right livelihood, right effort, right mindfulness, and right concentration."

The first part of the *Dhammacakkappavattana-sutta* proceeds similarly,[13] so that the main difference is that the Pāli version

12 The translated section is based on EĀ 19.2 at T II 593b25 to 593c5; see Anālayo 2016a: 268f.

13 SN 56.11 at SN V 421,2 (translated Bodhi 2000: 1844); for a comparative study of parallel versions to SN 56.11 and a critical examination of the hypothesis that the teaching of the four truths is a late element in early Buddhist thought see Anālayo 2015b: 347–88 and 2016a: 267–99.

continues right away with the delivery of the teaching on the four truths, which in the *Ekottarika-āgama* features in a separate discourse. The *Madhyama-āgama* parallel to the *Ariyapariyesanā-sutta* also just reports the teaching on the two extremes, without proceeding to the four truths. The implication of this difference appears to be that, after the Buddha had first delivered the teaching on the two extremes, a break occurred that would have afforded the five monastics time to reflect and digest this for them rather new perspective, after which only the Buddha disclosed to them the four truths. Two biographies preserved in Chinese translation in fact report that the Buddha, having clarified the two extremes, examined the minds of the five to see if they were ready for the teaching he was to give them next.[14]

In view of the earlier defiant attitude of the five monastics, it would indeed be meaningful if the Buddha were to portion out what he had to teach them in such a way that they could first mentally assimilate the notion of a middle path, before receiving further teachings. Such a suggestion need not be seen as standing in contrast to the *Dhammacakkappavattana-sutta*, which might simply be presenting the entire teaching together without explicitly marking that a break occurred between the clarification of the two extremes and the teaching on the four truths.

The nuance of a middle path aloof from the two extremes of sensual indulgence and self-tormenting appears to be well suited to the present occasion, enabling the five monastics to settle their doubts and realize that giving up asceticism does not equal giving up the path to liberation.

At the same time, however, the notion of a middle path of balance has wider implications. An illustrative example is the famous discourse to Kaccāyana, which takes up the two extremes of existence and non-existence.[15] This teaching was apparently of such renown already in early times that it was quoted on another occasion by Ānanda. This quote is addressed to Channa, who up to that point had been unable to gain deeper

14 T 189 at T III 644b18 and T 191 at T III 954a10.

15 SN 12.15 at SN II 17,8 (translated Bodhi 2000: 544) and its parallels SĀ 301 at T II 85c20 and a Sanskrit fragment version, Tripāṭhī 1962: 168; see also SHT X 3872+3981, Wille 2008: 203.

insight into the teachings. At the end of the discourse by Ānanda, however, Channa attains stream-entry. The *Saṃyukta-āgama* version proceeds in this way:[16]

> Formerly I heard this from the Buddha, an instruction given to Mahākaccāna: "People in the world are confused, depending on two extremes: existence and non-existence. People in the world cling to objects and conceive them in turn in the mind with attachment.
>
> "Kaccāna, if one does not accept, does not cling to, does not get established on, and does not conceive of a self, then when this dukkha arises, it [just] arises; when it ceases, it [just] ceases. Kaccāna, herein without doubt, without being puzzled, without needing to rely on others, one is able to understand this for oneself; this is called right view, as taught by the Tathāgata. Why is that?
>
> "Kaccāna, rightly contemplating the arising of the world as it really is, one will not give rise to the view of the non-existence of the world. Rightly contemplating the cessation of the world as it really is, one will not give rise to the view of the existence of the world.
>
> "Kaccāna, avoiding these two extremes the Tathāgata teaches the middle way, namely: because this exists, that exists; because of the arising of this, that arises; that is, conditioned by ignorance are formations, *conditioned by formations is consciousness, conditioned by consciousness is name-and-form, conditioned by name-and-form are the six sense-spheres, conditioned by the six sense-spheres is contact, conditioned by contact is feeling, conditioned by feeling is craving, conditioned by craving is clinging, conditioned by clinging is becoming, conditioned by becoming is birth, conditioned by* birth there arise old age, disease, death, worry, sorrow, vexation, and pain."

Both versions continue by presenting the cessation mode of dependent arising, where the cessation of ignorance leads via the cessation of the other links to the cessation of *dukkha*. In this way, the middle path practically implemented is the noble eightfold path, but from a doctrinal perspective the middle path is also dependent arising, which stays aloof from the two

16 The translated section is taken from SĀ 262 at T II 66c25 to 67a6, parallel to SN 22.90 at SN III 134,28 (translated Bodhi 2000: 947 and 544).

extremes of existence and non-existence. Instead of reifying things in either of these two modes, the middle path can be found by contemplating the process of conditionally arisen phenomena and the cessation of this process. Contemplating in such a way leads to letting go of the self-notion. As a result of being free from the conceit of a self, *dukkha* just arises and ceases, without creating the repercussions it did earlier. Such insight can be so powerful that, even in the case of someone like Channa, who earlier did not gain insight, it can lead to the breakthrough to stream-entry.

Another dimension of the middle path is the need for establishing balance in one's meditation practice, which requires neither striving too much nor becoming too slack. This finds expression in a dialogue between the Buddha and a *deva* on how the Buddha managed to cross the flood, a metaphor for liberation. The dialogue is found in a discourse in the *Saṃyutta-nikāya* with parallels in the two *Saṃyukta-āgamas*.[17] According to the *Saṃyutta-nikāya* discourse, in his reply to the *deva*'s query the Buddha pointed out two problems when crossing the flood. One is sinking, which happens when one stands still, and the other is being swept away, which occurs when one struggles excessively. Instead of either stagnation or else overexertion, a balanced mode of practice is what enables crossing the flood.

EXERCISE

As a practical implementation of a dimension of the middle path discovered by the Buddha, I would like to suggest bringing the theme of balance to bear on our meditation practice. This can be done particularly well with the awakening factors, already taken up in Chapter 13. Based on having aroused the seven awakening factors and maintaining a well-established foundation in mindfulness, the task now is to balance the two triads of investigation–energy–joy and tranquillity–concentration–equipoise. The first group of three is energizing and therefore to be given more emphasis when the mind is

17 SN 1.1 at SN I 1,1 (translated Bodhi 2000: 89), which has parallels in SĀ 1267 at T II 348b10 and SĀ² 180 at T II 438c15; see also Enomoto 1989: 28 (§13).

sluggish, the second group of three is calming and for this reason commendable when the mind is excited. Mindfulness provides the foundation for both, enabling us to recognize the condition of the mind in the first place.

From having experimented with mental balance in formal meditation, the same nuance can also be brought to bear on our daily activities, avoiding the extremes of sluggish slackness and of excessive agitation so as to find the middle path of balance in any situation, even in relation to the most mundane of activities. Another dimension of the same sense of balance can be found in recognizing how strengthening our sense of self can occur not only by way of indulging our whims, but also through taking pride in how hard we can be on ourselves. Both modes miss the middle path. Here, again, mindfulness provides the foundation for recognizing when balance has been lost.

XVI

THE FOUR TRUTHS

In this chapter I continue to examine the Buddha's first discourse. Having clarified his approach to involve a middle path between the two extremes of sensuality and asceticism, the next topic broached by the Buddha with his first five disciples concerns the four truths. As mentioned in the previous chapter, the *Ekottarika-āgama* presents the teaching of the two extremes and of the four truths as separate discourses, a feature also found in other versions of the Buddha's first sermon, presumably reflecting the idea that a break between the delivery of these two teachings would have allowed the five monastics to digest the notion of a middle path before being taught the four truths.

Another feature of the *Ekottarika-āgama* is that it does not employ the qualification "noble" when introducing the four truths. This, too, is a feature attested elsewhere. It suggests that at first this qualification was only used in specific instances and only later came to be applied to any reference to the four truths.[1] In view of their "ennobling" potential, such a more widespread application of the term "noble" to the four truths is hardly surprising.

Here is the relevant part of the *Ekottarika-āgama* account of the Buddha's first delivery of the teaching on the four truths:[2]

1 For a more detailed discussion see Anālayo 2016a: 239–48.

2 The translated part is based on EĀ 24.5 at T II 619a8 to 619a19 (translated Anālayo 2016a: 269f), parallel to SN 56.11 at SN V 421,19 (translated Bodhi 2000: 1844); for a comparative study of parallel versions to SN 56.11 see Anālayo 2015b: 347–88 and 2016a: 267–99.

> At that time the Blessed One said to the five monastics: "You should know that there are these four truths. What are the four? They are the truth of dukkha, the truth of the arising of dukkha, the truth of the cessation of dukkha, and the truth of the way out of dukkha.
>
> "What is reckoned to be that truth of dukkha? That is, birth is dukkha, old age is dukkha, disease is dukkha, death is dukkha, [as well as] grief, vexation, affliction, worry, and pains that cannot be measured; association with what is disliked is dukkha, dissociation from what is liked is dukkha, not getting what one wishes is also dukkha; stated in brief, the five aggregates of clinging are dukkha. This is reckoned to be the truth of dukkha.
>
> "What is that truth of the arising of dukkha? That is, it is grasping conjoined with craving that leads to acting carelessly with a mind that keeps being lustfully attached. This is reckoned to be the truth of the arising of dukkha.
>
> "What is that truth of the cessation of dukkha? It is being able to bring about the eradication and cessation without remainder of that craving, so that it will not arise again. This is reckoned to be the truth of the cessation of dukkha.
>
> "What is reckoned to be the way out of dukkha? That is, it is the noble eightfold path, namely right view, right thought, right speech, right action, right livelihood, right effort, right mindfulness, and right concentration.
>
> "This is reckoned to be the teaching of the four truths."

Appreciating this teaching of the four truths first of all requires gaining clarity about the implications of the term *dukkha*. Although this word can at times stand for pain and outright suffering, such nuances do not exhaust the range of implications of *dukkha*. In general it seems to me preferable to use the Pāli term, but, if a translation is needed, I would opt for "unsatisfactory" (unless the context is clearly specifying one of the three types of feelings).

According to the summary statement of the first truth, the five aggregates of clinging are *dukkha*. This can hardly mean that all of these five dimensions of personal experience, comprising body, feeling, perception, formations, and consciousness, are invariably painful or suffering.

The inapplicability of a translation as "suffering" could be illustrated with the second of these five aggregates. The early Buddhist analysis of feelings distinguishes three types: pleasant, painful, and what is literally "neither-painful-nor-pleasant", in short, neutral. When painful feelings manifest, one will probably suffer (but even that depends on one's mental attitude towards the pain), but when pleasant feelings are present, one will hardly be suffering. Of course, there is the fact of change. So when pleasant feelings change to one of the other types, one might suffer (but this again depends on one's attitude). When painful feelings change to one of the other two types, however, one will hardly suffer. Instead, the change of pain to neutral or pleasant feeling will be experienced as a relief. Thus when all types of feeling are qualified as *dukkha*, this cannot carry the sense that they are invariably "suffering" or "pain". It can only mean that they are "unsatisfactory". Due to their conditioned and changing nature, they can never yield lasting satisfaction.

The main import of the first truth thus would to be to draw attention to *dukkha* in the sense of the ultimately unsatisfactory nature of conditioned existence. This finds illustration in examples like disease, old age, and death, gaining freedom from which was central in the bodhisattva's motivation to set out on his quest for Nirvāṇa, as discussed in Chapter 1. The first truth thereby reiterates the Buddha's basic insight into human existence as *dukkha*. This holds however much at present one might be healthy, young, and alive, and thus prone to turn a blind eye to what will inevitably confront one sooner or later. The example set by the bodhisattva is to give full recognition to these dimensions of *dukkha*, as he did not allow his own health and youth to prevent him from recognizing the basic predicaments all humans eventually have to face in one way or another. In this way, the first truth confirms again the central directive that informed the Buddha's quest and teaching, namely to find what is free from disease, old age, and death.

The second truth then relates the arising of *dukkha* to grasping and craving which, according to the *Ekottarika-āgama* version's explanation, "leads to acting carelessly with a mind that keeps being lustfully attached". The *Dhammacakkappavattana-sutta* instead speaks of craving that leads to renewed becoming, and then distinguishes three types of craving: for sensual pleasures, for existence, and for non-existence.[3]

The relationship between craving and *dukkha* established in the second truth can be fleshed out with the help of dependent arising, discussed in Chapter 12. This teaching traces the conditioned arising of *dukkha* from its manifestation in old age and death via several intervening links to craving. Whereas the remainder of the series follows on its own, once craving is in place, the same is not the case for what functions as the condition for craving, which is feeling. Feeling can, but does not have to, lead to craving. This explains why the second truth points a spotlight on craving; this is the condition where mental culture and training can make a world of difference, by preventing the arising of *dukkha* and eventually eradicating this propensity for good. In terms of the *Ekottarika-āgama* version translated above, the task is to avoid acting carelessly with a mind under the influence of sensual lust. The *Dhammacakkappavattana-sutta*'s presentation additionally notes that the problem is not just sensuality, but also modes of craving related to existence and non-existence.

Regarding the case of craving for existence, a discourse in the *Aṅguttara-nikāya* and its *Madhyama-āgama* parallel clarify that such craving for existence has ignorance (the first of the conditions in dependent arising) as its nutriment. In agreement with its Pāli parallel, the *Madhyama-āgama* discourse presents the matter as follows:[4]

> Of craving for existence an ultimate beginning cannot be known, before which there was no craving for existence and at which instant craving for existence arose. [Yet], a condition for craving for existence can in turn be known. Craving for existence has its nutriment; it is not without nutriment. What is reckoned to be the nutriment for craving for existence? The answer is: ignorance is its nutriment.

---

3 SN 56.11 at SN V 421,27.

4 The translated part is based on MĀ 52 at T I 487c27 to 488a1 (translated Bingenheimer et al. 2013: 332), parallel to AN 10.62 at AN V 116,15 (translated Bodhi 2012: 1418), and T 36 at T I 819c23.

Thus the eradication of ignorance deprives craving for existence of its nutriment. In other words, with ignorance removed, such craving also comes to an end. According to another discourse in the *Saṃyutta-nikāya* and a parallel in a *Saṃyukta-āgama* collection (T 101) of which only a part has been preserved, insight into impermanence will bring craving to an end. The *Saṃyukta-āgama* version presents the matter for the first of the five aggregates of clinging as follows:[5]

> If one is able to understand that bodily form is impermanent and [subject to] destruction, if one is able to understand this truth and contemplate it, then craving for bodily form will depart. Craving for bodily form having been destroyed, then craving and lust will also be destroyed. Craving and lust having been destroyed, one will then be liberated.

The same holds for the other aggregates. The *Saṃyutta-nikāya* discourse expresses the same matter in slightly different terms, explaining that disenchantment towards bodily form leads to the destruction of delight and passion, which results in liberation.

Another discourse passage provides a perspective that leads beyond the arising of *dukkha* all the way up to liberation. Here is the *Madhyama-āgama* version of this presentation:[6]

> Conditioned by ignorance there are formations, conditioned by formations there is consciousness, conditioned by consciousness there is name-and-form, conditioned by name-and-form there are the six sense-spheres, conditioned by the six sense-spheres there is contact, conditioned by contact there is feeling, conditioned by feeling there is craving, conditioned by craving there is clinging, conditioned by clinging there is becoming, conditioned by becoming there is birth, conditioned by birth there are old age and death, conditioned by old age and death there is dukkha,[7]

---

5 The translation is based on SĀ[3] 12 at T II 496b25 to 496b27, parallel to SN 22.51 at SN III 51,12 (translated Bodhi 2000: 889).

6 The translated passage is taken from MĀ 55 at T I 491a4 to 491a11 (translated Bingenheimer et al. 2013: 349), parallel to SN 12.23 at SN II 31,26 (translated Bodhi 2000: 555) and D 4094 *ju* 51b2 or Q 5595 *tu* 56a2. For a study of the presentation in SN 12.23 see Bodhi 1980.

7 SN 12.23 at SN II 31,31 proceeds from birth directly to *dukkha*, without taking up old age and death.

> with the arising of dukkha there is then confidence, with the arising of confidence there is then right attention, with the arising of right attention there are then right mindfulness and right comprehension, with the arising of right mindfulness and right comprehension there is then the guarding of the faculties, *with the arising of guarding of the faculties there is then* the guarding of morality, *with the arising of guarding of morality there is then* the absence of regret, *with the arising of absence of regret there is then* delight, *with the arising of delight there is then* joy, *with the arising of joy there is then* tranquillity, *with the arising of tranquillity there is then* happiness, *with the arising of happiness there is then* concentration, *with the arising of concentration there is then* seeing as it really is and knowing as it really is, *with the arising of seeing as it really is and knowing as it really is there is then* disenchantment, *with the arising of disenchantment there is then* dispassion, *with the arising of dispassion there is then* liberation, and with the arising of liberation there is then the attainment of Nirvāṇa.

In this way the vista opens beyond *dukkha* to the arising of faith or confidence as the basis for cultivating those mental qualities that will eventually lead to realizing the end of *dukkha*. This is precisely the point made in the third noble truth, namely that the solution to the predicament of *dukkha* is to eradicate craving in such a way that it will not arise again. Notably, the quality that in the passage translated above leads over from *dukkha* to the series of conditions that culminate in the attainment of Nirvāṇa is confidence or faith.

The path to liberation then is the noble eightfold path. This path has right view as its first factor, and a regularly mentioned mode of right view is precisely understanding the four truths. Far from involving a tautology, the point is that some basic appreciation of the four truths is required for being motivated to set out on the path of practice at all. This mirrors the indication in the passage quoted above that *dukkha* is the condition for confidence or faith, *saddhā*, and thereby can lead to a whole series of conditions that issue in liberation. Without the minimum of confidence that a solution to *dukkha* can be found, and that a viable path to that solution exists, one will hardly do something about it.

Such a preliminary understanding of the four truths as a guiding principle for setting out on the path of practice is not identical with the level of insight into the four noble truths gained by a stream-enterer or even with full awakening. Instead, the first factor of the noble eightfold path, right view in the form of the four truths, can have a preliminary diagnostic function. It places the disconcerting recognition of the fact of *dukkha* within a framework that reveals its conditionality as well as the possibility of, and the means for, becoming free from it.

The basic scheme of the four truths mirrors a diagnostic scheme that appears to have been in use in ancient India.[8] Comparable to a scheme in current use in medical treatment called SOAP (Subjective, Objective, Assessment, and Plan),[9] the ancient Indian version requires a doctor to be skilled in knowing:[10]

- the disease,
- the source of the disease,
- the cure required for the disease,
- when the disease has been cured.

On being applied to the existential problem of *dukkha*, a shift in sequences occurs, such that the third and fourth in the medical scheme exchange their places. As a result of being adjusted in such a way that each of the two main issues, *dukkha* and its cessation, is followed by its respective conditions, the following pattern emerges:

- disease: *dukkha*,
- pathogen: craving,
- health: cessation of *dukkha*,
- cure: eightfold path.

The narrative setting that leads up to the teaching given to the first five monastics offers a background for appreciating the

8 See in more detail Anālayo 2015b: 27–40.

9 "Subjective" refers to the patient's subjective description of the ailment, "objective" documents the results from the medical check, "assessment" corresponds to the physician's diagnosis, and "plan" delineates the prescribed treatment; see Aming Tu in Anālayo 2016b: 254f.

10 SĀ 389 at T II 105a27f (translated Anālayo 2016b: 12).

employment of such a diagnostic scheme. As mentioned in the last chapter, on his way to Benares the recently awakened Buddha met the practitioner Upaka, who at first seemed quite impressed. Yet, on hearing that the Buddha claimed to be a supreme victor, Upaka appears to have lost whatever initial inspiration he may have had and just left. This narrative suggests the need for the Buddha to find a way of expressing his realization in such a way that others will acquire the basic confidence or faith needed for being willing to engage in the actual practice of what he has to offer. This holds in particular for his meeting with the five monastics, who at first were disinclined to believe his claim to have reached the final goal.

Given the Buddha's earlier ascetic practice of enduring pain and taking his body to the extremes of emaciation and a condition close to medical death, the nuance of a medical perspective on pain and disease is not surprising. In other words, the employment of a medical scheme of diagnosis in order to convey his realization to the five, who were not to be convinced easily, seems to stand in some degree of continuity with the pre-awakening narrative.

Moreover, in the ancient Indian setting, which the early discourses depict as teeming with various philosophers ready to debate their views, the choice of a medical analogy would have been sufficiently distinct from already existing philosophies to convey the novelty of his approach. At the same time, it would have enabled the Buddha to rely on something presumably known to the five already, in order to create a minimal sense of familiarity.

In addition, the four truths' formulation places emphasis on an analytical approach, which is indeed a distinct feature of the Buddha's teaching in general. The same formulation also conveys the eminent pragmatism with which he addressed the basic problem of *dukkha* and other issues. In fact the term "truth", *sacca*, used in the present context, does not imply a proclamation that just has to be believed as being true.[11] Instead,

---

11 Premasiri 2016: 325 and 330 explains that "the Buddha was not concerned with the search for absolute truth or absolute knowledge, but only knowledge that could free people from unwholesome tendencies and thereby free them from suffering."

the main point is that something is identified that one needs to realize oneself as being true.

In this way, when examined from the viewpoint of the narrative setting, the employment of a medical scheme of diagnosis seems a particularly skilful way of teaching the five monastics. It serves to convey axiomatic aspects of the Buddha's teaching and, with its mixture of familiar concepts and novelty, serves to inspire the needed confidence in his claim to have reached awakening and be able to teach the path to freedom, at the same time encapsulating this path in a nutshell.

EXERCISE

For actual practice I would like to recommend a simplified contemplation of the four noble truths, which can be applied to any situation with the mental question: "Does what I am about to do lead to *dukkha* or does it lead to liberation from *dukkha*?" According to situation and personal preference, we might give more emphasis to the first or to the second half of the question. Based on such a simple reflection, which could be put to good use also when we are in the midst of doing something and after we have completed an action, we increasingly learn to avoid doing what leads to an increase in *dukkha*, be this for ourselves or for others, and to pursue what leads to, at first temporary but eventually total, freedom from *dukkha*.

XVII

THE THREE TURNINGS

In this chapter I continue to explore the Buddha's first discourse, in particular the notion of three turnings that are to be applied to each of the four truths. The basic idea behind these three turnings is that each of the four truths requires first of all to be understood, which is the first turning; this understanding then needs to be followed by some implementation, the second turning; and this implementation has to be carried to its successful completion, the third turning. A *Saṃyukta-āgama* parallel to the *Dhammacakkappavattana-sutta* presents the second turning in the following manner (after having already described the first turning by way of an initial understanding of each of the four truths):[1]

> Again, the noble truth of dukkha should be further understood with knowledge, which is a teaching not heard before. When I gave proper attention to it, vision, knowledge, understanding, and realization arose [in me].
>
> [Again], having understood the noble truth of the arising of dukkha, it should be eradicated, which is a teaching not heard before. When I gave proper attention to it, vision, knowledge, understanding, and realization arose [in me].

1 The translated part is based on SĀ 379 at T II 103c17 to 103c24; parallel to SN 56.11 at SN V 422,3 (translated Bodhi 2000: 1845); for a comparative study and translations of parallel versions to SN 56.11 see Anālayo 2015b: 347–88 and 2016a: 267–99.

> Again, having understood this noble truth of the cessation of dukkha,[2] it should be realized, which is a teaching not heard before. When I gave proper attention to it, vision, knowledge, understanding, and realization arose [in me].
>
> Again, having understood this noble truth of the path to the cessation of dukkha, it should be cultivated, which is a teaching not heard before. When I gave proper attention to it, vision, knowledge, understanding, and realization arose [in me].

The discourse continues with the third turning, which requires the following in relation to each of the four truths:

- *dukkha*: to be understood completely,
- craving: to be eradicated completely,
- the cessation of *dukkha*: to be realized completely,
- the path to the cessation of *dukkha*: to be cultivated completely.

After the description of this third turning, the Buddha reportedly made the following statement:[3]

> [So long as] in regard to these four noble truths in three turnings and twelve modes I had not given rise to vision, knowledge, understanding, and realization, I had not yet attained deliverance, release, and liberation among the assemblies of those who listen to teachings: devas, Māra, Brahmā, recluses, brahmins; I had myself not realized the attainment of supreme and right awakening.

This is followed by the complementary statement that, once he had indeed completed the three turnings in relation to each truth, he did attain deliverance, release, and liberation. The *Saṃyutta-nikāya* presentation is similar overall, with the difference that, instead of applying one turning to all four truths and then moving on to the next turning, it rather applies all three turnings to one truth and then moves on to the next truth. This

---

2 The translation is based on an emendation by deleting a reference to "the cessation of the arisen *dukkha*", which appears to be the result of a transmission error; and it is also based on the adoption of a variant without a reference to "knowing".

3 The translation is taken from SĀ 379 at T II 104a2 to 104a5.

is a recurrent difference among the versions of this discourse.[4] Alongside such variation in presentation, however, the basic idea of three turnings to be applied to each truth is common ground among the parallels.

This notion of three turnings implies that there are different levels of profundity with each of these truths. This accords with a suggestion I made in the last chapter, in that the preliminary insight into the four truths that can function as a precursor to the noble eightfold path in the form of right view differs substantially from a realization of the four truths with full awakening. In other words, insight into the four truths is a matter of prolonged cultivation.

Another significant implication is that each of the truths is associated with a different task. Whereas *dukkha* requires "understanding", its arising calls for "eradication", its cessation needs "realization", and the path requires "cultivation". Although at first sight these might seem to be four different tasks resulting in four distinct insights, closer inspection shows that this is not the case.

For a proper appreciation of this point, the parallelism to the medical diagnostic scheme, mentioned in the previous chapter, is again relevant. In combination with the turnings to be applied to each truth, this results in the following presentation:

- disease (*dukkha*): to be understood,
- pathogen (craving): to be eradicated,
- health (cessation of *dukkha*): to be realized,
- cure (eightfold path): to be cultivated.

In a medical context, these are not four distinct matters, but rather four interrelated aspects of a single issue, namely a correct diagnosis of a patient's condition. Such a correct diagnosis involves not only recognizing the disease and identifying the pathogen, but also an assessment of the degree to which the patient can become healthy again and of what type of cure is required for that purpose. These four aspects are interrelated components of a single correct diagnosis.

---

4 For a survey of these different patterns see Anālayo 2016a: 298. In fact another parallel, EĀ 24.5 at T II 619b3, just mentions the three turnings and the resulting twelve modes, without working through them in detail.

The case of the four truths is similar. What the Buddha realized during the night of his awakening is Nirvāṇa. This was his realization of the third truth, the cessation of *dukkha*. With such realization of the cessation of *dukkha*, by dint of having once experienced its complete absence, *dukkha* is finally fully understood. This fulfils the first truth. With the same realization, the arising of *dukkha* has been eradicated for good. This fulfils the second truth. And with the same realization the path leading to the cessation of *dukkha* has been cultivated to its completion. This fulfils the fourth truth. In other words, the four truths describe a single realization experience.

Moreover, the four truths are not themselves the content of the realization – they do not imply that the Buddha was sitting under the tree of awakening and mentally saying to himself: "this is *dukkha*" etc. Instead, he realized Nirvāṇa. In order to express this realization in a way that can be easily understood by others in the ancient Indian setting, the four-truths scheme falls into place. It falls into place not only by way of conveying the actual realization, but also by way of encapsulating in a nutshell the whole progression of practice of which this realization is the culmination point.

Here the initial insight into *dukkha* is central to the bodhisattva's motivation to go forth, discussed in Chapter 1. This reaches its culmination point when he realizes what is entirely free from *dukkha*. Like knowing a house well but only from the inside, when one steps outside and knows its outer features, then one truly knows the house well. Similarly, full and penetrative understanding of *dukkha* requires that the recognition of its various manifestations be complemented by knowing what it means when *dukkha* is completely absent. This is similar to insight into dependent arising, discussed in previous chapters, where a gradually deepening understanding reaches its completion when the cessation of dependent arising is directly experienced. This takes place with the same experience of Nirvāṇa that also completes insight into *dukkha*.

The need to eradicate craving was also an integral dimension of the bodhisattva's going forth, where he decided to leave behind sensuality and to confront the arising of sensual desire in his mind. This reached its culmination point when he finally eradicated craving.

The quest to realize what is beyond old age, disease, and death was at the forefront of his aspiration from the outset, which neither the immaterial attainments nor asceticism had been able to fulfil. Only on the night of his awakening was the goal of his aspiration fully realized.

The path to such realization was a matter of continuous concern throughout his quest. The need for a moral foundation was clear to him from the outset, but the other requirements of this path, which he would eventually present as eightfold to his followers, only gradually became clear to him. With the attainment of awakening, he had reached the certainty of having brought this path to completion.

In this way the realization of Nirvāṇa is what underpins each of the four truths, what each truth converges on and where each truth reaches completion. The same realization also has a bearing on other aspects of early Buddhist doctrine. In fact, as already mentioned, the cessation mode of dependent arising similarly has the realization of Nirvāṇa as its reference point.

The discourses present various insights as having come to fulfilment with the Buddha's awakening. An example is insight into the true nature of feelings, already mentioned in Chapter 10.[5] Another is insight into the five aggregates of clinging, which a discourse in the *Saṃyutta-nikāya* and its *Saṃyukta-āgama* parallel relate to the Buddha's awakening. The *Saṃyukta-āgama* reports the following statement:[6]

> [So long as] I had not understood as it really is the gratification in relation to the five aggregates of clinging as gratification, the disadvantage as disadvantage, and the escape as escape, I was not liberated, was not released, had not been delivered, was continuously dwelling in [mental] distortion, and was unable to declare of myself among the assemblies of devas and humans – devas, Māra, Brahmā, recluses, brahmins – that I had attained supreme and right awakening.

5 See above p. 93 note 8.

6 The translated passage is taken from SĀ 14 at T II 2c23 to 2c27 (translated Anālayo 2012c: 24), parallel to SN 22.26 at SN III 28,19 (translated Bodhi 2000: 874f); see also above p. 109 note 10.

Next comes the assertion that, on having understood as it really is these different aspects in relation to the five aggregates of clinging, the Buddha did claim to have reached awakening. Needless to say, this does not stand in conflict with the association of the four truths to his realization, in the sense of offering a competing account of the Buddha's awakening. Instead, the passage translated above is best understood as showing one of the different facets of the penetrative understanding that has its source in the realization of Nirvāṇa.[7]

With the same converging point in the realization of Nirvāṇa, the four-truths scheme can be applied to different contexts and thus is not confined to *dukkha*. An example is the Buddha's insight into the "world", described in a discourse in the *Aṅguttara-nikāya* and its parallels in the *Madhyama-āgama* and the *Saṃyukta-āgama*. The *Madhyama-āgama* version proceeds in this way:[8]

> The Tathāgata has himself awakened to the world and he teaches this to others.[9] The Tathāgata has understood the world.
>
> The Tathāgata has himself awakened to the arising of the world and he teaches this to others. The Tathāgata has eradicated the arising of the world.
>
> The Tathāgata has himself awakened to the cessation of the world and he teaches this to others. The Tathāgata has realized the cessation of the world.
>
> The Tathāgata has himself awakened to the path [to the cessation] of the world and he teaches this to others. The Tathāgata has cultivated the path [to the cessation] of the world.

This presentation has much in common with the exposition of the four truths in the *Dhammacakkappavattana-sutta* and its parallels, with the difference that the main topic is the "world"

---

7 De Silva 1987: 49 compares what at first sight could appear to be different or even conflicting insights to a "circular vision, as when one is on top of a mountain ... however different the sceneries may be from the different directions, all the scenes constitute one integrated experience" for one who stands on the mountain's top.

8 The translated section is based on MĀ 137 at T I 645b12 to 645b16, parallel to AN 4.23 at AN II 23,21 (translated Bodhi 2012: 410); see also SĀ 894 at T II 224c29.

9 Here and below, AN 4.23 at AN II 23,21 does not mention that the Tathāgata teaches this to others.

instead of *dukkha*. Be it the world or *dukkha*, however, the underlying theme remains the realization of Nirvāṇa.

The central role of the Buddha's realization in relation to essential Buddhist doctrines emerges also from the ten powers of a Tathāgata, introduced in Chapter 6, which highlight various dimensions of his penetrative insight, culminating in the three higher knowledges he attained on the night of his awakening.

Another passage reflecting the centrality of the realization of Nirvāṇa occurs in a discourse in the *Saṃyukta-āgama*, which relates how the Buddha led his own son Rāhula to full liberation. Whereas the *Saṃyukta-āgama* account reports in detail what preceded the actual instruction given by the Buddha, which it then gives in abbreviated form, a parallel in the *Saṃyutta-nikāya* (also found in the *Majjhima-nikāya*) instead focuses on the actual instruction. Thus the two versions have a somewhat different coverage, and for this reason the passage to be discussed from the *Saṃyukta-āgama* version has no counterpart in its Pāli parallel.

According to the *Saṃyukta-āgama* account, Rāhula had approached the Buddha with the request to be given a teaching that would lead him to full awakening. The Buddha realized, however, that Rāhula's wisdom was not yet sufficiently matured. The Buddha told Rāhula that he should first teach others about the five aggregates of clinging. When Rāhula had done so, the Buddha told him that he should also teach the six sense-spheres and causality. When Rāhula had fulfilled this instruction and came back in the hope of finally getting instructions for his attainment of full awakening, the Buddha realized that he was still not sufficiently matured and told him to go into seclusion and reflect on the three doctrinal topics he had earlier taught to others. At this juncture, the *Saṃyukta-āgama* discourse continues in the following manner:[10]

> Then Rāhula, having received the Buddha's instruction and orders, contemplated and pondered the teachings as he had earlier heard them, the teachings he had [then] expounded, reflecting on their

10 SĀ 200 at T II 51b22 to 51b24 (translated Anālayo 2015b: 276); the report of Rāhula's eventual awakening is found in the parallel SN 35.121 at SN IV 107,28 (translated Bodhi 2000: 1196) or MN 147 at MN III 280,7 (translated Ñāṇamoli 1995/2005: 1127); see also Anālayo 2011: 836.

> meaning. He thought: "All these teachings proceed towards Nirvāṇa, flow towards Nirvāṇa, ultimately establish [one] in Nirvāṇa."

When Rāhula returned to the Buddha and reported his insight, the Buddha realized that his son was now finally ready to be led to full awakening and gave him the required teaching, which indeed resulted in Rāhula becoming an arahant.

Although the passage translated above is not found in the Pāli version, due to the different coverage of the two discourses already mentioned, its indication is in line with what emerges from a study of the three turnings to be applied to the four truths or from other passages that relate essential early Buddhist doctrines to the Buddha's awakening. All of these do indeed "proceed towards Nirvāṇa, flow towards Nirvāṇa, ultimately establish [one] in Nirvāṇa".

The same principle also underlies the association of the Buddha's first discourse with the idea of setting in motion the wheel of Dharma. As stated explicitly in a parallel to the *Dhammacakkappavattana-sutta*, found in the Dharmaguptaka *Vinaya*:[11]

> [When] the Tathāgata proclaims these four noble truths and there is nobody among the assemblies who realizes them, then the Tathāgata has not turned the wheel of Dharma for them.

Whereas the Buddha could ensure for himself that the three "turnings" in relation to each truth were fulfilled, his success in accomplishing the "turning" of the wheel of Dharma in the world required that someone else be able to follow suit. The *Dhammacakkappavattana-sutta* and its parallels report that this was indeed the case, as one of his five former companions by the name of Koṇḍañña attained stream-entry during the Buddha's disclosure of the four truths. The *Ekottarika-āgama* version reports this as follows:[12]

> At the time when this teaching was being spoken, Aññāta Koṇḍañña attained the pure eye of Dharma, eliminating all [mental] dust and stain. Then the Blessed One said to Koṇḍañña:

11 T 1428 at T XXII 788b18f (translated Anālayo 2016a: 286).
12 EĀ 24.5 at T II 619b6 to 619b9 (translated Anālayo 2016a: 271f).

> "Have you now reached the Dharma, have you attained the Dharma?"
>
> Koṇḍañña replied: "It is like this, Blessed One, I have attained the Dharma, I have reached the Dharma."

In this way the Buddha's choice of a medical scheme of diagnosis in order to convey his realization had been successful. It had enabled him not only to communicate his realization to those who at the outset were disinclined to place their trust in him, it had also fulfilled the function of leading one of his hearers to realizing the first stage of awakening himself. The four-truths scheme had fulfilled its purpose by enabling Koṇḍañña to find a refuge within.

The relationship between the four truths and the notion of refuge is expressed poetically in a set of verses in the *Udānavarga*. These build on the premise that one goes for refuge to the Buddha, the Dharma, and the Community, based on which one then comes to a realization of the four truths:[13]

> Seeing the four noble truths
> With wisdom:
> Dukkha, the arising of dukkha,
> The going beyond dukkha,
> And the noble eightfold path
> That leads to the stilling of dukkha.
> This indeed is a safe refuge,
> This is the best refuge,
> Having gone for this refuge
> One will be released from all dukkha.

EXERCISE

As a practical exercise, I would like to recommend inclining the mind towards Nirvāṇa and thereby towards the supreme freedom from all defilements and mental afflictions. The realization of such freedom is the ultimate aim and source of all the essential teachings of early Buddhism. Inclining the mind

---

13 The translation is based on Uv 27.33c+d and 27.34f, Bernhard 1965: 349f, parallel to Dhp 190c+d and 191f (translated Norman 1997/2004: 29); see also the Patna Dharmapada 218c+d and 219, Cone 1989: 160.

accordingly can be done by reflecting on and contemplating the following maxim:

> This is peaceful, this is sublime, namely: the calming of all constructions, the letting go of all supports, the extinguishing of craving, dispassion, cessation, Nirvāṇa.[14]

14 MN 64 at MN I 436,1 (translated Anālayo 2015a: 169).

XVIII

HONOURING THE DHARMA

From the first teaching given by the Buddha, which employs the scheme of four truths to communicate his realization, with the present chapter I turn to the Buddha's attitude and relationship towards the Dharma in general, after which in the next chapter I take up his teaching activities in general.

The Buddha's relationship to the Dharma comes to the fore in a discourse in the *Saṃyutta-nikāya* and its parallels. These report that, right after his awakening, the Buddha considered whom he should best honour, in awareness of the fact that (in the ancient Indian sociocultural context) not to pay homage to someone or something superior is inappropriate. The context gives the impression that this reflection should be placed before he engaged in teaching activities. The *Saṃyukta-āgama* version reports the conclusion he reached with his reflections in this way:[1]

> [Yet] there is no deva, Māra, Brahmā, recluse, brahmin, spirit, or person in the world who is able to be superior to me in the possession of morality, superior in concentration, superior in wisdom, superior in liberation, superior in knowledge and vision of liberation, causing me to honour and esteem him, to

1 The translated part is taken from SĀ 1188 at T II 321c27 to 322a3, parallel to SN 6.2 at SN I 139,5 (translated Bodhi 2000: 234); see also AN 4.21 at AN II 20,11 (translated Bodhi 2012: 406f), where the Buddha on a later occasion reports this reflection to the monastics, and for parallels to AN 4.21 Skilling et al. 2016.

> worship and support him, and to dwell in dependence on him. There is only the right Dharma which made me awaken myself and accomplish unsurpassed and right awakening. I should honour and esteem that, worship and support that, and dwell in dependence on that.

In agreement with its *Saṃyutta-nikāya* parallel, the *Saṃyukta-āgama* discourse continues by reporting that Brahmā, who had become aware of the Buddha's reflection, arrived to express his approval. Brahmā confirmed that previous Buddhas had done the same and future Buddhas would also act in this manner.[2] In this way the Dharma is what provides a reference point for those who have reached full awakening on their own – it is the Dharma to which they defer and pay respect.

The decision or perhaps recognition of the centrality of the Dharma and the implications this role has on matters of paying respect and worship provide some background to an episode reported in the *Aṅguttara-nikāya*, with parallels in a *Madhyama-āgama* discourse and another discourse preserved as an individual translation. A brahmin had censured the Buddha for not paying homage to elderly brahmins, according to what would have been the custom in the ancient Indian setting. Here is the *Madhyama-āgama* version's report of the Buddha's reply:[3]

> Brahmin, from the outset I do not see a deva, Māra, Brahmā, recluse, or brahmin, from humans to devas, who could expect that, on coming to approach me, he will make the Tathāgata pay homage and reverence, get up from the seat and invite him to sit down.

Hearing this reply, the brahmin concludes that the Buddha lacks taste, to which the Buddha agrees, explaining that he indeed lacks taste, although not in the way the brahmin thought:[4]

---

2 According to SĀ 1188 at T II 322a4, the Buddha himself had already been aware of the fact that former and future Buddhas act in this manner before Brahmā intervened; the same holds for another parallel to SN 6.2, SĀ² 101 at T II 410a17, and a parallel to AN 4.21, T 212 at T IV 718c4 (which in fact does not report Brahmā's intervention at all).

3 The translation is based on MĀ 157 at T I 679b13 to 679b15, parallel to AN 8.11 at AN IV 173,11 (translated Bodhi 2012: 1125) and T 75 at T I 882b2.

4 The translated passage stems from MĀ 157 at T I 679b19f.

> Whatever taste there is in forms, taste in sounds, taste in odours, [taste in flavours],[5] taste in tangibles, the Tathāgata has abandoned that with wisdom, has cut it off and extinguished it, has uprooted it so that it will not arise again.

By agreeing to the brahmin's conclusion that the Buddha's lack of respect for elderly brahmins showed his lack of taste, but then reinterpreting this allegation as an expression of his awakened status, the Buddha in a way conveyed to his visitor the reason that underpins the behaviour that the brahmin felt to be inappropriate. Simply stated, awakening overrules seniority based on age or caste membership.

The question of respectful behaviour towards those who are torchbearers of the Dharma also comes up in the *Vinaya* as part of recommendations on proper etiquette for monastics. Several specifications prevent a monastic from teaching the Dharma if the audience displays an attitude of lack of respect. In the ancient Indian setting this could take the form of sitting on a seat higher than that of a monastic, for example.[6] This has to be read in conjunction with the humble attitude expected of the same monastics when they go to beg for food. In other words, the issue at stake in such monastic teaching etiquette concerns a situation where they are acting as conduits of the Dharma. Due to the high respect that is to be given to the Dharma, to the extent that the Buddha himself decided to live by paying homage to it, monastics must ensure that their teaching of the Dharma is not received with disrespect.

In this way, the above exchange with the brahmin can be seen to exemplify a basic pattern evident in the Buddha's conduct in general, which conforms to the same principle as the conduct expected of monastics when teaching the Dharma, namely the priority given to honouring the Dharma. In fact at times the Buddha is shown to act in ways that at first sight could even

5 The absence of a reference to flavours can safely be taken to be a transmission error, wherefore I have supplemented it. Flavours are mentioned in AN 8.11 at AN IV 173,21, but are also missing in T 75 at T I 882b7.

6 Vin IV 204,22 (translated Horner 1942/1983: 149); for a survey of the corresponding stipulation in other *Vinaya*s see Pachow 1955: 205.

give the mistaken impression of arrogance, yet closer inspection shows that these are also best read as reflecting the honour he accorded to the Dharma.

One such episode occurs in the *Ariyapariyesanā-sutta* and its *Madhyama-āgama* parallel, when the Buddha approaches his five former companions. The parallel versions agree that, even though the Buddha had come all the way to teach them and was clearly aware of their initial diffidence, he right away asked them not to address him any longer as "friend" and by his personal name.[7] What lies behind this episode is that he was now an embodiment of the Dharma, a fully awakened one, a Tathāgata. Because of this, it was no longer appropriate for him to be addressed as "friend", or else for him to pay homage to elder brahmins, to return to the earlier example.

A succinct statement that relates the status of being a Tathāgata to the four noble truths (which the Buddha was about to teach to his five former followers) can be found in the *Saṃyutta-nikāya* and a parallel in the *Saṃyukta-āgama*. The latter proceeds as follows:[8]

> One who fully and rightly awakens to the four noble truths is called a Tathāgata, an arahant, a fully awakened one. What are the four? That is, they are the noble truth of dukkha, the noble truth of the arising of dukkha, the noble truth of the cessation of dukkha, and the noble truth of the path to the cessation of dukkha.

A complementary perspective on the Tathāgata can be gathered from a discourse in the *Aṅguttara-nikāya* and its *Madhyama-āgama* parallel, which place particular emphasis on his speaking what is true and real, thereby in a way fleshing out the sense that underlies his teaching of the four "truths" as something that accords with reality.[9] The *Madhyama-āgama* discourse states:[10]

---

7 MN 26 at MN I 171,33 (translated Ñāṇamoli 1995/2005: 264) and MĀ 204 at T I 777c12.

8 The translation is taken from SĀ 402 at T II 107c26 to 107c29, parallel to SN 56.23 at SN V 433,18 (translated Bodhi 2000: 1854).

9 See also above p. 150.

10 The translated extract stems from MĀ 137 at T I 645b18 to 645b21, parallel to AN 4.23 at AN II 24,2 (translated Bodhi 2012: 410).

> From the night in the past when the Tathāgata awakened to the supreme and unsurpassable awakening until the present day and night, and [until the time when] he will attain complete extinction in the element of Nirvāṇa without residue, throughout this period whatever words the Tathāgata speaks and the replies he gives, all of that is genuinely true and not false.

Thus it is the Tathāgata's role as one who reveals what is true, based on his own realization, that makes him deserve homage and respect. The homage and respect are due to him because of his role as the one who discovered and teaches the Dharma, as he did in the case of his five former companions by way of the four noble truths.

In fact alongside passages like the one from the *Ariyapariyesanā-sutta* and its parallel, other passages show the Buddha adopting an attitude of remarkable humility. One instance can be found in the report of a *Vinaya* observance in which monastics, at the end of the rainy-season retreat, invite each other to point out their respective shortcomings. Here is the *Ekottarika-āgama* report of an occasion where the Buddha did the same:[11]

> At that time the Blessed One, who had silently surveyed the monastics, said to the monastics in turn: "I now wish to undergo [the monastic observance of] invitation: 'Am I without fault in regard to the members of the community? Again, have I not offended by body, speech, or mind?'"
>
> When the Tathāgata had said these words, the monastics were silent and did not reply. Then again and a third time he said to the monastics:[12] "I now wish to undergo [the monastic observance of] invitation: 'Am I without fault in regard to the members of the community?'"

11 The translation is based on EĀ 32.5 at T II 677a6 to 677a11, parallel to SN 8.7 at SN I 190,30 (translated Bodhi 2000: 286), MĀ 121 at T I 610a13, T 61 at T I 858b22, T 63 at T I 861b23, SĀ 1212 at T II 330a14, SĀ² 228 at T II 457b8, and Uighur fragments, Zieme 1988: 453; for a comparative study of another aspect of this episode see Kuan 2013 and for a juxtaposition of the *Madhyama-āgama* and *Saṃyukta-āgama* versions Chung and Fukita 2011: 323–7. Some of the parallels no longer report that the Buddha openly invited his disciples to point out his shortcomings, which I take to reflect the unease felt by later generations at such display of humility by the Exalted One.

12 SN 8.7 at SN I 190,30 does not report that the Buddha repeated his invitation twice.

In view of the high regard accorded in the ancient Indian setting to a teacher, and the fact that the Buddha was not himself subject to the rules he had promulgated, for him to invite his own disciples to point out any shortcoming in accordance with the standard *Vinaya* procedure is certainly remarkable. As clarified by Sāriputta in reply, after the Buddha's third invitation, of course nobody had anything to criticize in regard to the Buddha. Sāriputta then invited the Buddha in turn to point out any shortcomings of his disciples.

The passage shows the Buddha acting with extraordinary humility on this occasion, thereby setting an example to his disciples. This further supports the impression that his expecting to be respected on other occasions is best understood as a reflection of the position of honour to be accorded to the Dharma. From the viewpoint of the role of being the one who had awakened to the Dharma on his own and was communicating it to others, he had to demand respect, but this does not mean that on other occasions he could not act with exemplary humility. In fact in a way genuine inner authority, through having realized the Dharma, goes hand in hand with true humility.

The way the Buddha accorded centrality to the Dharma can also be seen in another passage that concerns dependent arising. A discourse in the *Saṃyutta-nikāya* and its parallels, preserved in Chinese and Sanskrit, agree that the Buddha explained his role to be merely one of disclosing something that exists in its own right. The *Saṃyukta-āgama* version proceeds as follows:[13]

> Whether a Buddha emerges in the world or whether he has not emerged in the world, this Dharma remains invariable. The Dharma which remains, the element of the Dharma, is what the Tathāgata realizes himself by accomplishing right awakening.[14] He teaches it to people, elucidating and clarifying it, namely: conditioned by ignorance are formations ...

---

13 The translated part is based on SĀ 296 at T II 84b16 to 84b19, parallel to SN 12.20 at SN II 25,18 (translated Bodhi 2000: 551), a Sanskrit fragment version, Tripāṭhī 1962: 148 (§14.3), and D 4094 *ju* 137a2 or Q 5595 *tu* 157b1.

14 SN 12.20 at SN II 25,19 specifies that this refers in particular to the Dharma of specific conditionality, *idapaccayatā*.

The texts continue with an abbreviated reference to the remaining links of dependent arising up to old age and death. In this way, even with a doctrinal teaching as central as dependent arising, it is the Dharma which counts, at the centre of attention stands the Dharma, and the role of the Buddha is to realize and explain it to others.

Another passage depicts the Buddha as quite free from identifying with his role as a leader of the monastic community he had founded. The episode in question occurs in the *Mahāparinibbāna-sutta* and its parallels. The Buddha had been seriously sick and the worried Ānanda found some solace in the thought that the Buddha would not pass away without giving some final instructions to the community of his disciples. When the Buddha had recovered and Ānanda informed him of this reflection, according to the *Dīrgha-āgama* version the Buddha replied in this way:[15]

> What does the community of monastics expect from me? If someone were to say of himself: "I manage the community of monastics, I control the community of monastics", such a person should give a [final] instruction to the community.
>
> The Tathāgata does not say: "I manage the community of monastics, I control the community of monastics." Why should he give a [final] instruction to the community?
>
> Ānanda, the Dharma I have taught is already complete, within and without. I never kept to myself what I have seen and realized.

After this clarification, the Buddha described how one can become a refuge to oneself by undertaking the practice of the four *satipaṭṭhāna*s, namely mindful contemplation of the body, feelings, the mind, and dharmas.[16] It is through such contemplation that one can become a refuge for oneself:[17]

---

15 The translated passage is taken from DĀ 2 at T I 15a26 to 15b2 (translated Anālayo 2017c: 206), parallel to DN 16 at DN II 100,1 (translated Walshe 1987: 245) or else SN 47.9 at SN V 153,16 (translated Bodhi 2000: 1637), a Sanskrit fragment version, Waldschmidt 1951: 196 (§14.10f), and an individually translated discourse, T 6 at T I 180a20.

16 For an example of the full formula describing such practice see below p. 213.

17 The translation is based on DĀ 2 at T I 15b12 to 15b15.

> "Ānanda, this is reckoned being a light to yourself, a light in the Dharma, without another light, being a refuge to yourself,[18] a refuge in the Dharma, without another refuge."
>
> The Buddha said to Ānanda: "After my final Nirvāṇa, those who are able to cultivate this teaching are truly my disciples and foremost in the training."

In this way, the clarification that the Buddha did not identify with his guiding role in relation to the monastic community comes with a clear pointer regarding how one can become self-reliant, namely by cultivating the four *satipaṭṭhānas*. In other words, the Buddha directed attention away from himself and instead towards the Dharma and its practical implementation through the cultivation of mindfulness. It is the Dharma that lies behind and informs his own role. When he steps aside, the Dharma remains. Therefore establishing oneself in mindfulness is the way to take true refuge and become a light, or in some versions an island, to oneself.

EXERCISE

By way of putting into practice the eminent respect the Buddha himself accorded to the Dharma, I would like to recommend the practice of recollection of the Dharma. This could be undertaken regularly after formal meditation sessions or else in any other situation, whenever appropriate. It involves directing attention to the qualities of the Buddha's instructions as something that is directly visible, in the sense that they show results right here and now; they invite us to try them out, so to speak; and on engaging in their practice we can verify them for ourselves, we can personally experience them. This much can be confirmed by those who have seriously practised meditation in general and *satipaṭṭhāna* in particular in accordance with the canonical instructions. Over time genuine practice shows results and a gradual transformation towards the better manifests.

The recognition of the effect of such gradual transformation in turn inspires confidence in the Dharma and the wish to

---

18 Adopting a variant without a reference to "should".

understand it more deeply. Alongside sustained meditation practice, this also requires some degree of study in order to develop an increasing familiarity with the teachings in the form in which they are still available nowadays. Any improvement in our understanding through study can in turn serve to support our actual practice, as long as the study is undertaken in such a way that it relates to meditation. In this way study and practice of the Dharma can make their combined contribution to our personal transformation.

This in turn makes it indeed meaningful to accord respect to the Dharma. Here it can be helpful to consider the contrast between the Dharma and what usually inspires respect, be this physical beauty or material possessions, success in achieving power or acquiring wealth, etc. Instead, we now accord respect to what leads onwards on the path to freedom. According respect to the Dharma as the source of our own gradual change for the better can become a powerful support for generating the dedication and effort needed to sustain our practice against whatever challenges and obstructions might manifest until the time when we have realized the Dharma and become a conduit of Dharma ourselves.

XIX

TEACHING

Having studied the first teaching of the Buddha, with which he set in motion the wheel of Dharma, and his according the place of honour to the Dharma, I now proceed to a survey of his mode of teaching in general. A basic pattern here is that the Buddha taught based on his own practical experience and that he himself practised what he taught others. This integrity as a teacher finds expression in the following dictum in the *Dīrgha-āgama* parallel to the *Pāsādika-sutta*:[1]

> What the Tathāgata teaches is in accordance with his actions, and his actions are in accordance with what he teaches; for this reason he is called a Tathāgata.

The Buddha's teaching activities also relate to *satipaṭṭhāna*, which according to the passage taken up in the previous chapter is the chief resort for those who wish to become a refuge to themselves. Instead of the four *satipaṭṭhāna*s of contemplating the body, feelings, mind, and dharmas, however, in the case of the Buddha as a teacher this involves a set of three *satipaṭṭhāna*s. These three are described in the *Saḷāyatanavibhaṅga-sutta* and its parallels.[2]

---

1 The translated part is based on DĀ 17 at T I 75c9f, parallel to DN 29 at DN III 135,16 (Walshe 1987: 436 seems to have missed out on translating this part of the Pāli text, a rendering of which can be found in Rhys Davids and Rhys Davids 1921: 127).

2 MN 137 at MN III 221,3 (translated Ñāṇamoli 1995/2005: 1071), MĀ 163 at T I 693c23, and D 4094 *nyu* 59a1 or Q 5595 *thu* 101a8; for a comparative study see Anālayo 2011: 785–7.

Elsewhere I have already studied and translated the relevant part in the *Madhyama-āgama* parallel to the *Saḷāyatanavibhaṅga-sutta*,[3] wherefore in what follows I instead translate a discourse quotation of the same passage in the *Abhidharmakośabhāṣya*, preserved in Chinese. The passage describes what could happen when the Buddha gives teachings as follows:[4]

> The disciples in the assembly are entirely respectful and able to receive it properly. The Tathāgata does not give rise to elation because of it; he is equanimous and dwells at ease with right mindfulness and right comprehension. This is reckoned to be the first satipaṭṭhāna of the Tathāgata.
>
> The disciples in the assembly are solely disrespectful and do not receive it properly. The Tathāgata does not give rise to dejection because of it; he is equanimous and dwells at ease with right mindfulness and right comprehension. This is reckoned to be the second satipaṭṭhāna of the Tathāgata.
>
> Some disciples in the assembly are respectful and able to receive it properly, some are disrespectful and do not receive it properly. The Tathāgata does not give rise to elation or dejection because of it; he is equanimous and dwells at ease with right mindfulness and right comprehension. This is reckoned to be the third satipaṭṭhāna of the Tathāgata.

When engaging in the compassionate activity of teaching, the Buddha remains equanimous and will not be affected by how his teachings are received by his disciples. This combination of compassion with equanimity is a salient feature of his attitude when teaching in general.

Examples of the Buddha's equanimity can be seen when he is confronted with the anger of others. One such episode occurs in the *Mahāsaccaka-sutta* and its Sanskrit fragment parallel, where a debater notes that the Buddha, on being attacked in various ways, did not display any anger, in fact the colour of his skin

---

3 Anālayo 2013b: 240–3.

4 The translation is based on T 1558 at T XXIX 140c26 to 141a4. The Sanskrit version, Pradhan 1967: 414,11, abbreviates; another Chinese version can be found in T 1559 at T XXIX 292a6 and a Tibetan version at D 4090 *khu* 57a2 or Q 5591 *nyu* 65a8.

brightened and the colour of his face became clear.[5] I take it that this visible effect results from the Buddha reacting with *brahmavihāra* when faced with anger.

Another instance involves a brahmin and his wife, reported in the *Saṃyutta-nikāya* and the two *Saṃyukta-āgamas*. The wife had acquired firm confidence in the Buddha and on the occasion of a small mishap expressed her faith. The *Saṃyukta-āgama* version reports this as follows:[6]

> She held her palms together in the direction where the Tathāgata was dwelling and said three times: "Homage to the Buddha, the arahant, the fully awakened one, whose body has the colour of pure gold and a halo of one fathom, whose bodily proportions are replete like a Banyan tree, who well teaches the sublime Dharma, who is the most excellent one of sages and the foremost of seers; my great teacher."

In the *Saṃyutta-nikāya* version her expression of homage only corresponds to the first part of the above passage, thus she does not mention any of the qualities related to the Buddha's body or his teaching or else his excellence among sages and seers. The corresponding part in the other *Saṃyukta-āgama*, however, is about as detailed as the above passage.

Alongside such variations, this description is of interest in relation to the overall topic of recollection of the Buddha, to which I return in the concluding chapter.[7] It reflects a mode of recollecting the Buddha by way of a standardized formula of terms or epithets. The difference between the Pāli version and the two *Saṃyukta-āgama* versions gives the impression of a gradual growth of such formulas by incorporating additional

---

5 MN 36 at MN I 250,22 (translated Ñāṇamoli 1995/2005: 343) and fragment 339v2, Liu 2010: 243.

6 The translated part is based on SĀ 1158 at T II 308b26 to 308c1, parallel to SN 7.1 at SN I 160,10 (translated Bodhi 2000: 254) and SĀ² 81 at T II 401c25.

7 A similar way of expressing homage to the Buddha is on record in MN 100 at MN II 209,23 (translated Ñāṇamoli 1995/2005: 819) and its Sanskrit parallel, fragment 345r, Zhang 2004: 9 (see also SHT IV 33 fragment 29V and SHT IV 165 fragment 24R, Sander and Waldschmidt 1980: 172 and 199). The Sanskrit version is also more detailed than the Pāli passage, comparable to what is found in SĀ 1158 and SĀ² 81.

epithets or qualities. Even in the shorter Pāli version, however, the present passage clearly shows that the employment of such formulas, which is the standard mode of recollection of the Buddha in a traditional setting even today, is already attested in the early discourses.

The narrative in the above discourse continues by reporting that the husband was infuriated by the praise given in this way to the Buddha. After reprimanding his wife, he approached the Buddha with the apparent intent to challenge him. On meeting the Buddha, the brahmin expressed his challenge by asking in verse whom one should slay in order to sleep in peace and be without sorrow. The first part of the Buddha's reply to the brahmin takes the following form in the *Saṃyukta-āgama* version:[8]

> One who slays anger
> Gets to sleep in peace.
> The mind of one who slays anger
> Gets to be without sorrow.

This reply would have conveyed the gist of what it means to slay anger not only in words but also in deed, since by his calm reply the Buddha must have exemplified what it means to have slain anger. The brahmin was in fact deeply impressed by this reply, so much so that he eventually decided to go forth and in turn became an arahant.

The story does not end here, at least in the *Saṃyutta-nikāya*, as the next discourse in this collection reports that hearing about this brahmin's going forth infuriates another brahmin of the same clan, who also approaches the Buddha. Instead of posing a challenging question, however, he decides to abuse the Buddha. In reply, the Buddha calmly asks what the brahmin would do with what he has offered to guests but which has not been accepted by them. When the brahmin replies that such an offering remains with him, the Buddha clarifies that the same holds for the abuse the brahmin has just offered. Since the Buddha does not accept it, the abuse remains with

---

8 The translated verse occurs in SĀ 1158 at T II 308c16f, parallel to SN 7.1 at SN I 161,5 and SĀ^2 81 at T II 402a15.

the brahmin. The "other" *Saṃyukta-āgama* (T 100) reports this reply as follows:[9]

> As to the abuse and slander, the various modes of annoying that you have done in the face of the Tathāgata, the arahant, the fully awakened one, even though you gave them to me, I did not accept them.

Taken together, these two passages offer a practical option for following in the Buddha's footsteps by way of remaining with equanimity rather than getting irritated. This could even be considered an alternative approach to recollecting the Buddha, in addition to the formulaic homage expressed by the brahmin woman in the passage translated earlier. What one really needs to slay is not the other, but the enemy within. This enemy within is none other than anger itself. When confronted with the anger of others, one always has the option of not accepting the unwanted "gift" that has just been made. Often enough it seems so natural to accept such uninvited gifts and requite with more offerings of the same type. But this need not happen.

In other words, instead of reacting from the place of a hurt sense of ego and thereby a) accepting the "gift" and b) retaliating in kind, there is always in principle the possibility of remaining with equanimity, aided by recollecting the example set by the Buddha. All it takes is a moment of stepping back and reflecting on whether one really wants to be part of an exchange of gifts of anger that is about to take place.

The Buddha's lack of a sense of ego, which complements my discussion in the last chapter on his requesting others to respect him as a teacher of the Dharma, also comes to the forefront in descriptions of his approaching a monastic meeting place and noticing that the disciples inside are discussing the

---

9 The translation is based on SĀ^{2} 75 at T II 400b18 to 400b20, parallel to SN 7.2 at SN I 162,16 (translated Bodhi 2000: 256) and SĀ 1152 at T II 307a17. SĀ 1152 and SĀ^{2} 75 do not explicitly relate this brahmin's abusing the Buddha to his being irritated by the other brahmin's going forth. They also differ from SN 7.2 in not reporting that he eventually went forth and became an arahant (which in the case of SN 7.2 could in fact be the result of accidental copying of the conclusion of SN 7.1 during oral or written transmission).

Dharma. One such example can be found in the *Madhyama-āgama* parallel to the *Ariyapariyesanā-sutta*, which proceeds in this way:[10]

> Then the Blessed One, followed by the venerable Ānanda, went to the house of the brahmin Ramma[ka]. At that time, a group of many monastics were seated together in the house of the brahmin Ramma[ka] and discussing the Dharma. The Buddha stood outside the door, waiting for the monastics to finish their discussion of the Dharma. The group of many monastics, having completed their investigation and discussion of the Dharma, remained silent. On knowing this, the Blessed One coughed and knocked on the door. Hearing him, the monastics came and opened the door.

According to both versions, the monastics had actually assembled in the expectation of receiving a talk from the Buddha. Nevertheless, when he arrives to give them a teaching, the Buddha has the remarkable courtesy of waiting outside until they have finished their discussion. The image of the Buddha standing outside and waiting is a vivid reflection of his lack of ego as a teacher.

Other passages show the Buddha going out of his way in order to give timely instructions. Typical occurrences involve the sick, several instances of which I have surveyed in my study of *Mindfully Facing Disease and Death*.[11] Others concern his compassionate dispensing of the medicine of instructions to those who were in some way stuck in their meditation practice or understanding. Realizing that Mahāmoggallāna had problems with sleepiness during meditation, for example, the Buddha paid him a visit and delivered detailed instructions on how to deal with this problem.[12]

When Soṇa felt frustrated by his lack of progress in meditation and wanted to disrobe, the Buddha came to comfort

---

10 The translated passage is taken from MĀ 204 at T I 775c20 to 775c25, parallel to MN 26 at MN I 161,16 (translated Ñāṇamoli 1995/2005: 254); see also Anālayo 2011: 170.

11 Anālayo 2016b.

12 AN 7.58a at AN IV 85,17 (translated Bodhi 2012: 1059, referred to as discourse 61) and the parallels MĀ 83 at T I 559c5 and T 47 at T I 837a14.

and encourage him,[13] or else, according to some versions, the Buddha told another monastic to bring Soṇa to his presence.[14] In whatever way Soṇa came to be in the Buddha's presence, the ensuing encounter led to the delivery of the famous simile of the lute, whose strings should not be too tight or too loose. Similarly, Soṇa had to find a middle position of balance between excessive striving and giving up the practice altogether.

When Anuruddha reflected on seven qualities of the Dharma, the Buddha came to visit him in order to approve of the reflection and then offer an eighth quality to complement what Anuruddha had been reflecting on. This intervention appears to have been precisely what was required, as according to all versions of this discourse the practice undertaken by Anuruddha, after receiving this instruction, led him to full awakening.[15]

Another passage shows the Buddha giving a long teaching in the walking posture. According to the introductory narration, the Buddha had been in walking meditation when two of his monastic disciples approached him. He kept walking and delivered an exposition now found as one of the long discourses in the *Dīgha-nikāya* and its parallels.[16]

These examples point to the Buddha's readiness to teach in any situation. The same can also be seen in his impromptu use of suitable circumstances to deliver an instruction. One example involves a teaching to his son Rāhula. Having arrived and received water to wash his feet, the Buddha employed the

---

13 AN 6.55 at AN III 374,19 (translated Bodhi 2012: 933), with a discourse parallel in EĀ 23.3 at T II 612a29 and *Vinaya* versions in Vin I 182,11, T 1421 at T XXII 146a29, T 1425 at T XXII 481c18, and T 1428 at T XXII 844b13.

14 Waldschmidt 1968: 775, MĀ 123 at T I 612a8, SĀ 254 at T II 62b29, and Gnoli 1978: 142,16.

15 AN 8.30 at AN IV 235,17 (translated Bodhi 2012: 1165) and its parallels MĀ 74 at T I 542a16 and T 46 at T I 836c18. Another parallel, EĀ 42.6 at T II 754c13, concludes with Anuruddha's delight in receiving the Buddha's instruction and therefore does not report what, according to the other versions, happened after Anuruddha had undertaken a period of practice.

16 DN 27 at DN III 80,20 (translated Walshe 1987: 407) and its parallels DĀ 5 at T I 36c8, T 10 at T I 216c19, MĀ 154 at T I 673b24, and D 4094 *ju* 190a3 or Q 5595 *tu* 217a4 agree in reporting that, after paying homage, the two monastics joined the Buddha in walking up and down. Thus the whole discourse appears to have been delivered while the three were walking up and down.

very water vessel he had just used to illustrate his teaching to his son on the need to speak truthfully.[17]

Another teaching occasion involves fire. While on a journey with a group of monastics, the Buddha saw a great fire raging in the forest. He seized on the occasion by delivering a penetrative discourse on the dire consequences of breaches of morality, illustrated with comparisons with fire. The discourse reports that sixty monastics decided to disrobe as a result of this instruction, but another sixty monastics in the audience reached the final goal.[18]

These examples hardly suffice to give an adequate impression of the remarkable range of similes that the early discourses show the Buddha employing in his teaching activities; in fact to do so would require at least another chapter, if not more.[19] Nevertheless, the few cases mentioned exemplify his impromptu use of external circumstances as a support for expressing the Dharma. It seems that the Buddha immediately related virtually any event or circumstance to the Dharma, in one way or another.

EXERCISE

The cultivation of equanimity could serve as a convenient way of putting into practice a central theme of the Buddha's way of teaching, thereby at the same time providing a complement to the cultivation of compassion in Chapter 14. Here the formal cultivation of equanimity functions as the consummation of the four *brahmavihāras*.[20] For everyday practice, inspiration can be taken from the Buddha's own equanimity in the form of three *satipaṭṭhānas*, which in turn of course points to mindfulness.

17 MN 61 at MN I 414,11 (translated Ñāṇamoli 1995/2005: 523) and its parallels MĀ 14 at T I 436a20, T 211 at T IV 600a3, T 212 at T IV 668a10 (see also Balk 1984: 378,11), T 1442 at T XXIII 760c5, and D 3 *cha* 215b7 or Q 1032 *je* 200a4; for a comparative study see Anālayo 2011: 342f.

18 AN 7.68 at AN IV 135,5 (translated Bodhi 2012: 1094, referred to as discourse 72), which additionally reports that sixty monastics vomited hot blood, and its parallels MĀ 5 at T I 427a3 (translated Bingenheimer et al. 2013: 33) and EĀ 33.10 at T II 689c1.

19 A survey of Pāli similes can be found in Rhys Davids 1907 and 1908.

20 For practical instructions on the cultivation of the *brahmavihāras* see Anālayo 2015a: 151–62.

When we are established in mindfulness of the present moment, the arising of sensual lust or anger will more easily be recognized. At such time, recollecting the Buddha's attitude free from sensual lust or anger can serve as a source of inspiration for progressing ourselves in the same direction of inner freedom. In this way, in particular when faced with those who freely donate their defilements to others, we always have the option of not accepting such gifts by just remaining established in mindfulness and equanimity.

Another practical dimension emerges from the Buddha's impromptu use of whatever happens as a support for expressing the Dharma. The example set by him in this way could be taken as an inspiration to consider anything that happens or is at hand as a lesson with which to instruct ourselves in the Dharma. Whatever the situation in which we find ourselves may be, it does come with a potential seedling of insight. All it takes to discover this seedling and nourish its growth is mindfulness and equanimity.

XX

SEEING THROUGH VIEWS

The Buddha's ways of teaching, discussed in the previous chapter, lead me on to the topic of his attitude towards views and opinions held and debated in the ancient Indian setting. This attitude already becomes evident to some degree in his first teaching, where he apparently relied on an ancient Indian scheme of medical diagnosis to communicate his discovery to his first five disciples, as discussed above in Chapter 16. The implication appears to be that he needed to present matters in a way substantially different from current theories and philosophical standpoints in order to convey the novelty of his discovery.

The same also comes to the fore in his attitude towards a set of propositions that seem to have been of much interest among other wanderers and recluses. Judging from the discourses, the standard expectation was that one adopted any of the different standpoints among these propositions and thereby clarified where one stood and what view one followed. To the disappointment and even bewilderment of his contemporaries, the Buddha consistently refused to adopt any of these positions.

According to the *Cūḷamāluṅkya-sutta* and its *Madhyama-āgama* parallel, such disappointment even affected one of the Buddha's monastic disciples by the name of Māluṅkyaputta. The *Madhyama-āgama* version reports his reflection in this way:[1]

1 The translation is based on MĀ 221 at T I 804a25 to 804a29, parallel to MN 63 at MN I 426,9 (translated Ñāṇamoli 1995/2005: 533) and T 94 at T I 917b18; see also T 1509 at T XXV 170a8 and for a comparative study Anālayo 2011: 353f.

> There are these so-called views, which the Blessed One set aside and put away, without making a complete declaration about them, namely: Is the world eternal? Is the world not eternal? Is the world finite? Is the world infinite? Is the soul the same as the body? Is the soul different from the body? Does a Tathāgata come to an end? Does a Tathāgata not come to an end? Does a Tathāgata come to an end and not come to an end? Does a Tathāgata neither come to an end nor not come to an end?
>
> I do not like this, I cannot bear this, I do not approve of this.

Māluṅkyaputta got himself so worked up in his obsession with these proposals that he decided to confront the Buddha and either get a definite reply or else disrobe:[2]

> If the Blessed One definitely declares to me that this is true and the rest is all falsely stated, I will train in the holy life under him. If the Blessed One does not definitely declare to me that this is true and the rest is all falsely stated, having closely questioned him, I will abandon him and leave.

In the passage translated above, the views listed by Māluṅkyaputta revolve around the themes of the spatial and temporal dimensions of the world, the relationship between the soul and the body, and what happens to a Tathāgata at death. In order to appreciate the views listed, two aspects of this presentation require further discussion. One of these is the significance of the term Tathāgata, the other is why views concerning the Tathāgata are listed in four alternative modes rather than two, involving the so-called tetralemma.

In the context of the above views, the term Tathāgata refers to anyone who has reached full awakening. The more common use of the term in the early discourses, however, is when the Buddha is on record as employing the term Tathāgata to denote himself. This is noteworthy, as he is only rarely shown to refer to himself with the term Buddha.[3]

---

2 The translated part is taken from MĀ 221 at T I 804b5 to 804b9.

3 An example is AN 4.36 at AN II 39,3 (translated Bodhi 2012: 426) and parallels in a Gāndhārī fragment, Allon 2001: 121, SĀ 101 at T II 28b16, and SĀ[2] 267 at T II 467b23 (another parallel, EĀ 38.3, does not report such a reference).

The term Tathāgata itself can in principle be understood in two main ways: either as a combination of *tathā* and *āgata*, meaning "thus come", or of *tathā* and *gata*, meaning "thus gone". In line with another epithet of the Buddha as *sugata*, which combines *su* and *gata*, meaning "well gone", it seems probable that originally the more prominent nuance of Tathāgata would have been "thus gone".[4] The meaning "thus come" would presumably have become more prominent with the evolution of the idea that the Buddha had prepared himself over countless aeons for his task. In short, having "thus gone" beyond defilements and even a trace of identification with the five aggregates is a convenient way of summing up how the Buddha's nature can be understood and recollected.

Regarding the views listed, whereas the first topics are covered by stating two alternatives, the last involves four. This is an instance of the four propositions recognized in ancient Indian logic, the tetralemma. Instead of a black-and-white dichotomy, the tetralemma recognizes that at times something can be both black and white (such as when it is grey), or else neither black nor white (as in the case of being transparent).

The tetralemma is of considerable help not only in appreciating the ancient Indian setting and early Buddhist thought itself, but also by way of providing a practical guideline for approaching situations of conflict. Therefore in what follows I briefly explore the significance of the tetralemma before returning to Māluṅkyaputta.

An example of the use of the tetralemma can be found in a discourse in the *Aṅguttara-nikāya* and its parallel in Tibetan translation, which distinguish between four kinds of deeds.[5] Two of these are deeds that are either black or else white. These two types stand for actions that are entirely unwholesome or entirely wholesome. Another type is "black and white", which are deeds that are a mixture of wholesomeness and unwholesomeness.

4 Norman 1990/1993: 163 reasons, regarding the term Tathāgata, that one could "assume that *-gata* is used in the same way as in *sugata* and *duggata*"; see also Anālayo 2017d.

5 AN 4.232 at AN II 230,25 (translated Bodhi 2012: 601, referred to as discourse 233) and its parallel D 4094 *ju* 168a3 or Q 5595 *tu* 193b8 (translated Skilling 1979: 88f).

The fourth kind then is "neither black nor white", which refers to the abandoning of deeds, be these black or white or a mixture of both.

This example, chosen somewhat at random, serves to show in a practical manner that the tetralemma can offer a meaningful perspective, even though at first sight it might appear strange or even perplexing, given its divergence from the more familiar pattern of Western logic. Put into practice, the tetralemma can help to encourage an attitude where differences of views and opinions are not immediately seen as inevitably conflict-prone, in the sense that for someone to disagree with my view does not necessarily mean that I have to demolish the position of the other in order to ensure that I am right. Instead, it could be that the other and my own position are both true, in a way, or else we might also both be wrong. Keeping in mind these alternatives makes it easier to "agree to disagree", in the sense of being at ease with others who hold opinions quite different from one's own. Such an ability is as relevant to the ancient Indian setting as it is to the modern day.

Needless to say, this does not mean that one no longer has a clear opinion on certain matters. The point is only that one no longer feels such a strong urge to fight for one's opinion being right by way of tearing to pieces whatever disagrees with it. The resultant lack of contentiousness then directly feeds into the mental balance needed for successful progress to awakening.

Based on this appreciation of the term Tathāgata and the significance of the tetralemma, I now return to the episode concerning Māluṅkyaputta. In this episode, the Buddha not only refused to adopt the positions formulated in accordance with the dual logic, regarding the world and the soul, but he even did not take up any of the four proposals on the nature of an awakened one. Since these four proposals exhaust the positions that could be taken on this or any other topic according to ancient Indian logic, it is perhaps understandable why a refusal of all four options would have seemed to the Buddha's contemporaries to be in need of an explanation.

In order to appreciate the Buddha's attitude in this respect, the first two standpoints in the entire listing could be taken up, namely whether the world is eternal or not eternal. Given the recurrent emphasis in the early discourses on the impermanent nature of all conditioned phenomena, one would not expect the Buddha to have any qualms in stating that the world is not eternal. The reason for his refusal to take up both of the two positions must therefore be related to assumptions implicit in the use of the term "world". In the context of these two alternative proposals, the world was apparently conceived of as something self-existent, in its own right. This overlooks the subjective impact in the construction of a world as a dependently arisen experience. From an early Buddhist viewpoint, the term "world" is best used to refer to the conditioned interaction of the senses and their objects.[6] By affirming either of the two proposals, the Buddha would have implicitly acknowledged the appropriateness of a usage of the term "world" that conflicted with his own understanding of the constructed nature of the world of subjective experience.

Similarly, any statement about the relationship between soul and body implicitly affirms something that according to the early Buddhist analysis of reality does not exist in the first place.

The same holds for the four alternatives on an awakened one, where any underlying premise regarding the nature of a Tathāgata would have made it impossible for the Buddha to take up any of the four positions without incurring a conflict with his understanding of not-self. This becomes evident in another discourse where a monastic flatly states that a fully awakened one will be annihilated at death. On being interrogated by Sāriputta, the monastic had to admit that in truth and fact a Tathāgata is not identifiable with any of the five aggregates even while alive. This leaves hardly any room for being able to make a pronouncement about a Tathāgata after death.[7]

This makes it clear why Māluṅkyaputta's quest to get the Buddha to affirm one of these positions was from the outset bound to be unsuccessful. In reply to Māluṅkyaputta, the Buddha is reported to have delivered the famous simile of

6 SN 35.68 at SN IV 39,28 (translated Bodhi 2000: 1153) and its parallel SĀ 230 at T II 56a27.

7 SN 22.85 at SN III 112,5 (translated Bodhi 2000: 933) and its parallel SĀ 104 at T II 31b1 (translated Anālayo 2014b: 14).

the poisoned arrow. The simile describes someone struck by a poisonous arrow who refuses to let the arrow be removed until he has gathered a whole range of trivial information about the nature of the arrow, the archer, the bow, etc. The person will die of the poison that is spreading in his body before having received an answer to all of these questions.

The *Madhyama-āgama* parallel to the *Cūḷamāluṅkya-sutta* presents the Buddha's concluding statement in the following manner:[8]

> Because of what reason have I not definitely declared these [propositions]? These are not associated with benefit, not associated with Dharma, not associated with the foundation of the holy life, they do not lead to knowledge, do not lead to awakening, do not lead to Nirvāṇa. For this reason I have not definitely declared these [propositions].
>
> What is the teaching I have definitely declared? I have definitely declared what is beneficial: dukkha, the arising of dukkha, the cessation of dukkha, and the path to the cessation of dukkha. I have definitely declared this.

This shifts emphasis from upholding various views to viewing things rightly by way of the diagnostic scheme of the four truths. As the *Cūḷamāluṅkya-sutta* and its parallel declare, this is beneficial and leads to Nirvāṇa, unlike any of the views that Māluṅkyaputta was so obsessed with.

The Buddha's refusal to take up any of these standard propositions comes up again in the *Aggivacchagotta-sutta* and its parallels. The wanderer Vacchagotta was perplexed that the Buddha would not take up any of these alternative propositions. On being told that these views do not lead to the final goal, in what appears to be an expression of exasperation at what must have seemed to him incomprehensible evasiveness, he asked if the Buddha held any view at all. The Buddha's reply proceeds in this way in the *Saṃyukta-āgama* version:[9]

---

8 The translation is taken from MĀ 221 at T II 805b28 to 805c3.

9 The translated section is based on SĀ 962 at T II 245c21 to 245c25, parallel to MN 72 at MN I 486,11 (translated Ñāṇamoli 1995/2005: 592), SĀ[2] 196 at T II 445b8, and D 4094 *ju* 157b6 or Q 5595 *tu* 182a6; for a comparative study see Anālayo 2011: 392.

> The Tathāgata has already finished with what are views. Yet, wanderer Vacchagotta, the Tathāgata has "seen", namely he has seen that "this is the noble truth of dukkha", "this is the noble truth of the arising of dukkha", "this is the noble truth of the cessation of dukkha", and "this is the noble truth of the path to the cessation of dukkha."
>
> Having such knowledge and such vision, all views, all clinging, all rebirths, all views of a self and what belongs to a self, and underlying tendencies to being bound by attachment to the conceit of a self, [all these] have truly been exterminated, appeased, and become cool; and he has become liberated in this way.

The point made in this passage comes out with additional clarity in the Pāli terminology employed in the *Aggivacchagotta-sutta*, which contrasts the holding of a "view", *diṭṭhi*, to what the Buddha had "seen", *diṭṭha*. The etymologically close relationship between the two expressions involves a substantial shift in meaning, where the upholding of speculative views is replaced by the gaining of direct vision through seeing things as they really are. Whereas in the Pāli version this direct vision concerns the Buddha's insight into the true nature of the five aggregates, in the passage translated above and the other parallels it instead takes the form of the four truths.

In this way the Buddha as a Tathāgata is one who has "thus gone" completely beyond speculative "views" and realized the true "vision" of Nirvāṇa. This vision is eloquently expressed in the formulation of the four truths, which serves as right "view" for those willing to follow his example, thereby providing a diagnostic viewing of reality such that one can realize truth for oneself.

The *Aggivacchagotta-sutta* and its parallels agree that the Buddha illustrated the nature of a Tathāgata with the example of an extinguished fire. When a fire burns in front of oneself, it is possible to point out the fire and its fuel. But once the fire has become extinguished, it is not possible to point out the direction in which it has gone. Similarly to an extinguished fire, the Tathāgata has given up all clinging to any of the five aggregates. Since he no longer identifies with them, it is no longer possible to identify him with the five aggregates. Once he can no longer be identified with the five aggregates even while still alive, it is hardly possible to declare what will happen at death in terms of these five aggregates. This serves to reiterate the point made above, in that the four propositions regarding a Tathāgata involve a misconception of what the term Tathāgata, at least from the early Buddhist perspective, stands for.

The interrelationship between identifying with something and therefore becoming identifiable has significant implications, since it is precisely the fact of being identified with the aggregates that renders old age, disease, and death so fearful. Once by dint of full awakening all patterns of identification have been left behind, the problem of being afflicted by old age, disease, and death takes on an entirely different dimension, since there is no longer a reference point for feeling afflicted and becoming distressed.

EXERCISE

As a way of putting into practice the crucial distinction between holding on to views and cultivating a truthful vision of things as they really are, clinging to our own views offers itself as a convenient target for practice. In order to counter the affective investment we naturally have in our personal views and opinions, a helpful exercise could be to adopt the exact opposite view just for a moment in an attempt to appreciate whether there could be anything at all reasonable or even just understandable in that position.

Often enough it turns out that what earlier, when seen from our own viewpoint, seemed utterly unreasonable and incomprehensible, on being taken seriously even just for a short moment can reveal its inner rationale and meaningfulness. The point at issue here is not to throw overboard our own opinions completely, but only to suspend them for a moment and allow the opposite position sufficient mental space to be taken seriously. This can take us a long way in understanding better where our opponents come from and thereby make it possible to find a way of solving any disagreement that may have arisen out of conflicting views and opinions.

Another dimension of the same exercise is to shine the light of mindful investigation on the reassuring sense of kinship with those who have a similar view. The resultant sense of identity requires as a defining contrast others who hold the opposite view. In conjunction, such kinship and antagonism help to build up our own sense of identity, which lies at the root of clinging to views and opinions.

In terms of actual meditation practice, one of the perceptions listed in the *Girimānanda-sutta* and its Tibetan parallel could be taken up as a formal support for cultivating the appropriate attitude. This exercise comes as part of a set of perceptions that in one way or another point towards Nirvāṇa. The present perception is entitled "not delighting in the whole world", and it requires that we let go of any attachment to our positions and views, letting go of any instance of clinging to these building blocks of our sense of identity.[10]

10 See in more detail Anālayo 2016b: 227f.

XXI

DWELLING IN EMPTINESS

In the last chapter I took up the Buddha's transcendence of views and his role as a Tathāgata, a "thus gone one", who by dint of his realization of full awakening had gone beyond identifying with the five aggregates and thereby beyond being identified with them. This now leads me to the topic of emptiness.

The *Cūḷasuññata-sutta* and its parallels take as their starting point a short statement by the Buddha, according to which he often dwelled in emptiness.[1] This leads on to a detailed exposition on how such dwelling can be achieved in meditation practice. Since I have studied this in detail elsewhere, in what follows I merely provide a brief summary of chief aspects of the practice.[2]

The meditative progression in the *Cūḷasuññata-sutta* and its parallels proceeds through a series of perceptions, beginning with the monastery where the Buddha was staying at that time. This first perception requires seeing the monastery as devoid of the various types of animals and people that one would have encountered in a city in ancient India, but not devoid of the monastics who were staying there. The underlying pattern of the contemplation can best be presented with a statement made by

---

1 MN 121 at MN III 104,9 (translated Ñāṇamoli 1995/2005: 965) and its parallels MĀ 190 at T I 737a4 and Skilling 1994: 148,4; for a comparative study see Anālayo 2011: 683.

2 Anālayo 2015a: 83–169.

the Buddha after having introduced this first perception. Here is the *Madhyama-āgama* version of this statement:[3]

> Thus, Ānanda, whatever is not present, I therefore see as empty; and whatever else is present, I see as truly present. Ānanda, this is called truly dwelling in emptiness, without distortion.

This goes to show that truly dwelling in emptiness requires seeing things as they actually are, "without distortion". The contemplation of emptiness in the *Cūḷasuññata-sutta* and its parallels then proceeds from the first perception mentioned above via perceptions of the forest, of earth, and of the first three immaterial spheres, to signlessness.[4] The peak of emptiness is reached once the mind has become liberated from the influxes (*āsava*). The *Madhyama-āgama* version expresses this peak of emptiness in the following manner:[5]

> In this way one knows that this is empty of the influx of sensual desire, empty of the influx of existence, and empty of the influx of ignorance. Yet there is this non-emptiness: just this body of mine with its six sense-spheres and the life faculty.

The Buddha's dwelling in emptiness in relation to the six sense-spheres is the topic of a discourse in the *Saṃyutta-nikāya* and its *Saṃyukta-āgama* parallel. The parallel versions report that Sāriputta clarified, in a discussion with another monastic, that neither the senses nor their objects are fetters in themselves. To illustrate this, he employed the simile of two oxen that are yoked together. This image appears to have been taken from everyday life in ancient India, where oxen would have been regularly yoked together for tasks like ploughing or pulling carts. The point made by Sāriputta is that neither oxen is the fetter of the other. Instead, the fetter that keeps them in bondage is the yoke between the two. Similarly, the fetter is not in the senses or their objects per se, but is rather

---

3 The translation is based on MĀ 190 at T I 737a9 to 737a11 (translated Anālayo 2015a: 177).

4 The next step in MN 121 at MN III 107,10, which involves neither-perception-nor-non-perception, could be the result of a textual error; see Anālayo 2012b: 335–8 and 2015a: 134f.

5 The translated extract stems from MĀ 190 at T I 737c14 to 737c16.

to be found in desire and lust. In order to demonstrate that the experience of the six sense-spheres can take place without activating any fetter, Sāriputta then brings in the case of the Buddha. The *Saṃyukta-āgama* version proceeds like this:[6]

> The Blessed One sees with the eyes forms that are pleasing and that are displeasing, without giving rise to lustful desire. Yet other living beings, on seeing with the eyes forms that are pleasing and that are displeasing, do give rise to lustful desire. For this reason the Blessed One teaches them that they should abandon lustful desire so that their mind becomes liberated.[7]

The same applies to the other sense-spheres, be they the ears and sounds, the nose and odours, the tongue and flavours, the body and tangibles, or the mind and mind-objects. In each case, the Buddha experiences whatever happens without giving rise to lustful desire. This reveals an important dimension of his dwelling in emptiness, in that genuine insight into the empty nature of sense experience ensures that the mind remains empty of lustful desire in any situation.

Another dimension of the passage translated above is that compassion naturally arises out of such dwelling in emptiness. Such compassion then expresses itself in the willingness to teach others how to reach the same freedom from mental bondage.

This passage complements the profound meditative instructions in the *Cūḷasuññata-sutta* and its parallels, providing an example that can easily be related to everyday practice. Given that the fettering force is not to be found in the two oxen, the senses and their objects, the task is clearly not just to avoid sensory experience. This comes to the fore in a discussion between the Buddha and a brahmin student by the name of Uttara, reported in the *Indriyabhāvanā-sutta* and its *Saṃyukta-āgama* parallel. The title of the Pāli version announces the topic of the discussion, namely how to undertake the "cultivation",

6 The translated passage is taken from SĀ 250 at T II 60b17 to 60b20, parallel to SN 35.191 at SN IV 164,26 (translated Bodhi 2000: 1231, referred to as discourse 232).

7 SN 35.191 does not have a comparable remark on the Buddha teaching others.

bhāvanā, of the "sense faculties", *indriya*. The *Saṃyukta-āgama* version reports the relevant exchange as follows:[8]

> Uttara said to the Buddha: "My teacher Pārāsiya declares that not seeing forms with the eye and not hearing sounds with the ear is reckoned to be the cultivation of the faculties."
>
> The Buddha said to Uttara: "If it is as your [teacher] Pārāsiya declares, are the blind [then accomplished] cultivators of the faculties? Why [do I say] that? The blind just do not see forms with the eye."[9]

In the *Saṃyukta-āgama* discourse, Ānanda steps in at this point with the observation that the same holds for the deaf, as they do not hear. In the *Indriyabhāvanā-sutta* the Buddha himself brings up the example of the deaf and hearing.

Alongside such minor variation, the two versions agree that merely to avoid seeing and hearing as such is not the proper cultivation of the faculties, it fails to offer a solution to the problem of the fettering force of sensory experience. Lest this be misunderstood, however, the present passage needs to be read in conjunction with other passages that recommend dwelling in seclusion and engaging in formal meditation practice. In other words, it is indeed meaningful to live in seclusion and dedicate oneself to intensive practice in silence. However, the outer conditions for such practice are not an end in themselves, but only a means to an end. The true end is to learn to remain free from reacting to sense input with desire and aversion in any situation, whatever it may be.

This in turn serves as a touchstone for whatever formal meditation one regularly undertakes in silent seclusion. The challenge is to make sure that essential qualities from such practice carry over in one way or another to daily-life situations, that one somehow succeeds in bridging the two. Both are integral dimensions of progress on the path. If one were to give importance to only one of these two dimensions, at the

---

8 The translation is based on SĀ 282 at T II 78a28 to 78b2, parallel to MN 152 at MN III 298,13 (translated Ñāṇamoli 1995/2005: 1147); for a comparative study see Anālayo 2011: 849.

9 The translation is based on adopting a variant that dispenses with an occurrence of "if" at the outset of the last sentence.

expense of the other, then such lack of balance could easily become detrimental to one's overall actual progress.

The inner independence and balance that results from being able to dwell in emptiness in any situation finds expression in another exchange, this time between the Buddha and a *deva*, reported in a discourse in the *Saṃyutta-nikāya* with parallels in the two *Saṃyukta-āgama* collections. The relevant discourse in the "other" *Saṃyukta-āgama* (T 100) proceeds in this way:[10]

> A deva approached the Buddha and asked the Buddha: "Are you dejected?"
>
> The Buddha said: "I have not lost anything. For what reason should I be dejected?"
>
> The deva said again: "Are you elated?"
>
> The Buddha replied: "I have not acquired anything. For what reason should I be elated?"
>
> [The deva] said again: "Recluse, [so] you are neither dejected nor elated?"
>
> The Buddha said: "It is exactly as you said."

The above exchange brings out the Buddha's balance of the mind. Due to the absence of attachment and desire, there is no longer any loss or acquisition that could lead to reactions of dejection or elation. This is the balance of dwelling in emptiness. Again, as the previously translated passage makes clear, the indifference that comes from ignoring things misses the point. Instead, the equanimity that the present passage illustrates is the sublime internal equipoise of an awakened one with regard to whatever happens, which comes in conjunction with the compassionate disposition of being willing to lead others to the same superb inner balance.

Yet another dimension of dwelling in emptiness can be illustrated with the help of the *Mūlapariyāya-sutta* and its *Ekottarika-āgama* parallel. The *Mūlapariyāya-sutta* describes how a worldling constructs experience in a self-referential manner. From a simple apperception of earth as the first of

---

10 The translation is based on SĀ² 169 at T II 436c1 to 436c5, parallel to SN 2.18 at SN I 54,11 (translated Bodhi 2000: 150) and SĀ 585 at T II 155c3.

the four elements, for example, this leads to reifying earth and appropriating it as mine, with the final result of delighting in it. The same pattern holds for the other elements, various heavenly beings, the immaterial spheres, sensory experience, and even for the concept of Nirvāṇa.

In contrast to the predicament of the worldling, who easily succumbs to the powerful sway of such conceptual proliferations, a disciple in higher training avoids getting caught up in such a way. An accomplished arahant is then free from such reifications and conceptual proliferations. The same holds for the Buddha, of course, whose case the *Ekottarika-āgama* parallel presents in this way:[11]

> The Tathāgata, the arahant, the fully awakened one, is well able to distinguish earth; yet he does not attach to the earth element and does not give rise to those perceptions of the earth element. The reason is that all this results from his having smashed the net of craving, which has this outcome.
>
> In dependence on becoming there is birth, and in dependence on birth there is old age and death. All of this he has completely eliminated. The reason is that the Tathāgata has accomplished supreme and full awakening.

In this way, by having smashed the net of craving on the night of his full awakening, the Buddha had gone not only beyond old age and death but also beyond reifying and conceptually proliferating the raw data of sense experience.

Remaining with bare experience as it is, instead of giving rise to conceptual proliferations and their concomitant reifications, is a central theme of the instructions to the non-Buddhist wanderer Bāhiya. The discourse in the *Udāna* that records Bāhiya's instantaneous full awakening, after having received just a short but penetrative instruction to stay with bare experience, does not have a parallel.[12] However, a discourse in the *Saṃyutta-nikāya* that reports a similar instruction given to a monastic does

11 The translated section is taken from EĀ 44.6 at T II 766b11 to 766b14 (for an alternative translation see Pāsādika 2008: 145), parallel to MN 1 at MN I 5,34 (translated Ñāṇamoli 1995/2005: 89); for a comparative study see Anālayo 2011: 26.

12 Ud 1.10 at Ud 8,4 (translated Ireland 1990: 20).

have a parallel in the *Saṃyukta-āgama*.[13] The instructions given simply require one to limit sense experience to what is actually experienced, without proliferating in various ways.[14] This is how the two oxen can be unyoked, in a way; this is how one can indeed cultivate the faculties; and this is also how dejection and elation can be avoided. In sum, this is how one can avoid getting caught up in the pull of proliferation.

The key for putting this into practice is simply dropping back first of all into being in the present moment with receptive awareness rather than reactivity. The mental space created through such dropping back facilitates discerning the empty nature of the proliferations that usually occur when one reacts on the spot and without having established mindfulness. With some practice, such dropping back into the present moment in the face of whatever occurs will yield a subtle sense of joy, simply by dint of the mind not being drawn into reactivity and proliferation. This, in a way, is a taste of emptiness. Needless to say, stepping back for a moment from proliferation is not yet the final goal, and avoiding being caught in the net of craving does not equal its final and definite smashing. Nevertheless, every moment that one does not succumb to proliferation and thereby does not get caught in the net of craving is a step forward towards the realization of supreme emptiness, when the net of craving will be smashed once and for all.

The *Mahāsuññata-sutta* and its parallels show how the inner freedom of such dwelling in emptiness can be applied to various aspects of daily life.[15] They encourage maintaining equanimity, instead of desire and aversion, in any posture as one dimension of such dwelling in emptiness. In this way, dejection and elation can be avoided.

When thoughts arise, this is not a problem for one devoted to dwelling in emptiness. That is, such dwelling does not

13 SN 35.95 at SN IV 73,4 (translated Bodhi 2000: 1175) and its parallels SĀ 312 at T II 90a12 (translated Anālayo 2015a: 111) and D 4094 *ju* 241b3 or Q 5595 *tu* 276a2.

14 For a more detailed discussion see Anālayo 2015a: 110–14.

15 MN 122 at MN III 112,31 (translated Ñāṇamoli 1995/2005: 973) and its parallels MĀ 191 at T I 739a12 (translated Anālayo 2015a: 186) and Skilling 1994: 220,14; for a comparative study see Anālayo 2011: 694f and for a practical discussion 2015a: 115–23.

require keeping the mind void of any thought. In fact in daily life thoughts can hardly be avoided. One only needs to ensure that no unwholesome thoughts arise. If one becomes involved in conversations, another dimension of daily life that can hardly be avoided, the task is to keep away from talking about irrelevant and trivial matters. Instead, one tries to direct the course of conversation in such a way that it becomes beneficial and elevating for oneself and the other person, ideally by being related in some way, even if only implicitly, to the Dharma and progress towards awakening.

When sensually alluring objects are encountered, one just avoids succumbing to their attractive pull. A simple mode of implementing this is paying attention to their impermanent nature. Awareness of impermanence is also the antidote to identifications with any aspect of subjective experience (described in terms of the five aggregates affected by clinging).

In this way, according to the *Mahāsuññata-sutta* and its parallels, dwelling in emptiness can be fruitfully applied to various dimensions of daily-life experience, thereby providing support for formal meditation on emptiness as well as serving as the befitting expression of having successfully undertaken such practice.

EXERCISE

As a practical suggestion I would like to recommend dwelling in emptiness.[16] In Chapter 5 I already presented one mode of practice related in particular to the absence of self. Here I would like to focus on another of the steps in the gradual entry into emptiness, described in the *Cūḷasuññata-sutta* and its parallels, namely the perception of space.

In formal meditation, perception of space can serve as a mode of deconstructing the solidity of all aspects of material experience. Space is not only the visible absence of things, it also pervades whatever phenomenon we visually and tangibly experience as solid. As we know from quantum physics, all

16 For more detailed practical instructions that follow the model of the *Cūḷasuññata-sutta* and its parallels see Anālayo 2015a: 162–9.

these apparently solid phenomena are just energy processes in vast space.

One way in which this can be cultivated is to open our eyes briefly to become aware of the space between ourselves and whatever objects are in the field of our vision. Next we turn attention to space elsewhere, surrounding ourselves and any visual object. Closing our eyes while maintaining the sense of space we then allow the objects seen earlier to dissolve into space. They do occupy space, yet their true nature is to be indeed for the most part made of space. Finally, when we sit surrounded by space in all directions, we just make sure that even our own body is allowed to become part of that same perception by letting it also dissolve into space.

Awareness of the resultant perception of boundless space is best combined with the clear comprehension that all matter is empty by nature. Therefore all grasping and clinging to material things, including any discrimination and prejudices concerned with physical properties of human bodies, lack a solid foundation. They are, in short, empty.

The same perception can also be helpful in everyday life. Confronted by angry words, a moment of attention to the space between ourselves and the aggressor helps to give rise to the mental space needed to find the most skilful way possible to deal with this situation. This can be further strengthened by broadening attention from the space between ourselves and the other(s) to the abundance of space that exists all around.

Similarly, when crowded in by too many tasks and responsibilities, just a bit of attention to space right in front of our eyes as well as around ourselves can help to re-establish the degree of inner distance needed in order to be able to accomplish as much as possible without being thrown off balance and becoming a victim of anxiety. There is simply no limit to the transformative potential of dwelling in emptiness, as long as the practice itself is undertaken in a genuine manner and with sincere dedication.

XXII

DAILY CONDUCT

The topic of the Buddha's dwelling in emptiness in the last chapter led me from formal meditation on this theme to aspects of daily life. In the present chapter I further explore the latter topic by examining the everyday conduct of the Buddha in general. Although this book is a "meditator's life of the Buddha" and thus naturally focuses on meditation practices, in the early Buddhist frame of thought such practices are intimately interrelated with matters of daily life. It is by adopting a certain conduct that one builds the foundation for one's formal meditation practices and progress in their cultivation in turn shows in the way in which one behaves in everyday circumstances. Formal meditation practice is in fact not so much about attaining particular experiences, but about transforming oneself. For such transformation certain distinct experiences do offer a substantial contribution, no doubt. But in the final count their value rests in the degree to which they have led to an inner change, in particular to diminishing defilements and thereby gradually emerging from *dukkha*.

The daily conduct of the Buddha receives detailed coverage in the *Brahmāyu-sutta* and its parallels. The narrative context of this discourse features a brahmin who sends his student to investigate whether the good reputation he has heard about the Buddha is true. This brahmin student begins his investigation by ascertaining whether the Buddha is endowed with a set of marks that in the ancient Indian setting apparently represented exceptional bodily beauty. The way these marks have come down in the texts appears to be influenced by artistic depictions and conventions, as a result of which some are not easy to make sense of nowadays. However, close textual study shows that the original conception of these marks must have concerned rather subtle nuances that only someone trained in the lore of these marks could discern.[1] In other words, the Buddha is not being depicted as abnormal in any way, such as would make him easily distinguishable from others.

According to a recurrent specification in the texts, the possession of these marks implies that their bearer is destined to take a leading role either in secular society by becoming a wheel-turning king or else in the religious realm by becoming a Buddha. The early discourses regularly present concern with the possession of these marks as a preoccupation of brahmins, who on ascertaining that the Buddha had such marks become amenable to being taught by him. Such ascertaining of the presence of these marks requires the Buddha's cooperation, where he has to display the length of his tongue and the nature of his private parts; in regard to the latter it seems to me that the implication is that he was able to retract these.[2] This would then symbolize his asexual character; in fact among the whole set of marks only some are related to maleness and others rather to feminine qualities.

In the *Brahmāyu-sutta* and its parallels, once the brahmin student has ascertained that the Buddha indeed possesses these special physical marks, he follows him for some time to observe his daily conduct. According to the *Madhyama-āgama* version, when reporting his observations to his teacher, the brahmin student describes how the Buddha wears his robes as follows:[3]

> The recluse Gotama wears his robes in an orderly manner, not high up and not low down, not tightly on the body, [yet in such a way] that the wind is not able to blow the robe away from his body ...

---

1 For a more detailed discussion see Anālayo 2017a: 57–69.

2 See Anālayo 2017a: 132f.

3 The translated sections are taken from MĀ 161 at T I 687a3 to 687a5 and 687a9 to 687a11, parallel to MN 91 at MN II 139,20 (translated Ñāṇamoli 1995/2005: 748) and T 76 at T I 884b13; for a comparative study see Anālayo 2011: 539.

> He keeps robes not for the sake of ownership, not for the sake of pride, not for the sake of self-decoration, nor for the sake of adornment, but in order to protect himself against mosquitoes and gadflies, as well as the impact of wind and sun, and in order to cover the body out of a sense of modesty.

Alongside the emphasis given to dressing properly in this way, the above passage also mentions the appropriate attitude towards clothing.[4] This attitude is based on giving priority to the protective purpose of clothing, in contrast to a common tendency to show off with clothes, be this by wearing particularly expensive clothing or else dressing in a way that others will find sensually attractive.

A related topic taken up in the *Madhyama-āgama* discourse is the Buddha's way of walking, which is described in this manner:[5]

> When the recluse Gotama wishes to walk, he first raises his right foot, raising it straight and putting it down straight. He walks without disorderliness and also without disarray. When he walks, the two ankles never bump against each other.

The *Brahmāyu-sutta* is more detailed, mentioning other aspects of the Buddha's walking such as that he does not walk too quickly or too slowly, and that he puts his feet down neither too far nor too close. In sum, the Buddha walks in an orderly and balanced manner, exemplifying the balance of his mind.

Walking as one of the meditation postures is a recurrent feature in the early discourses as well as in modern practice. As mentioned in Chapter 19, the Buddha apparently even delivered a whole and rather long discourse in the walking posture. In the case of meditation undertaken in this posture, the standard descriptions speak of removing obstructive states

---

4 Although MN 91 does not mention the Buddha's attitude to robes, a comparable description can be found in MN 2 at MN I 10,4 (translated Ñāṇamoli 1995/2005: 94) as a way of removing influxes through proper usage, and according to MN 68 at MN I 464,13 (translated Ñāṇamoli 1995/2005: 567) the Buddha adopted such proper usage.

5 The translated part is from MĀ 161 at T I 687a13 to 687a15, parallel to MN 91 at MN II 137,12 and T 76 at T I 884a12.

from the mind.[6] Thus walking meditation seems to be simply a continuation of the basic practice undertaken in the sitting posture, done by just walking up and down in a normal manner, orderly and in a balanced way, comparable to the description in the extract above. In present-day meditation traditions, meditation in this posture can also involve specific modes of walking, such as slowing down and taking only very short steps, or else walking in a particular formalized manner.

Another aspect of the Buddha's conduct comes to the fore when he sits down to partake of food. The *Madhyama-āgama* version describes this as follows:[7]

> The recluse Gotama turns the body to the right, adjusts the seat, and sits on it. He does not sit down on the seat with excessive bodily force and he also does not support himself with his hands on the thighs when sitting on the seat. Having sat on the seat, he is not worried and not disturbed, and he is also not jolly ...
>
> The recluse Gotama forms the food into a ball in an orderly manner and slowly puts it into his mouth. He does not open the mouth until the ball of food has reached it. Once it is inside the mouth he chews it over thrice and swallows it, without any rice or soup being not broken up or remaining in the mouth when he further puts the next ball inside.[8]

In the ancient Indian setting one would have sat on the ground, so that the "seat" would have been a cloth or similar item spread on the floor. This explains the need to adjust the seat and then sit down on it, ideally without force and also without needing to support oneself. Another aspect of the same setting is that food is taken with one's hand, thus one needs to roll it into a ball and put it into the mouth properly.

---

6 An example is AN 3.16 at AN I 114,10 (translated Bodhi 2012: 212) and its parallel EĀ 21.6 at T II 604a15; see also Anālayo 2003a: 140.

7 The translated sections are taken from MĀ 161 at T I 687a25 to 687a28 and 687b1 to 687b4, parallel to MN 91 at MN II 138,1 and T 76 at T I 884a22.

8 The reference to chewing three times, or two to three times in MN 91 at MN II 138,22, could not imply that the Buddha only moves his mouth thrice, since that would hardly suffice for ensuring that the food is properly broken up and nothing remains in the mouth when the next mouthful is taken. I take it that it instead means two or three complete mastication cycles, each involving several chewing movements.

In agreement with its Pāli parallel, the *Madhyama-āgama* version continues by describing that the Buddha partakes of food just to maintain his bodily health and not for any other reason. Similar to the case of clothes, discussed above, the priority in matters of eating is the actual function of food to nourish the body and keep it healthy. The key aspect can best be summarized with the following statement in the *Madhyama-āgama* discourse:[9]

> [When] eating he consents to experiencing the taste, but he does not consent to being defiled by the taste.

The *Brahmāyu-sutta* makes a similar statement, according to which the Buddha experienced the taste of the food without experiencing lust for the taste. The experience of the taste is in fact an integral aspect of proper digestion during its preparatory phase, when the food is still in the mouth, leading to an increase in gastric secretion. Thus it is indeed meaningful to taste the food and there is nothing intrinsically wrong with just experiencing its taste. The problem rather lies in how to relate to the taste of food, where the challenge is to avoid craving and clinging.[10]

The *Madhyama-āgama* version reports what takes place after the meal in this way:[11]

> After the meal, at noon, he puts away his robe and bowl, washes his hands and feet, and with a sitting mat over his shoulder enters a hut to sit in meditation.

It is remarkable that the present passage, and the discourses in general, keeps referring to the Buddha's regular practice of formal sitting meditation. This even holds when he is called

---

9 The translation is based on MĀ 161 at T I 687b5, parallel to MN 91 at MN II 138,26. The Chinese phrase uses a term that can render *chanda* (as well as *kāma*, *rāga*, etc.), where my translation follows a sense this term has in some *Vinaya* contexts as "consent" or "agreement".

10 Ñāṇananda 2016: 15 notes that "the taste-buds of the Buddha are as acute as ours. They do not go inactive with the attainment of Buddhahood. But he has no attachment to taste ... this means that there is *Nibbāna* even at the tip of the tongue."

11 The translated extract stems from MĀ 161 at T I 687b23 to 687b25, parallel to MN 91 at MN II 139,25 and T 76 at T I 884b15.

to visit a seriously ill monastic, where he still does his daily meditation first and then goes to the sick.[12] Clearly, even a fully awakened one maintains formal sitting meditation as a daily habit and a befitting expression of his realization, hardly leaving an excuse for those less advanced on the path not to follow this example.

The *Brahmāyu-sutta* and its parallels agree that the Buddha's voice was endowed with exceptional qualities, making it not only a pleasure to listen to him, but also ensuring that what he said was clearly intelligible. The *Madhyama-āgama* version describes his actual engaging in teaching activity like this:[13]

> The sound of the recluse Gotama teaching the Dharma to an assembly remains just in the assembly and does not go beyond the assembly. He teaches others the Dharma to encourage and inspire them, to accomplish their delight. He teaches others the Dharma with innumerable skilful means. Having encouraged and inspired them, and accomplished their delight, he rises from his seat and returns to where he has been [staying] before.

Besides wearing robes, walking, sitting, eating, and speaking, another daily activity that merits attention is sleeping. Although this is not taken up explicitly in the *Brahmāyu-sutta* and its parallels, in what follows I survey selected passages relevant to this topic.

One passage reports that the debater Saccaka challenged the Buddha about taking a nap during the day in the hot season. In reply, according to the *Mahāsaccaka-sutta* and its Sanskrit fragment parallel the Buddha clarified that to do so is not in itself a sign of delusion.[14] In other words, even one who has removed defilements might sleep during the day, should that be what the body at that time requires.

Another similar challenge involves Māra, which is reported in a discourse in the *Saṃyutta-nikāya* and its *Saṃyukta-āgama*

---

12 See Anālayo 2016b: 171f.

13 The translated part is based on MĀ 161 at T I 687c3 to 687c6, parallel to MN 91 at MN II 140,1 and T 76 at T I 884b23.

14 MN 36 at MN I 250,1 (translated Ñāṇamoli 1995/2005: 342) and fragment 338v8, Liu 2010: 238.

parallels. The Buddha had spent the night in walking meditation and entered his hut to lie down to rest. Māra challenged him for sleeping when the sun was up. According to the partially preserved *Saṃyukta-āgama*, the Buddha replied:[15]

> Craving's net of attachment to all existences,
> Which covers all places everywhere,
> I have now destroyed that net.
> All craving has forever been abandoned,
> And all taking of birth has become extinct.
> I am stilled in Nirvāṇa's delight.
> Evil One, now what further
> Could you do in relation to me?

Needless to say, these two passages should not be taken as an encouragement to indulge in oversleeping. It can safely be assumed that the Buddha would have consistently practised wakefulness, with only the middle watch of the night spent in sleep. However, these two passages do clarify that sleeping as such is not problematic.

An additional perspective on the Buddha's sleep and his freedom from defilements emerges from his first meeting with Anāthapiṇḍika. The householder had come in the early morning and on arrival began their conversation by courteously asking whether the Buddha had slept well. The *Saṃyukta-āgama* version reports the Buddha's reply as follows:[16]

> A [true] brahmin who [has attained] Nirvāṇa
> Such a one is always at ease.
> Undefiled by craving and lust,
> Forever liberated without remainder,
> All longings being abandoned,
> The blazing flames in the mind being quelled,
> The mind has attained tranquil appeasement;
> And one who is appeased sleeps well.

---

15 The translated verses are taken from SĀ² 26 at T II 381c29 to 382a3 (for an alternative translation see Bingenheimer 2011: 132), parallel to SN 4.7 at SN I 107,23 (translated Bodhi 2000: 200) and SĀ 1087 at T II 285a26.

16 The translation is taken from SĀ 592 at T II 158a27 to 158b1, parallel to SN 10.8 at SN I 212,15 (translated Bodhi 2000: 313) or Vin II 156,25 (translated Horner 1952/1975: 219) and SĀ² 186 at T II 441a7.

Another exchange on the same topic of sleeping well can be found in a discourse in the *Aṅguttara-nikāya* and its *Ekottarika-āgama* parallel. In reply to a courteous enquiry as to whether he had slept well, the Buddha's affirmative reply leads his visitor to wonder how this could be so, given that the nights were cold and the Buddha only had straw or leaves to lie down on and only his robes as a cover. In reply the Buddha described a man in a luxurious house with all possible equipment and surrounded by female attendants. On hearing this description, the Buddha's visitor felt certain that such a man must sleep very well. According to the *Ekottarika-āgama* account, the Buddha continued in this way:[17]

> The Blessed One said: "Householder's son, how is it? If that man, who comfortably gets to sleep well, at that time gives rise to a mental condition of sensual desire, will he not get to sleep because of that mental condition of sensual desire?"
>
> The householder's son replied: "It is like this, Blessed One, if that man gives rise to a mental condition of sensual desire, he will then not get to sleep."
>
> The Blessed One said: "Now the Tathāgata has forever eradicated without remainder being like that person who is full of sensual desire, so that it has no further roots and can no more revive again."

The exchange in the two parallels continues by covering in the same way the possible impact of aversion and delusion, clarifying that the Buddha slept well because he had removed the three mental poisons. This is what ensures good sleep, even if outer conditions should be harsh.

In this way, the sublime condition of a mind free from all defilements has a range of repercussions, which show themselves in various dimensions of daily conduct and even have a beneficial impact on sleep.

---

17 The translation is based on EĀ 28.3 at T II 650b5 to 650b9, parallel to AN 3.34 at AN I 137,17 (translated Bodhi 2012: 233, referred to as discourse number 35) and SHT V 1343, Sander and Waldschmidt 1985: 232.

EXERCISE

As a practice related to the present chapter, I would like to recommend clear comprehension during various activities. This is an exercise found in the *Satipaṭṭhāna-sutta* and one of its parallels. The task is to train ourselves to be clearly aware and act with decorum in relation to a range of bodily activities, from walking and sitting to eating and going to sleep. As a basis for such practice, a helpful tool is whole-body awareness, which already came up in the exercise related to Chapter 11. Building on the continuity of such proprioceptive awareness, the task now is to allow the qualities cultivated in formal sitting meditation to express themselves in a dignified manner of acting and behaving in whatever situation.

In order to build up such practice gradually, it can be useful to pick out one particular aspect of our daily experience and make this the focus for some time. Thus we might, for example, for several days give emphasis to eating mindfully. This could be done by trying to eat experiencing the taste of the food but without experiencing lust for the taste, and also by chewing well, such that all food is well crushed up before swallowing and nothing remains in the mouth before the next bite is taken. Even with such a simple activity we can follow the example set by the Buddha.

After some time it can be useful to shift attention to something else (ideally maintaining fundamental aspects of the conduct established already for eating). Perhaps we could give attention to our walking for a change. Trying to walk centred and balanced, without disorderliness and without bumping into things. Other options will naturally present themselves, even if they have not been mentioned explicitly in this chapter. Any activity can become food for mindfulness and clear comprehension and thereby a way of emulating the Buddha.

XXIII

OLD AGE, DISEASE, AND DEATH

With the present chapter I am gradually coming closer to the end of my exploration of the Buddha's life; in the next chapter I will take up his passing away (as well as that of his foster mother). According to the Buddha's motivation to go forth, taken up in Chapter 1 of this study, he had set out in search of what is beyond old age, disease, and death. As explored in Chapter 13, he successfully achieved his aim by reaching full awakening. Although he had realized Nirvāṇa, which is beyond old age, disease, and death, his body was of course still subject to these. The freedom he had won was a mental one, a freedom from being affected by ageing or by becoming sick and, perhaps most important of all, he had won freedom from the fear of death.

The *Mahāparinibbāna-sutta*, the Discourse on the Great Final Nirvāṇa, and its parallels report a series of episodes that led up to the Buddha's passing away. In one such episode he had become quite sick and was apparently on the verge of death, but then recovered. In the *Dīrgha-āgama* version, he describes his own condition in this way:[1]

1 The translated passage is taken from DĀ 2 at T I 15b2 to 15b5, parallel to DN 16 at DN II 100,11 (translated Walshe 1987: 245) or SN 47.9 at SN V 153,26 (translated Bodhi 2000: 1637), a Sanskrit fragment version, Waldschmidt 1951: 198 (§14.19), and two individually translated discourses, T 5 at T I 164c14 and T 6 at T I 180a26; see also Anālayo 2017c: 206f.

> I am already old, having been eighty years for some time. My body is just like an old cart which by being expediently patched up and adjusted reaches the place to which it is going. By expedient strength I can maintain it alive a little [longer], through my own strength and energy, putting up with these painful feelings. When I do not give attention to any ⟨signs⟩ and enter ⟨signless⟩ concentration,[2] then my body is at ease and there are no afflictions.

It is perhaps noteworthy that in this passage the Buddha describes the deteriorating condition of his body to his attendant Ānanda, who was his constant companion. The fact that the Buddha needed to point this out gives the impression that he usually acted with such self-composure that even the one most regularly in contact with him had not fully noticed (or had been able to avoid noticing) the deteriorating condition of the Buddha's body and had to be told about it. In other words, the Buddha would have kept patching up the old cart of his body in such a way that its broken-down condition was not unmistakeably evident even to those close to him.

This in turn can be taken to exemplify how one best communicates one's own diseased or ageing condition. When this has a practical function, as in the present context, it is indeed meaningful to inform others of one's condition. Otherwise, however, one learns to bear up with the condition of the body without making a display of this in order to gain attention and sympathy.

In my study of advice from the early discourses on facing disease and death, I already took up another occasion when the Buddha was sick, at an earlier period of his life.[3] The Buddha's foot had been hurt, but he was able to endure the apparently quite strong pain with mindfulness. I argued that this shows that the potential of mindfulness in facing pain was already well recognized in early Buddhism, given that on this occasion

2 The translation is based on an emendation, following Weller 1939: 77 note 292. The original speaks of "unconscious" concentration rather than "signless" concentration. The emendation involves two Chinese characters that are easily confused with each other; for a survey of several instances of such confusion see Anālayo 2011: 274f note 54.

3 Anālayo 2016b: 59ff.

the Buddha (and on another occasion one of his accomplished disciples by the name of Anuruddha) did not simply opt out of the pain by entering a meditative condition known as the attainment of cessation. One who is in such an attainment no longer feels, so that entering this attainment would be a way of stopping painful feelings. Instead of adopting this mode of escaping from pain, however, the Buddha (and Anuruddha) decided instead to face pain with mindfulness.

The potential of mindfulness in facing the pain of disease has received widespread recognition in modern times. Particularly well-known in this respect is Mindfulness-based Stress Reduction. The basic principle in this approach appears to be the same as in the early Buddhist discourses, namely simply remaining aware of the pain with mindfulness as a more successful strategy than trying to distract oneself in one way or another.[4]

In the present passage, the challenge of facing disease comes together with the predicament of an old body that is kept going only with difficulty. According to the passage above, the Buddha's body was like an old cart kept going only by being patched up. In the modern setting one might think of a broken-down car that needs to be repaired and fixed continuously just to be able to drive a little further.

In this situation the Buddha opts for signless meditation as a way of easing the condition of his body. Signlessness, *animitta*, as a meditative practice requires not giving any attention to signs. Here a "sign", *nimitta*, is that by which one recognizes.[5] Ordinary experience involves the continuous activity of perception, which matches the raw data received by the senses with appropriate concepts and thereby enables its meaningful processing. By giving attention to signlessness, one no longer matches experience with concepts. The mind in a way steps back from its habitual involvement with experiencing.

A mental condition of signlessness as such does not necessarily imply that a level of awakening has been reached.[6] In the present case, however, it can safely be assumed that

4 Kabat-Zinn 1990/2013: 374.
5 See in more detail Anālayo 2015a: 136–43.
6 For a survey of signless meditations see Harvey 1986.

the Buddha's cultivation of signlessness was informed by his awakening realization of Nirvāṇa. One of the characteristics of the Nirvāṇa "experience", if it can be called such, is precisely signlessness (together with desirelessness and emptiness). On this understanding, a meditation that is based on a characteristic of Nirvāṇa, which the Buddha realized during the night of his awakening, furnished the appropriate medicine on this occasion of illness.

The *Mahāparinibbāna-sutta* and its Sanskrit fragment parallel agree with the passage translated above that the Buddha cultivated signlessness. The same holds for a parallel preserved as an individual translation, which mentions concentration without being aware of the multitude of signs. Another individual translation speaks of no longer giving mental attention to the condition of being "diseased", perhaps pointing to the same, in the sense that letting go of the perception of being sick eases a condition of illness.The parallels agree that the Buddha's physical condition improved. Thus the Buddha was able to patch up the old cart of his body and make it continue a bit longer.

The description that the Buddha would make an effort to maintain his body alive a little longer can be read alongside another episode, also found in the *Mahāparinibbāna-sutta* and its parallels, in which the Buddha deliberately let go of his life force. The narrative setting involves Māra, who approached the Buddha and reminded him of an earlier proclamation the Buddha had made. According to this earlier statement, the Buddha had said that he would not pass away until he had male and female disciples, both monastic and lay, who were sufficiently accomplished. This mission he had now completed. In the present episode, the Buddha in reply clarified that he would indeed pass away after a period of three months, whereupon Māra left. The *Dīrgha-āgama* continues in this way:[7]

---

7 The translation is based on DĀ 2 at T I 15c19 to 15c25, parallel to DN 16 at DN II 106,21 (translated Walshe 1987: 247), found again in SN 51.10 at SN V 262,21 (translated Bodhi 2000: 1725), AN 8.70 at AN IV 311,28 (translated Bodhi 2012: 1215), and Ud 6.1 at Ud 64,24 (translated Ireland 1990: 88), with parallels in Waldschmidt 1951: 212 (§16.14), T 5 at T I 165a23, T 6 at T I 180c6, and T 7 at T I 191c8; see also the *Divyāvadāna*, Cowell and Neil 1886: 203,7 (translated Rotman 2008: 340).

> Not long after Māra had left, being at the Capala shrine with a mind collected in concentration, the Buddha let go of his destiny to live a long life. Just at that time there was a great earthquake and in every country the people were all afraid such that the hair under their clothes stood on end. A great light came forth from the Buddha, shining penetratingly without limit, and all those in the dark realms were covered by brilliance so that they saw each other. Then the Blessed One said in verse:
>
> "What is" and "what is not" are both within [the domain of] formations,
> I now give up what is conditioned.
> Focused inwardly and collected in concentration,
> I am like a chick that emerges from its egg.

The narration continues with the Buddha explaining to Ānanda the different occasions when an earthquake can occur, which according to the traditional belief can mark special events in the life of a Buddha, including when he awakens, sets in motion the wheel of Dharma, gives up his life, and when he actually passes away.

In terms of the simile used earlier, the Buddha had decided no longer to patch up the old cart. His willingness to let go when the time for that had come puts into perspective his earlier efforts to keep himself alive. Clearly his earlier efforts were not motivated by any personal desire to stay alive, otherwise he would not have been ready to give up his life force on the present occasion. Read in conjunction, the two passages show the Buddha's inner freedom from attachment even in relation to what human beings cherish most: their own life. As long as this seemed meaningful, he kept the body going and continued teaching others. When the time had come to give up, he just let go of it all.

Another dimension of the Buddha's attitude towards death comes to the fore in relation to the passing away of others. In my study of what the early discourses have to offer for facing disease and death, I surveyed a range of passages that give advice on how to face one's own mortality and that of others, how to accompany those who are passing away, and how to face grief that arises when beloved ones succumb to the sweeping power of death.

In what follows I turn to another episode which reports the Buddha's reaction to the fact that his two chief disciples, Sāriputta and Mahāmoggallāna, have just passed away. Here is the first part of the *Saṃyukta-āgama* account:[8]

> At that time the Blessed One, having surveyed the community, said to the monastics: "Surveying the great community, I have seen it to be void, because Sāriputta and Mahāmoggallāna have [entered] final Nirvāṇa."

Clearly the Buddha is fully aware of the loss that has occurred and he openly addresses it. In both versions he continues by praising these two eminent disciples. This shows that mindful recognition of the loss that has taken place is there, but there is no grief. In fact the *Saṃyutta-nikāya* parallel explicitly states that the Buddha did not experience any grief. The same is implicit in the *Saṃyukta-āgama* account. In both versions the Buddha then continues by encouraging his disciples in the audience not to feel grief, keeping in mind that, whatever is of a nature to be born will inevitably pass away. The *Saṃyukta-āgama* version presents this advice as follows:[9]

> Monastics, do not give rise to sorrow and affliction. How could it be that, what is of a nature to be born, of a nature to arise, of a nature to be constructed, of a nature to be conditioned, of a nature to change, will not be obliterated? The wish to make it not be destroyed is for something that is impossible. Earlier I already told you: "Every one of the things that one can have affection towards will all come again to be lost." Now I myself will soon also pass away.
>
> For this reason you should know that by relying on yourself you have yourself as an island, by relying on the Dharma you have the Dharma as an island, having no other island and no other reliance.

---

8 The translated section is taken from SĀ 639 at T II 177a18 to 177a20, parallel to SN 47.14 at SN V 163,28 (translated Bodhi 2000: 1644).

9 The translated part is based on SĀ 639 at T II 177a27 to 177b7.

That is, be established in mindfulness by contemplating the body as a body internally, with energetic effort, right mindfulness, and clear comprehension, overcoming desire and discontent in the world. *Be established in mindfulness by contemplating the body* as a body externally, *with energetic effort, right mindfulness, and clear comprehension, overcoming desire and discontent in the world. Be established in mindfulness by contemplating the body* as a body internally and externally, *with energetic effort, right mindfulness, and clear comprehension, overcoming desire and discontent in the world.*

Be established in mindfulness by contemplating feelings *as feelings internally, with energetic effort, right mindfulness, and clear comprehension, overcoming desire and discontent in the world. Be established in mindfulness by contemplating feelings as feelings externally, with energetic effort, right mindfulness, and clear comprehension, overcoming desire and discontent in the world. Be established in mindfulness by contemplating feelings as feelings internally and externally, with energetic effort, right mindfulness, and clear comprehension, overcoming desire and discontent in the world.*

Be established in mindfulness by contemplating the mind *as mind internally, with energetic effort, right mindfulness, and clear comprehension, overcoming desire and discontent in the world. Be established in mindfulness by contemplating the mind as mind externally, with energetic effort, right mindfulness, and clear comprehension, overcoming desire and discontent in the world. Be established in mindfulness by contemplating the mind as mind internally and externally, with energetic effort, right mindfulness, and clear comprehension, overcoming desire and discontent in the world.*

Be established in mindfulness by contemplating dharmas as dharmas *internally, with energetic effort, right mindfulness, and clear comprehension, overcoming desire and discontent in the world. Be established in mindfulness by contemplating dharmas as dharmas externally, with energetic effort, right mindfulness, and clear comprehension, overcoming desire and discontent in the world. Be established in mindfulness by contemplating dharmas as dharmas internally and externally,* with energetic effort, right mindfulness, and clear comprehension, overcoming desire and discontent in the world.

This is called having yourself as an island by relying on yourself, having the Dharma as an island by relying on the Dharma, having no other island and no other reliance.

The *Saṃyutta-nikāya* version agrees in recommending that the disciples should become self-reliant by practising the four *satipaṭṭhāna*s, a minor difference being that it does not explicitly bring in the internal and external dimension of such mindfulness practice. The same can nevertheless safely be assumed to be implicit.

In this way the discourse on pain, grief, and death keeps coming back to one topic: become self-reliant through mindfulness. This is the practice that enables one to face disease and death, this is the best preparation for one's own last moments as well as for being with others who are sick or on the verge of death.

EXERCISE

As a practical exercise, I would like to bring in again the practice of mindfulness of the breath. In Chapter 7 I explored mindfulness of breathing in sixteen steps. Alternatively, mindfulness of the breath can also be yoked to awareness of our mortality as a way of preparing ourselves for what sooner or later will inevitably happen. As the discourse above states, how could what has been born and come into existence not change and eventually pass away? This holds for others; this holds for ourselves. The sooner we begin preparations for that final moment, the better we will be able to face it. In addition, the better we will be able to live now. By no longer ignoring our own mortality we gradually emerge from the need for all the suppressions and distractions usually employed to avoid the theme of death.

Elsewhere I have described this practice in more detail, hence in what follows I only delineate its main points.[10] The basic idea is to become mindful of the fact that our survival depends on a constant supply of oxygen through the process of breathing and that sooner or later this process will stop. Together with the certainty that it will stop comes the uncertainty about when this will happen, which could even be right in the next moment. In fact, death might be just one breath away from now.

Actual practice could be undertaken by relating this awareness of the precariousness of our own existence to awareness of the

10 Anālayo 2016b: 200–7.

inhalations in particular, whereas the exhalations could be made occasions for training ourselves in letting go. This allows balancing out the practice by giving more importance either to inhalations or to exhalations, depending on whether we are at a point where the mind needs to be energized or rather be made to relax.

To avoid facing our own mortality is a deeply ingrained habit. Going against this habit confronts ignorance head-on. Such confrontation will naturally lead to reactions, which can take the form of some degree of dullness in the mind, even leading to boredom. In such a case it is helpful to emphasize being in the present moment in order to restore clarity and liveliness to the practice. In the opposite case of fear and tension, emphasis on relaxing and letting go will help restore the lost balance.

Meditation practice undertaken in this way stands in close relationship to the reflection suggested in Chapter 1, where the task was to become aware of manifestations of old age, illness, and death throughout the day. From having established such all-round awareness, the task now is to make it indubitably clear to ourselves that our own body is most definitely of the same nature. A reflection recommended in the *Satipaṭṭhāna-sutta*, after having seen the corpse of another, is that this body of ours "is not exempt from that fate".[11]

Mindfulness of death has an immense transformative potential and can become a powerful mode of progressing towards the deathless, towards going completely beyond being affected by death through the full realization of Nirvāṇa.

---

11 Anālayo 2013b: 257.

XXIV

THE FINAL MEDITATION

In the present chapter I turn to the Buddha's last meditation, which forms the culmination of my exploration in the preceding chapters. A description of his meditative passing away can be found in the *Mahāparinibbāna-sutta* and its parallels. In what follows I translate the relevant part from the *Mahāparinirvāṇa-sūtra* preserved in Sanskrit fragments.[1]

> [The Buddha said]: "Indeed, monastics, cultivate silence. All formations are of a nature to decay." Such were the last words of the Tathāgata on that occasion.
>
> Having said this, the Blessed One attained the first absorption. Rising from the first absorption, he attained the second absorption. Rising from the second absorption, he attained the third absorption. Rising from the third absorption, he attained the fourth absorption.
>
> Rising from the fourth absorption, he attained the sphere of infinite space. Rising from the sphere of infinite space, he attained the sphere of infinite consciousness. Rising from the sphere of infinite consciousness, he attained the sphere of nothingness. Rising from the sphere of nothingness, he attained the sphere of

1 The translated passage is based on the edition by Waldschmidt 1951: 394–6 (§42.11–18), parallel to DN 16 at DN II 156,1 (translated Walshe 1987: 270), DĀ 2 at T I 26b19 (translated Anālayo 2016b: 194f), T 6 at T I 188b19, and T 7 at T I 205a2. For a comparative study of this episode see Waldschmidt 1948: 250–2 and Anālayo 2017c: 225–47.

neither-perception-nor-non-perception. Rising from the sphere of neither-perception-nor-non-perception, he attained the cessation of feeling and perception.

Then the venerable Ānanda said to the venerable Anuruddha: "Venerable Anuruddha, the Blessed One has [entered] final Nirvāṇa."

[The venerable Anuruddha replied]: "It is not like this, venerable Ānanda. The Buddha, the Blessed One, has attained the cessation of feeling and perception."

The venerable Ānanda said: "Venerable Anuruddha, [in fact] I heard it in the presence of the Blessed One, learning it from his own lips, that on having attained the fourth absorption, attaining the peace of imperturbability, those endowed with vision, Buddhas, Blessed Ones, [enter] final Nirvāṇa."

Then the Blessed One rose from the cessation of feeling and perception and attained the sphere of neither-perception-nor-non-perception. Rising from the sphere of neither-perception-nor-non-perception, he attained the sphere of nothingness. Rising from the sphere of nothingness, he attained the sphere of infinite consciousness. Rising from the sphere of infinite consciousness, he attained the sphere of infinite space.

Rising from the sphere of infinite space, he attained the fourth absorption. Rising from the fourth absorption, he attained the third absorption. Rising from the third absorption, he attained the second absorption. Rising from the second absorption, he attained the first absorption.

Rising from the first absorption, he attained the second absorption. Rising from the second absorption, he attained the third absorption. Rising from the third absorption, he attained the fourth absorption. Having attained the fourth absorption, endowed with vision, and with the peace of imperturbability attained, the Buddha, the Blessed One, [entered] final Nirvāṇa.

In my study *Mindfully Facing Disease and Death*, I translated the Chinese *Dīrgha-āgama* version of the Buddha's final words and meditation. There I proposed that key elements of this episode are a reminder of impermanence and the manifestation of meditative expertise and self-composure. Even on the eve of passing away, the Buddha was able to proceed through the whole range of concentrative attainments in forward and reverse order. From this viewpoint, the account of his final Nirvāṇa throws into relief the degree to which the Buddha had indeed reached the goal of his aspiration, taken up in the first chapter of the present book. Having reached complete liberation, his mind was unperturbed by the onset of death to such a degree that he was able to attain at will whatever level of concentrative depths he wished.

One might contextualize this description by noting how sometimes apprehensions of what is to come, even in relation to minor issues, can intrude on one's formal meditation session and unsettle the mind. Yet, as the present passage shows, by dint of practice the mind can evolve to a stage where even the onset of death no longer unsettles the mind. Such evolution stands in close relationship to insight into impermanence; in fact present-moment awareness of impermanence offers a powerful tool for facing one's own death.[2]

The texts do not associate such meditative mastery on the verge of death only with the Buddha. A discourse in the *Ekottarika-āgama*, with several parallels in Chinese translation as well as in the *Apadāna* collection, reports that the Buddha's foster mother Mahāpajāpatī Gotamī and her followers passed away in a comparable manner. In the remainder of this chapter I translate and study this account by way of complementing the account of the Buddha's decease. This also serves to make up for the inevitable focus on the Buddha as a male protagonist throughout this book by directing attention to portrayals of highly accomplished female saints.

According to the *Ekottarika-āgama*'s narration of what happened before the episode translated below, Mahāpajāpatī Gotamī had heard that the Buddha would soon pass away. She approached the Buddha and requested permission to precede him into final Nirvāṇa, which the Buddha readily granted. Having returned to the nunnery, she informed the other nuns of her intention to enter final Nirvāṇa. Having heard this, the other nuns also approached the Buddha and requested permission as well to precede him into final Nirvāṇa, which the Buddha again

2 See Anālayo 2016b: 240.

readily granted. Once the nuns had returned to the nunnery, Mahāpajāpatī Gotamī and her following of highly accomplished nuns entered final Nirvāṇa in the following way:[3]

> Then Mahāpajāpatī closed the door of the lecture hall, struck the gong, put down her sitting cloth in an open place, and soared up into the empty sky. [While] sitting, lying down, standing, and walking in the empty sky, [from her body] burning flames came out; from her lower body smoke came out; from her upper body fire came out; from her lower body water came out; from her upper body smoke came out; her whole body released flames; her whole body released smoke; from the left side of her upper body water came out; from the right side of her upper body fire came out; from the right side of her upper body water came out; from the left side of her upper body fire came out;[4] from the front [of her body] fire came out; from the back [of her body] water came out; from the front [of her body] water came out; from the back [of her body] fire came out; from her whole body fire came out; and from her whole body water came out.
>
> When Mahāpajāpatī had performed many transformations, she returned to her original seat to sit down cross-legged with straight body and straight mind, collecting mindfulness in front. She entered the first absorption. Rising from the first absorption, she entered the second absorption. Rising from the second absorption, she entered the third absorption. Rising from the third absorption, she entered the fourth absorption.
>
> Rising from the fourth absorption, she entered the sphere of [infinite] space. Rising from the sphere of [infinite] space, she entered the sphere of [infinite] consciousness. Rising from the sphere of [infinite] consciousness, she entered the sphere of nothingness. Rising from the sphere of nothingness, she entered the sphere of neither-perception-nor-non-perception. Rising from the sphere of neither-perception-nor-non-perception, she entered the cessation of perception and knowing.
>
> Rising from the cessation of perception and knowing, she

3 The translated text is taken from EĀ 52.1 at T II 822a3 to 822b3; a translation and a more detailed study, together with a survey of the parallel versions, can be found in Anālayo 2016a: 367–80; on the Mūlasarvāstivāda *Vinaya* version see Dhammadinnā 2015.

4 The translation is based on adopting the variant "fire" instead of "smoke".

entered the sphere of neither-perception-nor-non-perception. Rising from the sphere of neither-perception-nor-non-perception, she entered the sphere of nothingness. Rising from the sphere of nothingness, she entered the sphere of [infinite] consciousness. Rising from the sphere of [infinite] consciousness, she entered the sphere of [infinite] space. Rising from the sphere of [infinite] space, she entered the fourth absorption.

Rising from the fourth absorption, she entered the third absorption. Rising from the third absorption, she entered the second absorption. Rising from the second absorption, she entered the first absorption.

Rising from the first absorption, she entered the second absorption. Rising from the second absorption, she entered the third absorption. Rising from the third absorption, she entered the fourth absorption. Having entered the fourth absorption, she in turn entered complete extinction.

At that time there was a great earthquake in the world. The east rose up and the west sank down, the west rose up and the east sank down. The four sides rose up and the centre sank down, and on all four sides a cool breeze arose. [Some] devas in the sky danced and made music. [Some] devas of the sensual sphere were crying in grief, which was like a timely rain that falls from the sky in a month of the spring season. The sublime devas scattered various lotus fragrances and various [kinds of] sandalwood powder on her [body].

At that time the nun Khemā, the nun Uppalavaṇṇā, the nun Kisāgotamī, the nun Sakulā, the nun Sāmā, the nun Paṭācārā, the nun [Bhaddā] Kaccānā, the nun [Vi]jayā, being at the head of the five hundred nuns, each put down their sitting cloths in an open place and soared up into the empty sky.

[While] sitting, lying down, standing, and walking in the empty sky,[5] *from their bodies burning flames came out; from their lower bodies smoke came out; from their upper bodies fire came out; from their lower bodies water came out; from their upper bodies smoke came out; their whole bodies released flames; their whole bodies released smoke; from*

5 EĀ 52.1 at T II 822b2 abbreviates and just mentions that "they performed eighteen transformations", after which the text indicates that the ensuing meditative progression should be supplemented up to their final Nirvāṇa, including their attainment of the cessation of perception and knowing.

the left side of their upper bodies water came out; from the right side of their upper bodies fire came out; from the right side of their upper bodies water came out; from the left side of their upper bodies fire came out; from the front of their bodies fire came out; from the back of their bodies water came out; from the front of their bodies water came out; from the back of their bodies fire came out; from their whole bodies fire came out; and from their whole bodies water came out.

When they had performed many transformations, they returned to their original seats to sit down cross-legged with straight body and straight mind, collecting mindfulness in front. They entered the first absorption. Rising from the first absorption, they entered the second absorption. Rising from the second absorption, they entered the third absorption. Rising from the third absorption, they entered the fourth absorption.

Rising from the fourth absorption, they entered the sphere of infinite space. Rising from the sphere of infinite space, they entered the sphere of infinite consciousness. Rising from the sphere of infinite consciousness, they entered the sphere of nothingness. Rising from the sphere of nothingness, they entered the sphere of neither-perception-nor-non-perception. Rising from the sphere of neither-perception-nor-non-perception, they entered the cessation of perception and knowing.

Rising from the cessation of perception and knowing, they entered the sphere of neither-perception-nor-non-perception. Rising from the sphere of neither-perception-nor-non-perception, they entered the sphere of nothingness. Rising from the sphere of nothingness, they entered the sphere of infinite consciousness. Rising from the sphere of infinite consciousness, they entered the sphere of infinite space. Rising from the sphere of infinite space, they entered the fourth absorption.

Rising from the fourth absorption, they entered the third absorption. Rising from the third absorption, they entered the second absorption. Rising from the second absorption, they entered the first absorption.

Rising from the first absorption, they entered the second absorption. Rising from the second absorption, they entered the third absorption. Rising from the third absorption, they entered the fourth absorption. Having entered the fourth absorption, each of them in turn entered complete extinction.

According to the above *Ekottarika-āgama* passage, Mahāpajāpatī Gotamī and her following of nuns performed the twin miracle before passing away. The twin miracle requires the simultaneous manifestation of fire and water, a feat that according to the Theravāda tradition only a Buddha can perform.[6] Although the *Apadāna* parallel to the above passage does not involve an actual performance of the twin miracle, it does report that Mahāpajāpatī Gotamī manifested fire and water, with the difference that these manifestations did not take place simultaneously.[7] Another difference is that the *Apadāna* does not mention the attainment of cessation, so that in its account Mahāpajāpatī Gotamī's meditative tour before passing away only proceeds up to the sphere of neither-perception-nor-non-perception.[8]

Nevertheless, the *Apadāna* notes that her passing away was even more remarkable than that of the Buddha.[9] Moreover, according to the *Apadāna* account the Buddha had explicitly requested that Mahāpajāpatī Gotamī perform supernormal feats, which she should do to dispel the view of those foolish ones who doubt that women can reach full realization of the Dharma.[10]

Mahāpajāpatī Gotamī's spectacular passing away throws into relief the same basic quality of complete meditative expertise and self-composure as manifest in the Buddha's final meditation. Her mind was just as unperturbed by the prospect of death as the mind of the Buddha. The same also holds for her following of nuns, mentioned in the passage translated above. This highlights the degree to which through meditation practice the mind can evolve to a stage where even the onset of death is no longer unsettling and one maintains one's meditative ability and equipoise unperturbed up to one's very last breath. It also

---

6 See the discussion in Skilling 1997: 303–15 and Dhammadinnā 2015: 42–5; on the twin miracle in general see also Anālayo 2009.

7 Ap 17.85+88 at Ap 536,7 (translated Walters 1995: 127) and Thī-a 146,3 (translated Pruitt 1998/1999: 193).

8 Ap 17.146 at Ap 540,10 and Thī-a 151,4.

9 Ap 17.173 at Ap 542,13 and Thī-a 153,13. Shaw 2006/2007: 151 explains that "her achievements exceeded those of Shakyamuni in one area, for the Buddha was not followed into parinirvāṇa by any of his disciples, whereas five hundred of Gotamī's congregation of nuns ... accompanied her on her final journey."

10 Ap 17.79 at Ap 535,24 and Thī-a 145,13. Dhirasekera 1967: 157 comments that "when Mahapajapati Gotami visits the Buddha to bid him farewell, he calls upon her to give proof of the religious attainments of the Bhikkhunis in order to convince the disbelieving sceptics."

shows the remarkable extent to which these female disciples had been able to emulate the supreme inner balance and freedom of the Buddha.

Regarding the nuns mentioned by name in the passage translated above, according to the listing of outstanding nuns in the *Aṅguttara-nikāya* and its parallel in the *Ekottarika-āgama*, Khemā was foremost in wisdom just as Uppalavaṇṇā was foremost in supernormal powers.[11] Kisāgotamī was an eminent practitioner of asceticism and Sakulā was outstanding in the exercise of the divine eye. The *Ekottarika-āgama* version reckons Sāmā as exceptional in the ability to enter concentration without her mind being scattered. According to both versions, Paṭācārā was renowned for upholding the monastic discipline. The *Aṅguttara-nikāya* list of outstanding nuns considers Bhaddā Kaccānā eminent in supernormal knowledge, whereas its *Ekottarika-āgama* parallel praises her for being liberated by confidence or faith. The *Ekottarika-āgama* list presents Vijayā as particularly apt in the analytical knowledges (*paṭisambhidā*).

These nuns, mentioned by name from the substantial group (literally "five hundred") that followed Mahāpajāpatī Gotamī's example, embodied a range of exceptional qualities. These span from wisdom and analytical knowledge to supernormal powers and deep concentration, together with asceticism and upholding the monastic discipline. For any of these nuns to be reckoned eminent in respect to one of these qualities, there must have been a number of other nuns who also cultivated the same quality, albeit not to the high degree of perfection attained by those mentioned above.

Alongside this impressive display of various role models of female sainthood, the passage translated above also drives home again the truth of impermanence. Just as the Buddha passed away, so too these eminent female disciples all have passed away. "All formations are of a nature to decay."

---

11 My indications here and in what follows are based on the listing of outstanding nuns in the *Aṅguttara-nikāya* and the *Ekottarika-āgama*, AN 1.14.5 at AN I 25,17 (translated Bodhi 2012: 111, referred to as the "fifth subchapter") and EĀ 5.1 to 5.5 at T II 558c20 (translated and studied in Anālayo 2016a: 301–24). For a detailed study of several of these nuns see also Collett 2016.

EXERCISE

As a practical exercise I would like to recommend recollecting the Community of Noble Disciples using as example Mahāpajāpatī Gotamī or any of the eminent nuns mentioned in the passage above. The purpose of such recollection is to give attention to particularly inspiring qualities as a way of rousing inspiration and encouraging our own cultivation of the same qualities. By inviting even my male readers to undertake this type of recollection with the help of one of the female saints of early Buddhism, I hope to make up to some extent for the inevitable focus on a male protagonist in a book concerned with aspects of the life of the Buddha.

Needless to say, the final aim of practice is to go beyond gendered notions. In order to do so, however, for males it can be helpful to put themselves at least once into the situation that females experience with depressing regularity in Buddhist texts and traditions, due to the overall tendency to prioritize male role models.

In the end, however, whether embodied by a male or a female, the qualities of an awakened one as such are what really counts. Here neither gender nor race etc. is of any relevance. The possibility to awaken is open to all those who seriously dedicate themselves to the appropriate practices. In times of difficulty and struggle it can be helpful to recollect our own potential in this respect, and perhaps also that, as amply shown by the different abilities of the accomplished nuns, each of us has a particular strength on which we can rely. Even though we might feel at times far away from the final goal of full liberation from all defilements, certainly there must be at least one quality related to progress to awakening on which we can count. Recollecting this quality can serve as a bridge between ourselves and the Community of Noble Disciples.

CONCLUSION

As mentioned briefly in Chapter 19, bringing to mind the Buddha with the help of a series of epithets or qualities is already attested in the early discourses.[1] Reflecting on and reciting such epithets is the traditional form of recollection of the Buddha.[2] As a way of further enriching ways of making the Buddha a presence in one's life, in addition to the traditional approach, the foregoing twenty-four chapters of my exploration are meant as an invitation to engage in various meditation practices related to the Buddha. Several exercises in the previous chapters are also related to the other five out of the standard set of six recollections. The whole set of six takes the following objects:

- the Buddha,
- the Dharma taught by the Buddha,
- the Community of Noble Disciples of the Buddha,
- one's own accomplishment in morality,
- one's own accomplishment in generosity,
- one's own accomplishment in qualities that are similar to those of *deva*s.

Recollection of the Buddha forms a continuous theme throughout the preceding chapters. Recollection of the Dharma came up in Chapter 18, recollection of the Community in Chapter 24,

1 See above p. 173–4.

2 A detailed exegesis on the standard epithets employed for such recollection can be found in Vism 198,1 (translated Ñāṇamoli 1991: 192ff).

recollection of morality in Chapter 2, recollection of generosity in Chapter 8, and recollection of *deva*s in Chapter 4.

The function of recollection of the Buddha, a central theme in my exploration, can be illustrated with a passage that involves Mahānāma, who had just heard that the Buddha and his monastic disciples were about to depart, after having completed the rainy-season retreat. According to the *Saṃyukta-āgama* account, he approached the Buddha and stated the following:[3]

> "Blessed One, I am no [longer] in control of my four limbs, I am losing the [sense of the] four directions, and I am forgetting the teachings I have learned, as I heard from a group of many monastics who had assembled in the refectory to sew the Blessed One's robes that soon the Blessed One, the rainy-season retreat being completed and his robes having been made, will take his robes and bowl to journey among the people. For this reason now I am reflecting: 'When will I get to see the Blessed One again and the monastics with whom I am acquainted?'"
>
> The Buddha said to Mahānāma: "Whether you see the Blessed One or you do not see the Blessed One, see the monastics with whom you are acquainted or do not see them, you should just be mindful of five qualities and make an effort to cultivate them.
>
> "Mahānāma, you should rely on giving precedence to right confidence, not absence of right confidence, be endowed with morality, endowed with learning, endowed with generosity, and endowed with wisdom as being essential, not being without wisdom. In this way, Mahānāma, in reliance on these five qualities, you [should] cultivate the six recollections."

In the Pāli version Mahānāma just asks for advice and does not describe his apprehensions regarding the Buddha's impending departure in a comparable manner. In a version of the present discourse in the partially preserved *Saṃyukta-āgama*, however, he similarly expresses his dismay. The description in these two versions serves to highlight a basic predicament: how to make the Buddha a presence in one's life when he is not there?

---

3 The translated section is taken from SĀ 932 at T II 238b15 to 238b24, parallel to AN 11.12 at AN V 328,19 (translated Bodhi 2012: 1564) and SĀ[2] 157 at T II 433b16.

The Buddha's reply shifts attention to qualities that Mahānāma can cultivate within himself. The Pāli version's set of such qualities differs, as it lists the five faculties of confidence, energy, mindfulness, concentration, and wisdom. The somewhat different listings thus agree on confidence and wisdom as the foundation for practising the six recollections. It is particularly noteworthy that wisdom serves as a foundation in this respect, showing that in early Buddhist thought the practice of recollection is considered as something that bears a relation to wisdom.

Regarding confidence or faith as a faculty, another discourse in the *Saṃyukta-āgama* offers the following definition:[4]

> What is the faculty of confidence? Here a noble disciple has gained in the mind serene confidence in the Tathāgata's awakened mind.

Although this discourse does not seem to have a Pāli parallel,[5] a comparable phrase can be found in a number of other Pāli discourses,[6] which also speak of having confidence in the awakening of the Tathāgata.

A crucial ingredient required for engaging in the actual practice of the liberating teachings is precisely some degree of confidence that the Buddha indeed realized awakening.[7] The five companions from his ascetic times at first lacked such confidence and it took some convincing on the part of the Buddha for them to acquire sufficient trust to be willing to listen to him.

---

4 The translation is based on SĀ 659 at T II 184a10 to 184a12. Notably, this discourse relates all of the faculties to the Buddha's awakening.

5 SN 48.50 seems too different from SĀ 659 to be reckoned a parallel properly speaking.

6 The Pāli phrase is *saddahati tathāgatassa bodhiṃ*. Here is just a single example from each of the four *Nikāyas*: DN 33 at DN III 237,6 (translated Walshe 1987: 496), MN 53 at MN I 356,2 (translated Ñāṇamoli 1995/2005: 462), SN 48.9 at SN V 196,26 (translated Bodhi 2000: 1671), and AN 4.61 at AN II 66,22 (translated Bodhi 2012: 449).

7 Gethin 2016: 185 explains that "Buddhist texts understand faith in the Buddha, Dharma and Sangha not so much as a question of belief that certain propositions about the world are true, [but] as a trust, confidence, affection, and devotion inspired by the person of the Buddha, his teachings and followers – a confidence that there is indeed a path leading to the cessation of suffering which has been walked by the Buddha and at least some of his followers."

In modern times the notion that asceticism is a requirement for being able to awaken is no longer of such general appeal as it appears to have been for the Buddha's five companions. Therefore to acquire the basic confidence in the Buddha's awakening is not so much a matter of having to accept that awakening does not require ascetic practices. However, other obstructions to granting the minimum of initial trust to be able to dedicate oneself to the actual practice present themselves. One example is the belief that awakening is no longer possible nowadays, that this was only an option to be pursued in ancient times. Another example is a tendency to reinterpret descriptions of awakening and the realization of Nirvāṇa in rather mundane terms, assuming that they merely stand for a momentary experience of ease rather than a thorough transformation of the mind that culminates in a condition of total absence of defilements. Such assumptions can easily become a self-fulfilling prophecy, as the very lack of confidence in the possibility of awakening will stop one from pursuing the practices that can lead to awakening.

When the Buddha himself set out on his quest, there was no one who could have served as an example in which to place such trust. He could only have had the confidence in the very possibility of awakening. Even that much was sufficient to sustain him in his prolonged quest, which eventually led him to the final goal.

His disciples from ancient to modern times are in a more fortunate position, since they have predecessors to look up to. Of course, this is first and foremost the Buddha himself, but also any of his disciples who have reached one of the four levels of awakening. Each of the Buddha's awakened disciples, past, present, and future, is a corroboration of the fact that it is meaningful to place one's confidence in the Buddha's awakening. Such initial trust is what enables one to engage seriously in the path of practice, which on being undertaken properly will sooner or later show results that corroborate to oneself that this is indeed a path of increasing inner freedom from detrimental habits, a mode of practice that is for one's own welfare and that of others. With this personal and direct corroboration gained, one's confidence in the Buddha's awakening becomes strengthened in turn, until one eventually realizes one of the levels of awakening oneself. At that point, one's confidence has become unshakeable. It has become unshakeable simply because by now one knows for oneself.

Regarding the above discourse to Mahānāma, a central message would be that, being unable to meet the living Buddha, one can fill the resultant absence by cultivating central qualities he recommended, especially confidence in the possibility of awakening and the type of wisdom that leads to it. Based on this foundation one then recollects him as well as his teaching, those who follow his teaching, etc., that is, one engages in the six recollections.

A passage in another discourse in the *Aṅguttara-nikāya* sets such meditative practice within the context of the natural tendency of the human mind to recollect things. Although no parallel to this discourse has been preserved in the Chinese *Āgamas*, a parallel can be found as a discourse quotation in the *Saṅgītiparyāya*, which proceeds as follows:[8]

> Here certain types of person recollect wife and children, or recollect wealth, or recollect relatives, or recollect recluses and brahmins who have developed wrong view, who cultivate wrong view, or their wrong teachings. Although they do recollect – it is not that they do not recollect – I say that such types [of recollection] are of an inferior nature and worldly, it is not an ennobling recollection.
>
> If one cultivates and establishes pure confidence and affection, being able to recollect the Tathāgata and the Buddha's disciples, I say that such types of recollection are supreme, one is capable of benefiting oneself, capable of being at ease oneself, capable of making oneself dwell with one's whole being at peace, transcending the worries caused by misfortune and extinguishing all distress and affliction, being quickly able to realize and gain the truth of the essential teachings. This is called the supreme recollection.

The *Aṅguttara-nikāya* parallel applies to this type of recollection the same phrase used in the *Satipaṭṭhāna-sutta* for the four *satipaṭṭhāna*s, according to which these serve "for the purification

8 The translated section is taken from T 1536 at T XXVI 433c26 to 434a4 (see Stache-Rosen 1968: 173), parallel to AN 6.30 at AN III 328,26 (translated Bodhi 2012: 894).

of beings, for the surmounting of sorrow and lamentation, for the disappearance of *dukkha* and discontent, for acquiring the right method, for the realization of Nirvāṇa".[9] Although in the present case it is only the Pāli version which makes such an indication, another discourse in the *Saṃyukta-āgama* does introduce the practice of recollection as the "direct path" for the purification of beings, thereby using the counterpart to the expression with which the *Satipaṭṭhāna-sutta* introduces the four *satipaṭṭhānas*.[10] In short, these discourses present recollection of the Buddha and his disciples in terms similar to the potential they accord to *satipaṭṭhāna* meditation.

The contrast set in the present passage between worldly types of recollection and the commendable form of practice that takes the Buddha or his disciples as objects conveys the sense that, with this mode of meditation, a natural tendency of the mind is put to good use. It is natural for the mind to recollect things, to have fond memories of one's possessions and family members, etc. This propensity of the mind can be harnessed to progress to liberation simply by being directed towards a suitable object of the mind. In the form of the six recollections, this inclination of the mind to reminisce can become a vehicle for advancing to the final goal.

Another point worthy of note is that the present passage, in line with the reference to wisdom already mentioned above, hints at the insight potential of the practice of recollection with its reference to realizing the truth of the teachings. How the practice of recollecting the Buddha can become a vehicle for insight can be seen in another discourse to Mahānāma in the *Aṅguttara-nikāya* and its parallels. Here is the relevant part from the *Saṃyukta-āgama* version:[11]

---

9 MN 10 at MN I 55,31 (translated Anālayo 2013b: 253).

10 SĀ 550 at T II 143b22; on the peculiar translation employed in this discourse for the "direct path" see the discussion in Nattier 2007: 187f. The parallel AN 6.26 at AN III 314,22 (translated Bodhi 2012: 885) does not use the phrase *ekāyano maggo*, but has the remainder of the statement found also in AN 6.30; a parallel extant in a Sanskrit fragment, MS 2380/1/1+2 recto1, Harrison 2007: 202, has preserved *ekāyano mārgaḥ*.

11 The translation is based on SĀ 931 at T II 237c21 to 237c29, parallel to AN 6.10 at AN III 285,3 (translated Bodhi 2012: 862), SHT IV 623 folio 40R, Sander and Waldschmidt 1980: 256, and SĀ[2] 156 at T II 432c10.

> A noble disciple recollects with the Tathāgata as the object: "The Tathāgata is an arahant, fully awakened, endowed with knowledge and conduct, a well-gone one, a knower of the world, a supreme person, a tamer of persons, a teacher of devas and humans, a Buddha, a Blessed One."
>
> At the time of recollecting in this way, the noble disciple does not give rise to the entanglement of lustful desires and does not give rise to a mind of anger or delusion. That mind is straight and upright, having reached the significance of the Tathāgata and reached [the significance of] the right teachings of the Tathāgata. The mind gains delight in relation to the Tathāgata and in relation to the right teachings of the Tathāgata. The mind having become delighted, it becomes joyful. Having become joyful, the body is pleasantly calm. The body having become pleasantly calm, one experiences happiness. The mind of one having experienced happiness becomes concentrated. The mind having become concentrated, the noble disciple, [even] being among ferocious living beings, is not obstructed and has entered the stream of Dharma up to Nirvāṇa.

In a way this is a mode of overcoming the hindrances that circumvents them, rather than confronting them head-on, and by dint of the inner joy that comes from recollection easily leads over to the type of happiness and tranquillity that can then be harnessed to progress to liberating insight.

EXERCISE

A basic practice that sums up not only the present chapter but in a way this whole book is simply to make the Buddha a presence in our life. Through the selected aspects of his conduct and his qualities explored in the previous chapters, it becomes possible to develop some degree of familiarity with him, and based on such familiarity we can recollect him and perhaps pose ourselves questions like: "In this situation, what would the Buddha have done?" or else: "What would the Buddha recommend I do in this type of condition; what would he approve of?"

By way of support for such enquiry, the exercises described in the preceding chapters can be combined. In what follows I present just one possible way of joining these exercises, in the hope that this will stimulate the creativity of practitioners to find their own way of bringing some or all of them together (or devising their own exercises, based on relevant canonical passages) in the way best suited to their inclinations and needs. The key aspect is simply to undertake various practices in awareness of the fact that these bear a relation to the Buddha. By engaging in these practices, in one way or another we follow in his footsteps. The joy and inspiration that can arise from such reflection have the potential, as the discourse to Mahānāma translated above shows, to become a vehicle for progress to liberation.

As a starting point, a foundational reflection for anything we decide to do could be the simple question: "Does what I am about to do lead to *dukkha* or away from it?" (Chapter 16). Whenever challenges arise in our interactions with others, recollecting our morality (Chapter 2) can become a powerful support for withstanding the temptation of doing what is not wholesome. The same can also be accomplished by recollecting other accomplished practitioners whose example we would like to follow (Chapter 24).

Special challenges can be faced by becoming aware of space in front of ourselves and thereby broadening our mental condition (Chapter 21), employing this as an entry door into emptiness (Chapter 5), or alternatively by creating inner distance through attending to the reciprocal interrelationship between consciousness and name-and-form (Chapter 12). Any success we have with such practice serves to corroborate that the Dharma is indeed directly visible and can be experienced here and now (Chapter 18).

Eating can become an occasion for cultivating contentment (Chapter 8). This can lead over to mindfulness in relation to various daily activities (Chapter 22). Any such activity can serve as an opportunity to become aware of the subtle mental pleasure of being in the present moment (Chapter 10). Throughout the day, a clear distinction between wholesome and unwholesome thoughts, recalled briefly during moments that allow even a split second's time of introspection, builds up familiarity with what happens in our own mind (Chapter 3). Should the mind be overwhelmed by one of the hindrances, we can employ one of five methods to come out of obsessive thoughts (Chapter 6). When the mind is no longer overwhelmed by the hindrances, this can be made an occasion for arousing the joy of seeing the mind free from the hindrances (Chapter 4), and the conscious cultivation of such joy can become an integral part of our path in any situation (Chapter 9).

A clear formulation of our motivation (Chapter 1), ideally in a form that gives room to compassion (Chapter 14), could be recollected every time we start formal meditation practice (Chapter 10). Such formal meditation could begin with the *brahmavihāra*s up to equanimity (Chapter 19). This could then be followed by the sixteen steps of mindfulness of breathing (Chapter 7), the practice which the Buddha himself appears to have favoured. The breath on its own can also serve to recollect death (Chapter 23). The sixteen steps, however, are a mode of bringing into being all four *satipaṭṭhāna*s (Chapter 11). These can profitably be used as a basis for arousing and cultivating the awakening factors in dependence on seclusion, dispassion, and cessation, leading to letting go (Chapter 13), based on finely balancing these factors with each other (Chapter 15). In this way we increasingly learn to let go of all our attachments (Chapter 20) and the mind inclines ever more towards Nirvāṇa (Chapter 17), the supreme happiness, peace, and freedom.

REFERENCES

Allon, Mark 2001: *Three Gāndhārī Ekottarikāgama-type sūtras, British Library Kharoṣṭhī Fragments 12 and 14*, Seattle: University of Washington Press.

Anālayo 2003a: *Satipaṭṭhāna, the Direct Path to Realization*, Birmingham: Windhorse Publications.

— 2003b: "Nimitta", in *Encyclopaedia of Buddhism*, W.G. Weeraratne (ed.), 7/1: 177–9, Sri Lanka: Department of Buddhist Affairs.

— 2009: "Yamakapāṭihāriya", in *Encyclopaedia of Buddhism*, W.G. Weeraratne (ed.), 8/3: 776–7, Sri Lanka: Department of Buddhist Affairs.

— 2010: *The Genesis of the Bodhisattva Ideal*, Hamburg: Hamburg University Press.

— 2011: *A Comparative Study of the Majjhima-nikāya*, Taipei: Dharma Drum Publishing Corporation.

— 2012a: *Excursions into the Thought-world of the Pāli Discourses*, Washington: Pariyatti.

— 2012b: *Madhyama-āgama Studies*, Taipei: Dharma Drum Publishing Corporation.

— 2012c: "On the Five Aggregates (1) – A Translation of Saṃyukta-āgama Discourses 1 to 32", *Dharma Drum Journal of Buddhist Studies*, 11: 1–61.

— 2013a: "On the Five Aggregates (3) – A Translation of Saṃyukta-āgama Discourses 59 to 87", *Dharma Drum Journal of Buddhist Studies*, 13: 1–65.

— 2013b: *Perspectives on Satipaṭṭhāna*, Cambridge: Windhorse Publications.

— 2014a: "On the Five Aggregates (4) – A Translation of Saṃyukta-āgama Discourses 33 to 58", *Dharma Drum Journal of Buddhist Studies*, 14: 1–71.

— 2014b: "On the Five Aggregates (5) – A Translation of Saṃyukta-āgama Discourses 103 to 110", *Dharma Drum Journal of Buddhist Studies*, 15: 1–64.

— 2015a: *Compassion and Emptiness in Early Budddhist Meditation*, Cambridge: Windhorse Publications.

— 2015b: *Saṃyukta-āgama Studies*, Taipei: Dharma Drum Publishing Corporation.
— 2016a: *Ekottarika-āgama Studies*, Taipei: Dharma Drum Publishing Corporation.
— 2016b: *Mindfully Facing Disease and Death, Compassionate Advice from Early Buddhist Texts*, Cambridge: Windhorse Publications.
— 2016c: "On the Six Sense-spheres (1) – A Translation of Saṃyukta-āgama Discourses 188 to 229 (Fascicle 8)", *Dharma Drum Journal of Buddhist Studies*, 18: 1–61.
— 2017a: *Buddhapada and the Bodhisattva Path*, Bochum: Projekt Verlag.
— 2017b: *Early Buddhist Meditation Studies*, Barre: Barre Center for Buddhist Studies.
— 2017c: *Dīrgha-āgama Studies*, Taipei: Dharma Drum Publishing Corporation.
— 2017d: "Some Renditions of the Term Tathāgata in the Chinese Āgamas", *Annual Report of the International Research Institute for Advanced Buddhology at Soka University*, 20: 11–21.
— 2017e: *Vinaya Studies*, Taipei: Dharma Drum Publishing Corporation.
— forthcoming: *Mindfulness of Breathing, A Practice Guide, Study and Translations.*
Balk, Michael 1984: *Prajñāvarman's Udānavargavivaraṇa, Transliteration of Its Tibetan Version (Based on the Xylographs of Chone/Derge and Peking)*, Bonn: Indica et Tibetica.
Bapat, P.V. 1950 (part 1): "The Arthapada-sūtra Spoken by the Buddha", *Visva-Bharati Annals*, 3: 1–109.
Bareau, André 1963: *Recherches sur la biographie du Buddha dans les Sūtrapiṭaka et les Vinayapiṭaka anciens: de la quête de l'éveil à la conversion de Śāriputra et de Maudgalyāyana*, Paris: École Française d'Extrême-Orient.
— 1974: "La jeunesse du Buddha dans les Sūtrapiṭaka et les Vinayapiṭaka anciens", *Bulletin de l'École Française d'Extrême-Orient*, 61: 199–274.
— 1988: "Les débuts de la prédication du Buddha selon l'Ekottara-āgama", *Bulletin de l'École Française d'Extrême-Orient*, 77: 69–96.
Bernhard, Franz 1965 (vol. 1): *Udānavarga*, Göttingen: Vandenhoeck & Ruprecht.
Bingenheimer, Marcus 2011: *Studies in Āgama Literature, with Special Reference to the Shorter Chinese Saṃyuktāgama*, Taiwan: Shin Weng Feng Print Co.
Bingenheimer, Marcus, Bh. Anālayo, and R. Bucknell 2013 (vol. 1): *The Madhyama Āgama (Middle Length Discourses)*, Berkeley: Numata Center for Buddhist Translation and Research.
Blomfield, Vishvapani 2011: *Gautama Buddha, The Life and Teachings of the Awakened One*, London: Quercus.
Bodhi, Bhikkhu 1980: *Transcendental Dependent Arising, A Translation and Exposition of the Upanisa Sutta*, Kandy: Buddhist Publication Society.

— 2000: *The Connected Discourses of the Buddha, A New Translation of the Saṃyutta Nikāya*, Boston: Wisdom Publications.

— 2012: *The Numerical Discourses of the Buddha, A Translation of the Aṅguttara Nikāya*, Boston: Wisdom Publications.

— 2017: *The Suttanipāta: A Collection of the Buddha's Discourses Together with Its Commentaries*, Boston: Wisdom Publications.

Bongard-Levin, Grigorij Maksimovic, D. Boucher, T. Fukita, and K. Wille 1996: "The Nagaropamasūtra: An Apotropaic Text from the Saṃyuktāgama, A Transliteration, Reconstruction, and Translation of the Central Asian Sanskrit Manuscripts", in *Sanskrit-Texte aus dem buddhistischen Kanon, Folge 3*, 7–103, Göttingen: Vandenhoeck & Ruprecht.

Bopearachchi, Osmund 2016: *Seven Weeks after the Buddha's Enlightenment, Contradictions in Text, Confusions in Art*, New Delhi: Manohar.

Boucher, Daniel 2008: *Bodhisattvas of the Forest and the Formation of the Mahāyāna, A Study and Translation of the Rāṣṭrapālaparipṛcchā-sūtra*, Honolulu: University of Hawai'i Press.

Brahm, Ajahn 2006: *Mindfulness, Bliss, and Beyond, A Meditator's Handbook*, Boston: Wisdom Publications.

Bronkhorst, Johannes 1993/2000: *The Two Traditions of Meditation in Ancient India*, Delhi: Motilal Banarsidass.

Carrithers, Michael 1983: *The Buddha*, Oxford: Oxford University Press.

Chung, Jin-il and T. Fukita 2011: *A Survey of the Sanskrit Fragments Corresponding to the Chinese Madhyamāgama, Including References to Sanskrit Parallels, Citations, Numerical Categories of Doctrinal Concepts and Stock Phrases*, Tokyo: Sankibo Press.

Collett, Alice 2016: *Lives of Early Buddhist Nuns: Biographies as History*, Delhi: Oxford University Press.

Cone, Margaret 1989: "Patna Dharmapada", *Journal of the Pali Text Society*, 13: 101–217.

Coomaraswamy, Ananda K. 1916: *Buddha and the Gospel of Buddhism*, New York: Harper Torchbooks.

Cousins, L.S. 1973: "Buddhist jhāna: Its Nature and Attainment According to the Pali Sources", *Religion*, 3: 115–31.

Cowell, E.B. 1895/2000 (vol. 1): *The Jātaka or Stories of the Buddha's Former Births, Translated from the Pāli by Various Hands*, Delhi: Asian Educational Services.

Cowell, E.B. and R.A. Neil 1886: *The Divyāvadāna, A Collection of Early Buddhist Legends, Now First Edited from the Nepalese Sanskrit Mss. in Cambridge and Paris*, Cambridge: Cambridge University Press.

de Silva, Lily 1987: "The Buddha and the Arahant Compared (A Study Based on the Pali Canon)", in *Pratidāna Mañjarī, Papers on Buddhism and Sri Lankan Studies in Commemoration of Gate Mudaliyar W.F. Gunawardhana*, M.H.F. Jayasuriya (ed.), 37–52, Dehiwala: Gate Mudaliyar W.F. Gunawardhana Commemoration Committee.

Dhammadinnā, Bhikkhunī 2015: "The Parinirvāṇa of Mahāprajāpatī Gautamī and Her Followers in the Mūlasarvāstivāda Vinaya", *Indian International Journal of Buddhist Studies*, 16: 29–61.

Dhirasekera, Jotiya 1967: "Women and the Religious Order of the Buddha", *The Maha Bodhi*, 75/5/6: 154–61.

Durt, Hubert 1982: "La 'visite aux laboureurs' et la 'méditation sous l'arbre jambu' dans les biographies sanskrites et chinoises du Buddha", in *Indological and Buddhist Studies, Volume in Honour of Professor J.W. de Jong on His 60th Birthday*, L.A. Hercus (ed.), 95–120, Canberra: Faculty of Asian Studies.

Dutoit, Julius 1905: *Die duṣkaracaryā des Bodhisattva in der buddhistischen Tradition*, Strasburg: Karl J. Trübner.

Dutt, Nalinaksha 1940: "Place of Faith in Buddhism", *Indian Historical Quarterly*, 639–46.

Enomoto, Fumio 1989: "Śarīrārthagāthā, A Collection of Canonical Verses in the Yogācārabhūmi", in *Sanskrit-Texte aus dem Buddhistischen Kanon: Neuentdeckungen und Neueditionen Folge 1*, 1: 17–35, Göttingen: Vandenhoeck & Ruprecht.

Foucher, Alfred 1949: *La vie du Bouddha, d'après les textes et les monuments de l'Inde*, Paris: Payot.

Freiberger, Oliver 2006: "Early Buddhism, Asceticism, and the Politics of the Middle Way", in *Asceticism and Its Critics: Historical Accounts and Comparative Perspectives*, O. Freiberger (ed.), 235–58, New York: Oxford University Press.

Gethin, Rupert 1997: "Cosmology and Meditation: From the Aggañña-Sutta to the Mahāyāna", *History of Religions*, 36: 183–217.

— 2016: "The Buddhist Faith of Non-Buddhists: From Dual Belonging to Dual Attachment", in *Buddhist Christian Dual Belonging: Affirmations, Objections, Explorations*, G. D'Costa and R. Thompson (ed.), 179–95, Farnham: Ashgate.

Giustarini, Giuliano 2012: "The Role of Fear (bhaya) in the Nikāyas and in the Abhidhamma", *Journal of Indian Philosophy*, 40/5: 511–31.

Glass, Andrew 2007: *Four Gāndhārī Saṃyuktāgama sūtras: Senior Kharoṣṭhī Fragment 5*, Seattle: University of Washington Press.

Gnoli, Raniero 1977 (part 1) and 1978 (part 2): *The Gilgit Manuscript of the Saṅghabhedavastu, Being the 17th and Last Section of the Vinaya of the Mūlasarvāstivādin*, Rome: Istituto Italiano per il Medio ed Estremo Oriente.

Harrison, Paul 2007: "A Fragment of the *Saṃbādhāvakāśasūtra from a Newly Identified Ekottarikāgama Manuscript in the Schøyen Collection", *Annual Report of the International Research Institute for Advanced Buddhology at Soka University*, 10: 201–11.

Hartmann, Jens-Uwe 1991: *Untersuchungen zum Dīrghāgama der Sarvāstivādins*, unpublished habilitation thesis, Göttingen: Georg-August-Universität.

Harvey, Peter 1986: "'Signless' Meditations in Pāli Buddhism", *Journal of the International Association of Buddhist Studies*, 9/1: 25–52.

Hecker, Helmuth 1972: *Wegweiser zu den Lehrreden des Buddha, Ein Kommentar zu den 152 Reden der Mittleren Sammlung in der Übersetzung von Karl Erich Neumann*, Herrnschrot: Beyerlein & Steinschulte.

Hoernle, A.F. Rudolf 1916/1970: *Manuscript Remains of Buddhist Literature Found in Eastern Turkestan, Facsimiles of Manuscripts in Sanskrit, Khotanese, Kuchean, Tibetan and Chinese with Transcripts, Translations and Notes, Edited in Conjunction with Other Scholars, with Critical Introduction and Vocabularies*, Amsterdam: St. Leonards Ad Orientem.

Horner, I.B. 1942/1983 (vol. 3), 1951/1982 (vol. 4), and 1952/1975 (vol. 5): *The Book of the Discipline (Vinaya-Piṭaka)*, London: Pali Text Society.

Horsch, P. 1964: "Buddha's Erste Meditation", *Asiatische Studien*, 17: 100–54.

Ireland, John D. 1990: *The Udāna, Inspired Utterances of the Buddha*, Kandy: Buddhist Publication Society.

— 1991: *The Itivuttaka, The Buddha's Sayings*, Kandy: Buddhist Publication Society.

Johnston, Edward Hamilton 1936/1995 (vol. 1): *Aśvagoṣa's Buddhacarita or Acts of the Buddha, Sanskrit Text with English Translation, Cantos I to XIV Translated from the Original Sanskrit and Cantos XV to XXVIII Translated from the Tibetan and Chinese Versions Together with an Introduction and Notes*, Delhi: Munshiram Manoharlal.

Jones, J.J. 1952/1976 (vol. 2) and 1956/1978 (vol. 3): *The Mahāvastu, Translated from the Buddhist Sanskrit*, London: Pali Text Society.

Jurewicz, J. 2000: "Playing with Fire: The Pratītyasamutpāda from the Perspective of Vedic Thought", *Journal of the Pali Text Society*, 26: 77–103.

Kabat-Zinn, Jon 1990/2013: *Full Catastrophe Living, Using the Wisdom of Your Body and Mind to Face Stress, Pain, and Illness*, New York: Bantam Books.

Karetzky, Patricia Eichenbaum 1992: *The Life of the Buddha, Ancient Scriptural and Pictorial Traditions*, Lanham: University Press of America.

Krueger, Joel 2012: "Seeing Mind in Action", *Phenomenology and the Cognitive Sciences*, 11: 149–73.

Kuan, Tse-fu 2013: "The Pavāraṇā Sutta and 'Liberation in Both Ways' as against 'Liberation by Wisdom'", *Bulletin of the School of Oriental and African Studies*, 76/1: 49–73.

Kudo Noriyuki and M. Shono 2015: "The Sanskrit Fragments Or. 15009/601–678 in the Hoernle Collection", in *Buddhist Manuscripts from Central Asia, The British Library Sanskrit Fragments*, S. Karashima, J. Nagashima, and K. Wille (ed.), 3: 419–74, Tokyo: International Research Institute for Advanced Buddhology, Soka University.

Lefmann, S. 1902: *Lalita Vistara, Leben und Lehre des Çâkya-Buddha, Textausgabe mit Varianten-, Metren- und Wörterverzeichnis*, Halle: Verlag der Buchhandlung des Waisenhauses.

Liu, Zhen 2010: *Dhyānāni tapaś ca*, 禅定与苦修, Shanghai: 古籍出版社.

Martini, Giuliana 2012: "The 'Discourse on Accumulated Actions' in Śamathadeva's Abhidharmakośopāyikā", *Indian International Journal of Buddhist Studies*, 13: 49–79.

Melzer, Gudrun 2009: "The Sanskrit Fragments Or. 15009/151–200 in the Hoernle Collection", in *Buddhist Manuscripts from Central Asia, The British Library Sanskrit Fragments*, S. Karashima and K. Wille (ed.), 2: 199–226, Tokyo: International Research Institute for Advanced Buddhology, Soka University.

Nagashima, Jundo 2009: "The Sanskrit Fragments Or. 15009/51–90 in the Hoernle Collection", in *Buddhist Manuscripts from Central Asia, The British Library Sanskrit Fragments*, S. Karashima and K. Wille (ed.), 2: 128–59, Tokyo: International Research Institute for Advanced Buddhology, Soka University.

Nakamura, Hajime 2000 (vol. 1): *Gotama Buddha, A Biography Based on the Most Reliable Texts*, Tokyo: Kosei Publishing Co.

Ñāṇamoli, Bhikkhu 1972/1992: *The Life of the Buddha According to the Pali Canon*, Kandy: Buddhist Publication Society.

— 1991: *The Path of Purification (Visuddhimagga) by Bhadantācariya Buddhaghosa*, Kandy: Buddhist Publication Society.

— 1995/2005: *The Middle Length Discourses of the Buddha, A Translation of the Majjhima Nikāya*, Bhikkhu Bodhi (ed.), Boston: Wisdom Publications.

Ñāṇananda, Bhikkhu 2015 (vol. 1): *The Law of Dependent Arising (Paṭicca Samuppāda), The Secret of Bondage and Release*, Sri Lanka: Pothgulgala Dharmagrantha Dharmasravana Mādhya Bhāraya.

— 2016: *The Miracle of Contact*, Sri Lanka: Kaṭukurunde Ñāṇananda Sadaham Senasun Bhāraya.

Nattier, Jan 2007: "'One Vehicle' (一乘) in the Chinese Āgamas: New Light on an Old Problem in Pāli", *Annual Report of the International Research Institute for Advanced Buddhology at Soka University*, 10: 181–200.

Norman, K.R. 1990/1993: "Pāli Lexicographical Studies VIII", in *Collected Papers*, K.R. Norman (ed.), 4: 155–63, Oxford: Pali Text Society.

— 1997/2004: *The Word of the Doctrine (Dhammapada)*, Oxford: Pali Text Society.

Obermiller, E. 1932/1986: *The History of Buddhism in India and Tibet by Bu-ston*, Delhi: Sri Satguru.

Pachow, W. 1955: *A Comparative Study of the Prātimokṣa, on the Basis of Its Chinese, Tibetan, Sanskrit and Pali Versions*, Santiniketan: Sino-Indian Cultural Society.

Park, Jungnok 2012: *How Buddhism Acquired a Soul on the Way to China*, Sheffield: Equinox.

Pāsādika, Bhikkhu 2008: "The Ekottarāgama Parallel to the Mūlapariyāyasutta", *Indian International Journal of Buddhist Studies*, 9: 141–9.

Pradhan, P. 1967: *Abhidharmakośabhāṣya of Vasubandhu*, Patna: K.P. Jayaswal Research Institute.

Premasiri, P.D. 2016: "Early Buddhist Concept of Truth: A Study Based on the Pali Canonical Sources", *Anveṣaṇā*, 7: 313–37.

Pruitt, William 1998/1999: *The Commentary on the Verses of the Therīs (Therīgāthā-aṭṭhakathā, Paramatthadīpanī VI) by Ācariya Dhammapāla*, Oxford: Pali Text Society.

Rhys Davids, C.A.F. 1907 and 1908: "Similes in the Nikāyas", *Journal of the Pali Text Society*, 5: 52–151 and 6: 180–8.

Rhys Davids, T.W. and C.A.F. Rhys Davids 1921 (vol. 3): *Dialogues of the Buddha, Translated from the Pāli of the Dīgha Nikāya*, London: Oxford University Press.

Rotman, Andy 2008: *Divine Stories, Divyāvadāna, Part 1*, Boston: Wisdom Publications.

Sander, Lore and E. Waldschmidt 1980: *Sanskrithandschriften aus den Turfanfunden, Teil IV*, Stuttgart: Franz Steiner.

— 1985: *Sanskrithandschriften aus den Turfanfunden, Teil 5*, Stuttgart: Franz Steiner.

Schmithausen, Lambert 1991: "Buddhism and Nature", in *Proceedings of an International Symposium on the Occasion of EXPO 1990*, 22–34, Tokyo: International Institute for Buddhist Studies.

— 1997: *Maitrī and Magic: Aspects of the Buddhist Attitude Towards the Dangerous in Nature*, Vienna: Verlag der Österreichischen Akademie der Wissenschaft.

Senart, Émile 1890 (vol. 2) and 1897 (vol. 3): *Le Mahāvastu, texte sanscrit publié pour la première fois et accompagné d'introductions et d'un commentaire*, Paris: Imprimerie Nationale.

Shaw, Miranda 2006/2007: *Buddhist Goddesses of India*, Delhi: Munshiram Manoharlal.

Silverlock, Blair 2009: *An Edition, Translation and Study of the Bodha-sūtra from the Manuscript of the Gilgit Dīrghāgama of the (Mūla-)Sarvāstivādins*, BA thesis, University of Sydney.

Skilling, Peter 1979: "Discourse on the Four Kinds of Karma", *The Journal of Religious Studies*, 7/1: 86–91.

— 1981: "Uddaka Rāmaputta and Rāma", *Pāli Buddhist Review*, 6: 99–104.

— 1994 (vol. 1) and 1997 (vol. 2): *Mahāsūtras: Great Discourses of the Buddha*, Oxford: Pali Text Society.

Skilling, Peter, Saerji, and P. Assavavirulhakarn 2016: "A Possible Sanskrit Parallel to the Pali Uruvelasutta", in *Buddhist Manuscripts Volume IV*, J. Braarvig (ed.). 159–82, Oslo: Hermes Publishing.

Stache-Rosen, Valentina 1968 (vol. 1): *Dogmatische Begriffsreihen im älteren Buddhismus II; Das Saṅgītisūtra und sein Kommentar Saṅgītiparyāya*, Berlin: Akademie Verlag.

Stevenson, Ian 1983: *Cases of the Reincarnation Type, Volume IV, Twelve Cases in Thailand and Burma*, Charlottesville: University Press of Virginia.

— 1987/2001: *Children Who Remember Previous Lives, A Question of Reincarnation, Revised Edition*, Jefferson: McFarland & Company.

Strong, John S. 2001: *The Buddha, A Short Biography*, Oxford: Oneworld.

Thomas, E.J. 1927/2003: *The Life of Buddha as Legend and History*, Delhi: Munshiram Manoharlal.

Tripāṭhī, Chandrabhāl 1962: *Fünfundzwanzig sūtras des Nidānasaṃyukta*, Berlin: Akademie Verlag.

— 1995: *Ekottarāgama-Fragmente der Gilgit-Handschrift*, Reinbek: Verlag für Orientalistische Fachpublikationen.

Vetter, Tilman 1996: "Das Erwachen des Buddha", *Wiener Zeitschrift für die Kunde Südasiens*, 40: 45–85.

Vijitha, Moragaswewa 2015: "The Biography of the Buddha as Depicted in the Pāli Canon", *Sri Lanka International Journal of Buddhist Studies*, 4: 56–67.

Waldschmidt, Ernst 1929/1982: *Die Legende vom Leben des Buddha, in Auszügen aus den heiligen Texten, aus dem Sanskrit, Pali und Chinesischen übersetzt und eingeführt*, Graz: Verlag für Sammler.

— 1948 (vol. 2): *Die Überlieferung vom Lebensende des Buddha, Eine vergleichende Analyse des Mahāparinirvāṇasūtra und seiner Textentsprechungen*, Göttingen: Vandenhoeck & Ruprecht.

— 1951 (vol. 2): *Das Mahāparinirvāṇasūtra, Text in Sanskrit und tibetisch, verglichen mit dem Pāli nebst einer Übersetzung der chinesischen Entsprechung im Vinaya der Mūlasarvāstivādins, auf Grund von Turfan-Handschriften herausgegeben und bearbeitet*, Berlin: Akademie Verlag.

— 1956 (vol. 2): *Das Mahāvadānasūtra, ein kanonischer Text über die sieben letzten Buddhas, Sanskrit, verglichen mit dem Pāli nebst einer Analyse der in chinesischer Übersetzung überlieferten Parallelversion, auf Grund von Turfan-Handschriften herausgegeben*, Berlin: Akademie Verlag.

— 1957 (vol. 2): *Das Catuṣpariṣatsūtra, eine kanonische Lehrschrift über die Begründung der buddhistischen Gemeinde, Text in Sanskrit und tibetisch, verglichen mit dem Pāli nebst einer Übersetzung der chinesischen Entsprechung im Vinaya der Mūlasarvāstivādins, auf Grund von Turfan-Handschriften herausgegeben und bearbeitet*, Berlin: Akademie Verlag.

— 1968: "Ein Beitrag zur Überlieferung vom Sthavira Śroṇa Koṭiviṃśa", in *Mélanges d'indianisme à la mémoire de Louis Renou*, 773–87, Paris: Éditions de Boccard.

Waldschmidt, Ernst, W. Clawiter, and L. Holzmann 1965: *Sanskrithandschriften aus den Turfanfunden, Teil I*, Wiesbaden: Franz Steiner.

— 1971: *Sanskrithandschriften aus den Turfanfunden, Teil 3*, Wiesbaden: Franz Steiner.

Walshe, Maurice 1987: *Thus Have I Heard; The Long Discourses of the Buddha*, London: Wisdom Publications.

Walters, Jonathan S. 1995: "Gotamī's Story", in *Buddhism in Practice*, D.S. Lopez (ed.), 113–38, Princeton: Princeton University Press.

Weller, Friedrich 1928: "Die Überlieferung des älteren buddhistischen Schrifttums", *Asia Major*, 5: 149–82.

— 1939: "Buddhas Letzte Wanderung, Aus dem Chinesischen übersetzt", *Monumenta Serica*, 4: 40–84.

Wille, Klaus 2008: *Sanskrithandschriften aus den Turfanfunden Teil 10*, Stuttgart: Franz Steiner.

Wynne, Alexander 2007: *The Origin of Buddhist Meditation*, London: Routledge.

Zhang, Lixiang 2004: *Das Śaṃkarasūtra: Eine Übersetzung des Sanskrit-Textes im Vergleich mit der Pāli Fassung*, MA thesis, Munich: Ludwig-Maximilians-Universität.

Zieme, Peter 1988: "Das Pravāraṇā-sūtra in alttürkischer Überlieferung", in *A Green Leaf, Papers in Honour of Professor Jes P. Asmussen*,W. Sunderman, J. Duchesne-Guillemin, and F. Vahman (ed.), 445–53, Leiden: Brill.

LIST OF ABBREVIATIONS

AN	*Aṅguttara-nikāya*
Ap	*Apadāna*
D	Derge edition
DĀ	*Dīrgha-āgama* (T 1)
Dhp	*Dhammapada*
Dhp-a	*Dhammapada-aṭṭhakathā*
DN	*Dīgha-nikāya*
EĀ	*Ekottarika-āgama* (T 125)
It	*Itivuttaka*
It-a	*Itivuttaka-aṭṭhakathā*
Jā	*Jātaka*
MĀ	*Madhyama-āgama* (T 26)
Mil	*Milindapañha*
MN	*Majjhima-nikāya*
Nidd	*Niddesa*
Ps	*Papañcasūdanī*
Q	Peking edition
SĀ	*Saṃyukta-āgama* (T 99)
$SĀ^2$	*Saṃyukta-āgama* (T 100)
$SĀ^3$	*Saṃyukta-āgama* (T 101)
SHT	Sanskrithandschriften aus den Turfanfunden
SN	*Saṃyutta-nikāya*
Sn	*Sutta-nipāta*
Spk	*Sāratthappakāsinī*
Sv	*Sumaṅgalavilāsinī*
T	Taishō edition (CBETA)
Thī-a	*Therīgāthā-aṭṭhakathā* (1998 edition)
Ud	*Udāna*
Uv	*Udānavarga*
Vin	*Vinaya*
Vism	*Visuddhimagga*
〈 〉	emendation
[]	supplementation

SUBJECT INDEX

INTRODUCTORY NOTE

References such as '178–9' indicate (not necessarily continuous) discussion of a topic across a range of pages. Wherever possible in the case of topics with many references, these have either been divided into sub-topics or only the most significant discussions of the topic are listed.

INDEX LOCORUM

WINDHORSE PUBLICATIONS

Windhorse Publications is a Buddhist charitable company based in the UK. We place great emphasis on producing books of high quality that are accessible and relevant to those interested in Buddhism at whatever level. We are the main publisher of the works of Sangharakshita, the founder of the Triratna Buddhist Order and Community. Our books draw on the whole range of the Buddhist tradition, including translations of traditional texts, commentaries, books that make links with contemporary culture and ways of life, biographies of Buddhists, and works on meditation.

As a not-for-profit enterprise, we ensure that all surplus income is invested in new books and improved production methods, to better communicate Buddhism in the 21st century. We welcome donations to help us continue our work – to find out more, go to windhorsepublications.com.

The Windhorse is a mythical animal that flies over the earth carrying on its back three precious jewels, bringing these invaluable gifts to all humanity: the Buddha (the 'awakened one'), his teaching, and the community of all his followers.

Windhorse Publications
169 Mill Road
Cambridge CB1 3AN
UK
info@windhorsepublications.com

Perseus Distribution
210 American Drive
Jackson TN 38301
USA

Windhorse Books
PO Box 574
Newtown NSW 2042
Australia

THE TRIRATNA BUDDHIST COMMUNITY

Windhorse Publications is a part of the Triratna Buddhist Community, an international movement with centres in Europe, India, North and South America and Australasia. At these centres, members of the Triratna Buddhist Order offer classes in meditation and Buddhism. Activities of the Triratna Community also include retreat centres, residential spiritual communities, ethical Right Livelihood businesses, and the Karuna Trust, a UK fundraising charity that supports social welfare projects in the slums and villages of India.

Through these and other activities, Triratna is developing a unique approach to Buddhism, not simply as a philosophy and a set of techniques, but as a creatively directed way of life for all people living in the conditions of the modern world.

If you would like more information about Triratna please visit thebuddhistcentre.com or write to:

London Buddhist Centre
51 Roman Road
London E2 0HU
UK

Aryaloka
14 Heartwood Circle
Newmarket NH 03857
USA

Sydney Buddhist Centre
24 Enmore Road
Sydney NSW 2042
Australia